COUNTRY LIVING

The New Flavors of
Country Cooking

COUNTRY LIVING

The New Flavors of
Country Cooking

FROM THE EDITORS OF COUNTRY LIVING

Hearst Books
A Division of Sterling Publishing Co., Inc.
New York

Country Living
Editor-in-Chief: Nancy Mernit Soriano
Food Editor: Cheryl Slocum

Library of Congress Cataloging-in-Publication Data
Country living the new flavors of country cooking / edited by
Cheryl Slocum.
    p. cm.
  ISBN 1-58816-291-5
  1. Cookery. I. Title: New flavors of country. II. Cheryl Slocum.
III. Country living (New York, N.Y.)
  TX714.C6986 2004
  641.5--dc22

                              2003018685

10 9 8 7 6 5 4 3 2 1

Supplemental text by Victoria Spencer

Book design by Alexandra Maldonado

Published by Hearst Books
A Division of Sterling Publishing Co., Inc.
387 Park Avenue South, New York, NY 10016

Country Living is a trademark owned by Hearst Magazines
Property, Inc., in USA, and Hearst Communications, Inc., in
Canada. Hearst Books is a trademark owned by Hearst
Communications, Inc.

www.countryliving.com

Distributed in Canada by Sterling Publishing
c/o Canadian Manda Group, One Atlantic Avenue, Suite 105
Toronto, Ontario, Canada M6K 3E7

Distributed in Australia by Capricorn Link (Australia) Pty. Ltd.
P.O. Box 704, Windsor, NSW 2756 Australia

Printed in China

ISBN 1-58816-291-5

TABLE OF CONTENTS

FOREWORD   6

INTRODUCTION   7

Chapter 1 > > SOUPS AND STARTERS   9

Chapter 2 > > CHICKEN, DUCK, AND TURKEY   27

Chapter 3 > > BEEF, PORK, AND LAMB   47

Chapter 4 > > SEAFOOD   67

Chapter 5 > > PASTA AND GRAINS   83

Chapter 6 > > VEGETABLES   99

Chapter 7 > > SALAD   121

Chapter 8 > > BREADS AND MUFFINS   137

Chapter 9 > > SAUCES, PRESERVES, AND CONDIMENTS   163

Chapter 10 > > CAKES AND COOKIES   175

Chapter 11 > > PIES AND TARTS   199

Chapter 12 > > DESSERTS   219

INDEX   238

PHOTOGRAPHY CREDITS   240

FOREWORD

There are a handful of activities that *Country Living* readers are truly passionate about, and cooking is right up at the top of the list. It's not hard to understand why. Preparing a meal for family and friends is more than an opportunity to nourish the ones you love, it's also a chance to be creative by trying a new recipe or adding a fresh twist to an old favorite. I know this from experience: One of my greatest joys is seeing my husband's and son's faces light up when a well-loved dish is set on the table or when a stove-top experiment turns out to be a hit.

American cooking has come a long way since *Country Living* first appeared on newsstands in 1978. Ingredients that seemed exotic back then—arugula, balsamic vinegar, and porcini mushrooms to name a few—can be found at just about every supermarket across the country today. *Country Living New Flavors of Country Cooking* embraces this trend. Between these covers you'll find delicacies infused with roasted garlic, maple syrup, sage, cilantro, and curry. You'll also find tried-and-true recipes like Chicken Potpie and Chocolate Cake. After all, some flavors never go out of style.

—NANCY MERNIT SORIANO, Editor-in-Chief

| INTRODUCTION

Compiling a collection of *Country Living* recipes for *The New Flavors of Country Cooking* has certainly been one of the more enjoyable projects I've undertaken as food editor. It was a trip down memory lane—affording me the opportunity to revisit some of my favorite recipes and reflect on how our food from the *Country Living* test kitchen has evolved over the past twenty-five years. So this collection includes not only classic country dishes but also recipes that fit into the busy lives we all lead. And, all are recipes that uphold our philosophy of offering homemade dishes made with fresh ingredients that are also delicious and satisfying.

Here you will find recipes such as Spicy Southern Fried Chicken, Blueberry-Peach Pie, and Prized Family Meatloaf—the kind of simple country fare that reflect time-honored traditions and evoke comforting emotions about home and health. As technology brings the world around us closer, faraway places offer inspiration. You will find evidence in many of our dishes, such as Moroccan Lamb Kebabs, Chicken and Manchego Empanadas, and artisan-style breads, including Olive Fougasse. Contemporary touches, such as adding an unusual combination of spices or an exotic ingredient (as we did with Pumpkin Seed Pesto, cinnamon-infused Hot Chocolate Snacking Cake, and T-Bone Steaks with North African Spices) will let you update traditional recipes with ease.

But no matter what the influence, inspiration, or origin, certain threads remain constant in our *Country Living* recipes: It is our goal to create dishes that stimulate and excite by providing our readers with new ideas, simplified cooking methods and shortcuts, information about the highest-quality ingredients and, at all times, top-notch results. There is something for everyone in *The New Flavors of Country Cooking*. The well-seasoned cook, versed in many methods, ingredients, and cuisines, will find recipes impressive enough to include in a treasured collection of favorite dishes. The avid weekend cook, who loves to experiment, will find stimulating ideas, unusual ingredients and innovative cooking methods. And families with children and busy schedules can count on our one-dish meals and simpler preparations when good, wholesome, easy-to-prepare family-friendly fare fits the bill.

I hope you will enjoy making these recipes as much as we have enjoyed creating them for you. And, most of all, I hope they bring the comfort and joy of country cooking to your kitchen.

—CHERYL SLOCUM, Food Editor

SOUPS AND STARTERS

COLD AVOCADO SOUP

Perfect for summer, this creamy soup spiked with lime juice requires no cooking. Just place the ingredients in the blender and buzz.

- 1 avocado (about ½ pound), halved, pitted, and peeled
- ¾ cup buttermilk
- ½ cup low-sodium chicken broth
- ¼ cup plus 2 tablespoons chopped green onions
- ½ clove garlic
- ½ cup water
- 1 tablespoon fresh lime juice
- ½ teaspoon salt
- ⅛ teaspoon ground red pepper
- ¼ cup shredded radishes (about 4 large)

MAKE THE SOUP: In a blender, combine the avocado, ½ cup buttermilk, chicken broth, 2 tablespoons green onions, and garlic and process until very smooth. Transfer the soup to a large bowl and, while stirring, add the rest of the buttermilk, water, lime juice, salt, and ground red pepper. Divide among 4 bowls and serve immediately or chill for up to eight hours. Garnish with 1 tablespoon each of radish and green onion.

Nutrition information per serving—protein: 3.2 g; fat: 8.4 g; carbohydrate: 7.5 g; fiber: 2.5 g; sodium: 337 mg; cholesterol: 2.2 mg; calories: 109.

MAKING THE MOST OF BUTTERMILK

Contrary to its name, buttermilk contains no butter at all. The name reflects its origins as the liquid by-product of churned butter, but today, buttermilk is usually made by adding live cultures to nonfat milk. Most cooks use buttermilk when making pancakes or baking, but it can also be used to great effect in salad dressing and soups, both chilled and hot (see Creamy, Carrot and Parsnip Soup (page 12) and Cold Avocado Soup (above)). Buttermilk imparts a rich, slightly tangy flavor without the added calories of cream of milk. It is low in fat and a good source of calcium. Stored in a tightly covered container in the refrigerator, buttermilk will keep for about 2 weeks.

CHILLED FRESH PEA SOUP > >

This refreshing soup, with its cool green hue, offers a powerful antidote to summer's sizzle.

- 2 tablespoons unsalted butter
- ¾ cup thinly sliced leeks
- ¼ cup diced peeled carrots
- 1 tablespoon fresh thyme leaves
- 2 cups chopped iceberg lettuce (about ½ head)
- 1 cup fresh or frozen green peas
- ½ pound sugar snap peas, strings removed
- 1½ teaspoons salt
- ⅛ teaspoon ground white pepper
- 2 cups water
- 6 fresh mint leaves, coarsely chopped
- 2½ teaspoons fresh lime juice
- 1 tablespoon grated lime zest (about 1 lime)
- 8 tablespoons crème fraîche (optional)

1 COOK THE SOUP: In a large saucepan, melt the butter over medium heat. Add leeks, carrots, and thyme and cook until the leeks are translucent and the carrots are tender—about 8 minutes. Add the lettuce and green peas and continue to cook for 5 more minutes. Stir in the sugar snap peas, salt, pepper, and water. Increase heat to medium high and cover. Cook until the liquid simmers and the snap peas are tender—about 5 minutes. Remove from heat.

2 FINISH THE SOUP: Make an ice bath by setting a bowl large enough to hold the soup over another bowl filled with ice and a small amount of water. In small batches, carefully puree the soup in a blender or food processor until very smooth, then pour into the chilled bowl. Add the mint, lime juice, and zest to the last batch. Stir the soup to cool it quickly. Remove the bowl of soup from the ice bath, cover with plastic wrap, and refrigerate until thoroughly chilled. Ladle soup into chilled soup bowls. Garnish each with a tablespoon of crème fraîche, if desired.

Nutrition information per serving—protein: 2.4 g; fat: 3 g; carbohydrate: 8.8 g; fiber: 2.7 g; sodium: 439 mg; cholesterol: 7.7 mg; calories: 70.

CREAMY CARROT AND PARSNIP SOUP

Fresh horseradish can be hard-to find, if you substitute prepared horseradish be sure to look at the expiration date as it will spoil. Prepared horseradish is less pungent than fresh, so taste and adjust the amount to suit you palate.

- 2 pounds carrots, peeled and coarsely chopped (about 8 cups)
- 2 pounds parsnips, peeled and coarsely chopped (about 8 cups)
- 3 cups water
- 3 cups low-sodium chicken broth
- 2 teaspoons sugar
- 1 teaspoon salt
- 3 tablespoons butter
- 1 medium onion, finely chopped (about 1 cup)
- 4 cloves garlic, crushed with the side of a large knife
- 2 cups buttermilk
- 1 teaspoon freshly grated horseradish
- 1 teaspoon grated peeled fresh ginger
- 1 tablespoon crème fraîche or sour cream (optional)
- 1 tablespoon chopped fresh dill (optional)

1 COOK THE VEGETABLES: In a large stockpot, combine carrots, parsnips, water, broth, sugar, and salt, over medium-high heat. Boil gently until vegetables are tender—about 15 minutes. Melt the butter in a 10-inch skillet over medium heat. Add the onion and sauté until translucent—about 5 minutes. Add the garlic and cook for 2 to 3 more minutes.

2 MAKE THE SOUP: Using a slotted spoon, remove the carrots and parsnips from the stockpot. In a blender or food processor with the metal blade attached, puree the vegetables in batches. Add the onion and garlic and puree until smooth. Return the mixture to the stockpot, add the buttermilk, and heat until warm but not boiling.

3 TO SERVE: Stir in grated horseradish and ginger; garnish with crème fraîche or sour cream and a sprinkling of dill, if desired.

Nutrition information per 1-cup serving—protein: 5.3 g; fat: 6.9 g; carbohydrate: 38 g; fiber: 8.8 g; sodium: 758 mg; cholesterol: 15.7 mg; calories: 226.

SPRING-GREENS SOUP

Any combination of fresh greens can be used in this soup; just be sure the total weight amounts to $1^1/2$ pounds.

- 2 tablespoons olive oil
- 1 large onion, chopped (about $1^1/2$ cups)
- 1 large bulb fennel, chopped
- $1/2$ pound dandelion greens, cleaned and chopped
- $1/2$ pound mustard greens, cleaned and chopped
- $1/2$ pound baby spinach leaves, cleaned
- 4 cloves garlic
- 6 cups low-sodium chicken broth
- $1/4$ teaspoon salt
- $1/4$ teaspoon ground white pepper
- 1 cup half-and-half
- Sprouts (optional)

1 MAKE THE SOUP: In a 4-quart saucepan, heat oil over medium heat. Add onion and fennel; sauté until vegetables soften and are lightly browned—about 10 minutes. Add dandelion greens, mustard greens, spinach, and garlic. Cook, stirring occasionally, until greens wilt—about 5 minutes. Add chicken broth, salt, and pepper. Increase heat to high and bring to a boil. Reduce heat to low, cover, and simmer 20 minutes. Remove from heat; let cool 15 minutes.

2 FINISH THE SOUP: In a blender, puree the soup in small batches. Transfer the pureed soup to a 3-quart saucepan. Stir in half-and-half and reheat over low heat. When ready to serve, divide soup among bowls and garnish with sprouts, if desired.

Nutrition information per serving—protein: 6 g; fat: 8 g; carbohydrate: 9 g; fiber: 3 g; sodium: 576 mg; cholesterol: 12 mg; calories: 117.

ROASTED GARLIC SOUP

For a crispy accompaniment, top soup with cheese croutons: Broil sliced rounds of French bread topped with grated cheese until golden brown.

- 2 large whole unpeeled garlic heads, plus 1 clove, minced
- 3 tablespoons olive oil
- 2 bay leaves
- 1 tablespoon unsalted butter
- 2 medium onions, minced (about 2 cups)
- 1 cup minced peeled carrots
- 1 large potato, peeled and cubed (1¼ cups)
- 4 cups low-sodium chicken broth
- ½ cup dry white wine
- 1 teaspoon salt
- ½ teaspoon ground black pepper
- ¼ cup heavy cream

1 ROAST THE GARLIC: Preheat oven to 350°F. Using a serrated knife, cut the top off each garlic head so that the tip of each clove is exposed. Place the garlic heads on a large piece of aluminum foil and drizzle with 2 tablespoons of olive oil. Add the bay leaves and fold the foil to form a packet. Place the packet in the oven and bake for 45 minutes. Remove from oven and let cool slightly. In a small bowl, squeeze the garlic head until all of the roasted flesh is released. Discard outer husks and bay leaves.

2 MAKE THE SOUP: In a large heavy-duty saucepan, heat the remaining olive oil and butter; add onions, and cook over medium heat until translucent—about 4 minutes. Add the carrots and continue to cook for 5 more minutes. Add the minced garlic and cook for 2 minutes. Stir in the potato, chicken broth, white wine, roasted garlic, salt, and pepper. Cover and bring the soup to a boil. Reduce heat to medium low and continue to cook for 35 minutes.

3 FINISH THE SOUP: In a blender, puree the soup in small batches until smooth. Return the soup to the saucepan over medium heat and whisk in the heavy cream. Heat until warmed. Do not boil. Keep warm until ready to serve.

Nutrition information per serving—protein: 2.2 g; fat: 11.4 g; carbohydrate: 11.8 g; fiber: 1.4 g; sodium: 778 mg; cholesterol: 16.6 mg; calories: 164.

TOMATO-FENNEL SOUP

Pair this fresh, creamy tomato soup with grilled cheese sandwiches for a satisfying meal that can be prepared in about an hour.

- 2 tablespoons olive oil
- 1 clove garlic, minced
- 1½ cups chopped fennel bulb (about ½ bulb)
- 1 medium onion, chopped (about 1 cup)
- 2 28-ounce cans whole tomatoes, drained, liquid reserved
- 1 tablespoon grated lemon zest
- 1 tablespoon chopped fresh rosemary leaves
- ½ teaspoon crushed red pepper
- 1 teaspoon packed light brown sugar
- ½ teaspoon salt
- ¼ cup chopped fresh parsley
- 1 teaspoon fresh thyme leaves
- ⅓ cup heavy cream

1 MAKE THE SOUP: In a large Dutch oven, heat the oil over medium-high heat. Add the garlic and cook until softened—about 2 minutes. Add the fennel and onions and cook until onions are translucent—about 5 more minutes. Add the tomatoes, zest, rosemary, and red pepper flakes and cook for 5 minutes. Add the reserved tomato liquid, 2 cups of water, sugar, and salt. Reduce heat to low, cover, and simmer until fennel is very tender—about 45 minutes.

2 FINISH THE SOUP: In a blender or food processor fitted with the metal blade, transfer the soup in small batches and puree until smooth. Add the parsley and thyme to the last batch and puree until smooth. Return the soup to the Dutch oven and stir in the heavy cream. Ladle hot soup into bowls and serve immediately.

Nutrition information per serving—protein: 3.5 g; fat: 10.2 g; carbohydrate: 16.9 g; fiber: 3.9 g; sodium: 628 mg; cholesterol: 17.9 mg; calories: 160.

CRAB BISQUE

MAKES 8 SERVINGS

This rich soup makes an impressive start to any dinner party. If you don't have brandy on hand, sherry is a delicious alternative.

STOCK:

¼ cup coarsely chopped peeled carrot

1 medium onion, coarsely chopped (about 1 cup)

1 stalk celery, coarsely chopped

1 teaspoon fresh thyme leaves

1 bay leaf

10 whole black peppercorns

1 48-ounce can (6 cups) low-sodium chicken broth

2 8-ounce bottles clam juice

½ cup dry white wine

BISQUE:

¼ cup (½ stick) butter

1 medium onion, diced (about 1 cup)

½ cup diced peeled carrot

¾ cup diced celery

1 clove garlic, minced

1 tablespoon chopped fresh parsley

¼ cup all-purpose flour

½ teaspoon chopped fresh thyme leaves

2 tablespoons tomato paste

1 teaspoon salt

½ teaspoon ground black pepper

½ pound fresh crabmeat, picked over and shell pieces discarded

⅛ teaspoon ground red pepper

¼ cup brandy

8 shelled crab claws for garnish

½ cup fresh flat-leaf parsley for garnish

1 MAKE THE STOCK: In a 4-quart stockpot, add all stock ingredients and bring to a boil, then lower heat and simmer for 20 minutes. Strain through a meshed sieve into a large bowl and discard the solids. Cover the liquid and set aside.

2 MAKE THE BISQUE: In a stockpot, melt the butter over medium-high heat. Add the onion, carrot, and celery and cook, stirring occasionally, until softened—about 10 minutes. Add the garlic and cook for 2 more minutes. Stir in the parsley, flour, thyme, tomato paste, salt, and black pepper. Cook and continue to stir for 1 minute. Stir in the stock and bring to a boil. Reduce heat to medium-low and allow mixture to simmer for about 20 minutes. Stir in the crabmeat and red pepper and simmer for about 10 minutes. Add brandy. Keep warm.

3 SERVE THE BISQUE: When ready to serve, transfer to a tureen or rimmed soup bowls. Garnish with crab claws and parsley leaves.

Nutrition information per serving—protein: 9.4 g; fat: 7.9 g; carbohydrate: 10.2 g; fiber: 2 g; sodium: 601 mg; cholesterol: 49 mg; calories: 183.

ROASTED BUTTERNUT SQUASH AND PEAR SOUP

MAKES 9 CUPS

A thermos of this velvety soup makes a great accompaniment for picnic sandwiches. Any leftover soup (unlikely!) can be frozen for up to 1 month.

1 large or 2 small butternut squash (3–4 pounds)

1 tablespoon vegetable oil

2 medium onions, chopped (about 2 cups)

1 shallot, chopped (about 2 tablespoons)

1 tablespoon chopped peeled fresh ginger

1 fresh jalapeño pepper, seeded and chopped (about 1 tablespoon)

1¼ teaspoons salt

¼ teaspoon ground black pepper

2 ripe pears, peeled, cored, and cut into chunks (about 2 cups)

6 cups low-sodium chicken broth

1 tablespoon honey

1 teaspoon fresh thyme leaves

¼ cup heavy cream

1 ROAST THE SQUASH: Preheat oven to 400°F. Cut the squash in half lengthwise and place cut side down on a nonstick baking pan. Pour ¼ cup water into the pan and roast for 45 minutes or until the squash is tender when pricked with a fork. Remove from the oven and allow to cool. (This step may be done the day before preparing the soup.)

2 MAKE THE SOUP: Remove the seeds and peel from the roasted squash. Place the cooked squash in a medium bowl and mash coarsely. Set aside. In a 6-quart saucepan, heat the oil over medium-high heat. Add the onion, shallot, ginger, jalapeño, salt, and pepper, and cook until onion is soft and begins to turn light brown—about 10 minutes. Add the pears and cook another 5 minutes. Measure 3 cups of the cooked, mashed squash and add to the saucepan. Stir in the broth, honey, and thyme and bring to a boil. Reduce heat and simmer, covered, for 15 minutes. In a blender or food processor fitted with the metal blade, puree the soup in batches. Return the soup to the saucepan. Stir in the cream and keep warm. Do not boil. Serve warm.

Nutrition information per 1-cup serving—protein: 4.3 g; fat: 6 g; carbohydrate: 30 g; fiber: 6.7 g; sodium: 381 mg; cholesterol: 12 mg; calories: 169.

WINTER ROOT VEGETABLE SOUP

MAKES 10 CUPS (8 SERVINGS)

Top this hearty soup with a dollop of sour cream and a sprinkling of chives.

2 tablespoons olive oil

1 large onion, coarsely chopped (about 1½ cups)

2 tablespoons finely chopped garlic

6 cups low-sodium chicken broth

2 tablespoons cider vinegar

1 pound celery root, peeled and diced (about 2½ cups)

¾ pound baking potatoes, peeled and diced (about 2⅓ cups)

¾ pound sweet potatoes, peeled and diced (about 2⅓ cups)

½ pound parsnips, peeled and diced (1¾ cups)

½ pound carrots, peeled and diced (1⅓ cups)

¼ pound turnips, diced (2 cups)

½ teaspoon minced peeled fresh ginger

½ teaspoon salt

¼ teaspoon ground cumin

¼ teaspoon curry powder

¼ teaspoon ground cinnamon

⅛ teaspoon ground red pepper

1 MAKE THE SOUP: In a pressure cooker, heat the oil over high heat. Add the onions and sauté until soft—about 3 minutes. Add the garlic and sauté 1 more minute. Add the remaining ingredients, seal the pressure-cooker lid, and bring the cooker to high pressure. Reduce the heat just enough to maintain high pressure and cook for 8 minutes. Release pressure using the quick-release method and carefully remove lid.

2 FINISH THE SOUP: In a blender or food processor fitted with the metal blade, puree the soup in batches until smooth. Serve hot.

Nutrition information per serving—protein: 4 g; fat: 6.9 g; carbohydrate: 32.2 g; fiber: 6.3 g; sodium: 957 mg; cholesterol: 3.8 mg; calories: 198.

HOLIDAY OYSTER STEW

MAKES 8 SERVINGS

In many homes, this stew is traditionally served on Christmas Eve. For even richer flavor, substitute light cream for the half-and-half.

3 tablespoons unsalted butter

2 shallots, minced

1 medium onion, minced (about 1 cup)

½ cup minced celery

4 cups half-and-half

4 cups milk

¼ teaspoon ground red pepper

1 teaspoon salt

1 teaspoon cracked black pepper

2 pints freshly shucked oysters, liquor reserved

2 tablespoons 1-inch-long pieces chives (optional)

MAKE THE SOUP: In a large saucepan, melt butter over medium heat. Sauté the shallots, onions, and celery until soft—about 5 minutes. Stir in half-and-half, milk, red pepper, salt, and black pepper. Heat to just under a boil. Add oysters and their liquor. Simmer just until the oysters begin to curl on the edges—about 5 minutes. Ladle into soup bowls and sprinkle with chives, if desired.

Nutrition information per serving—protein: 16.8 g; fat: 25.4 g; carbohydrate: 18.4 g; fiber: .6 g; sodium: 645 mg; cholesterol: 138 mg; calories: 367.

GOUGÈRES

MAKES ABOUT TWENTY 2-INCH GOUGERES

A French favorite, these crispy bite-sized puffs of cheesy choux pastry are wonderful with drinks. You can make them ahead and them serve at room temperature, and they'll taste great—but they're at their best when warm.

1 cup water

6 tablespoons (¾ stick) butter

½ teaspoon salt

1 cup all-purpose flour

1 ½ cups grated Gruyère cheese (about 3½ ounces)

2 teaspoons Dijon mustard

5 large eggs

3 tablespoons grated domestic Parmesan cheese (for tops)

1 MAKE THE CHOUX PASTRY: Preheat oven to 450˚F. In a small saucepan, combine water, butter and salt and bring to a boil. Remove from heat and, while whisking, add flour. Return pan to low medium heat and with a wooden spoon stir constantly until batter has thickened and is pulling away from the sides and the bottom of the pan, 4 to 5 minutes. Remove pan from heat and stir in Gruyère and mustard until well incorporated. Stir in 4 eggs, one at a time until each is incorporated.

2 BAKE THE GOUGÈRES: Place choux pastry in a large resealable plastic bag and cut the corner. Pipe 2-inch diameter rounds onto a parchment-lined baking sheet, at least one inch apart and 2-inches in diameter. In a small bowl, beat remaining egg. Brush tops with egg and sprinkle with Parmesan cheese. Set baking sheets in center rack in oven and bake until gougères are puffed and well-browned, 20 to 25 minutes. Serve immediately or at room temperature.

Nutritional information per gougere—protein: 5.4 g; fat: 7.7 g; carbohydrate: 7.4 g; fiber: .3 g; sodium: 127 mg; cholesterol: 72.2 mg; calories: 122.

CHICKEN AND MUSHROOM NOODLE SOUP >>

MAKES 6 SERVINGS

Lemongrass is the key ingredient here, adding sparkling flavor to this Asian-style chicken-and-noodle soup. For best results, use fresh lemongrass, which is found in most Asian markets along with chili paste and somen noodles.

8 cups low-sodium chicken broth

6 green onions, cut into 1-inch pieces, white and green parts separated

2 teaspoons peeled chopped fresh ginger

1 1$\frac{1}{2}$-inch piece fresh lemongrass, chopped (or 1 tablespoon dried)

1 1-pound boneless chicken breast

$\frac{1}{2}$ pound assorted mushrooms (such as shiitake, oyster, and cremini), sliced

2 tablespoons low-sodium soy sauce

$\frac{1}{2}$–1 teaspoon chili paste

3$\frac{1}{2}$ ounces thin somen or ramen noodles, cooked and drained

2 ounces baby spinach, cleaned

1 POACH THE CHICKEN: In a large stockpot, combine broth, the white bottoms of the green onion, ginger, and lemongrass and bring to a boil. Add the chicken, reduce heat to medium, and cook until chicken is done—about 20 minutes. Remove the chicken and skim the broth. Shred the chicken and set aside.

2 MAKE THE SOUP: Strain the broth through cheesecloth or a very fine sieve and return it to the stockpot. Add mushrooms and green-onion tops to the broth and simmer for 10 minutes. Return chicken to the broth, stir in the soy sauce and chili paste, and simmer for 10 more minutes. Divide the noodles and spinach among 6 bowls and ladle the soup into the bowls. Serve immediately.

Nutrition information per serving—protein: 23.3 g; fat: 4 g; carbohydrate: 11g; fiber: 2.3 g; sodium: 466 mg; cholesterol: 53 mg; calories: 162.

WARM AGED-GOUDA CUSTARD WITH ROASTED TOMATOES

MAKES 6 SIDE-DISH OR APPETIZER SERVINGS

Aging makes the flavor of Gouda stronger and nuttier—the perfect complement to sweet, oven-roasted tomatoes. If you can't find aged Gouda, substitute Asiago or Parmesan.

1$\frac{1}{4}$ cups heavy cream

$\frac{3}{4}$ cup milk

1$\frac{1}{4}$ cups grated aged Gouda, Asiago, or Parmesan cheese

1 cup fresh bread crumbs

3 large egg yolks

1$\frac{1}{4}$ teaspoons salt

1$\frac{1}{4}$ teaspoons ground black pepper

4 plum tomatoes, quartered

2 tablespoons balsamic vinegar

2 tablespoons olive oil

1 MAKE THE CUSTARD: In a small saucepan, heat the cream and milk over medium heat until it just simmers. Add the cheese and stir over low heat until the cheese has melted—about 4 minutes. Add the bread crumbs and set aside, allowing the crumbs to soften in the milk mixture for 30 minutes. Generously coat 6 four-ounce ramekins with vegetable oil and set aside.

2 COOK THE CUSTARD: Preheat oven to 300°F. Pour 1 inch hot water into a roasting pan, place it on a baking sheet, and set aside. In a medium bowl, gently whisk the egg yolks, the milk mixture, $\frac{1}{4}$ teaspoon salt, and $\frac{1}{4}$ teaspoon pepper together until thoroughly combined. Pour about $\frac{1}{3}$ cup custard into each ramekin. Bake in the prepared roasting pan on the center rack of the oven until a toothpick inserted into the center of the custard comes out clean—about 1$\frac{1}{4}$ hours. Remove from oven, place on a wire rack to cool for at least 10 minutes.

3 ROAST THE TOMATOES: Increase oven temperature to 450°F. Place the tomatoes, balsamic vinegar, olive oil, and remaining salt and pepper in a roasting pan, toss to coat, and cook until browned—15 to 20 minutes. Set aside. Gently run a knife around the outside of each custard and invert ramekin onto a serving plate. Top each custard with the tomatoes and serve immediately.

Nutrition information per serving—protein: 13.1 g; fat: 33 g; carbohydrate: 11.2 g; fiber: .7 g; sodium: 912 mg; cholesterol: 195 mg; calories: 391.

GRILLED CHICKEN WITH CITRUS SAUCE

< <

These tasty chicken kabobs are perfect cocktail party food—guests can hold the skewer in one hand and a drink in the other. No knives and forks needed!

¼ cup extra-virgin olive oil

¼ cup fresh lemon juice

3 tablespoons chopped fresh oregano leaves

¾ teaspoon salt

½ teaspoon ground black pepper

1 pound boneless, skinless chicken breast halves, cut into ¼-inch-wide strips

1 cup plain yogurt

1 teaspoon grated orange zest

2 teaspoons fresh orange juice

1 small clove garlic, minced

1/2 teaspoon ground cumin

1 MARINATE THE CHICKEN: In a large bowl, combine olive oil, 2 tablespoons lemon juice, 2 tablespoons oregano, ½ teaspoon salt, and pepper. Add the chicken and marinate for 20 minutes.

2 MAKE CITRUS SAUCE: In a medium bowl, stir together the remaining ingredients. Cover and refrigerate.

3 COOK THE CHICKEN: Heat grill to medium high. Run skewers through chicken pieces and grill for about 4 minutes, turn over, and grill until cooked through—about 4 more minutes. Serve with citrus sauce.

Nutrition information per skewer—protein: 5.7 g; fat: 3.4 g; carbohydrate: 1.1 g; fiber: 0 g; sodium: 101 mg; cholesterol: 14.7 mg; calories: 58.2.

"BEDEVILED" EGGS

We made this summer picnic favorite a bit exotic by adding a touch of the Middle Eastern spices fenugreek and coriander.

12 hard-cooked large eggs, peeled

½ cup plus 2 tablespoons mayonnaise

½ teaspoon hot pepper sauce

2 tablespoons finely diced cornichon or dill pickle relish

¼ cup finely diced onion

2 tablespoons finely chopped fresh parsley

2 teaspoons ground coriander

1 teaspoon ground fenugreek

1 teaspoon salt

¼ teaspoon ground red pepper

1 MAKE THE FILLING: Slice eggs in half lengthwise and remove yolks; set egg whites aside. In a medium bowl, use a fork to mix the yolks, mayonnaise, and hot pepper sauce together. Stir in the cornichon, onion, parsley, coriander, fenugreek, salt, and red pepper.

2 FILL THE EGGS: Fill a large zip-top plastic bag with the yolk mixture. Cut one corner of the bag to make a small hole (about 1 inch in diameter). Squeeze about 1 tablespoon of the filling into each egg-white half. Cover and chill until ready to serve.

Nutrition information per serving—protein: 3.3 g; fat: 7 g; carbohydrate: 1.2 g; fiber: .15 g; sodium: 163 mg; cholesterol: 109 mg; calories: 84.

SHRIMP MOUSSE

This traditional Gulf Coast appetizer can be made up to 2 days in advance. Cooked lobster or crabmeat makes an excellent substitute for the shrimp.

  1 envelope unflavored gelatin

  1/4 cup water

  1 10 3/4-ounce can condensed tomato
    soup

  8–ounce package cream cheese,
    softened

  1/2 cup finely chopped celery

  1/2 cup finely chopped green onions

  1/4 cup finely chopped green bell pepper

  1 cup mayonnaise

  2 teaspoons fresh lemon juice

  1/4 teaspoon Cajun seasoning

  1/4 teaspoon Worcestershire sauce

  1/4 teaspoon hot pepper sauce

  1/8 teaspoon ground black pepper

  3/4 pound cooked shrimp, shelled,
    deveined, and chopped

1 MAKE THE MOUSSE: In a saucepan, sprinkle gelatin into water. Stir to dissolve and gently heat until clear. Add soup and cream cheese and cook over low heat, stirring until mixture is smooth. Remove from heat and fold in remaining ingredients.

2 Pour into a lightly greased 6-cup mold. Cover and chill until set—about 4 hours. Unmold and serve with crackers.

Nutrition information per serving—protein: 12.9 g; fat: 33 g; carbohydrate: 8 g; fiber: .5 g; sodium: 623 mg; cholesterol: 130 mg; calories: 374.

CITRUS GRAVLAX

Our version of the Swedish delicacy gravlax, (salmon cured in a sugar, salt, and herb mixture), is flavored with lemon, lime, and lemongrass. Slice it thinly and serve with pumpernickel bread or crackers.

  1 2-pound center-cut salmon fillet,
    skin on

  1 cup chopped fresh dill

  1/2 cup kosher salt

  1/2 cup sugar

  2 tablespoons cracked black pepper

  2 tablespoons vodka

  1 tablespoon dried lemongrass

  1/2 orange, grated zest of

  1 lemon, grated zest of

  1 lime, grated zest of

CURE THE SALMON: Place the salmon, skin-side down, on a large piece of plastic wrap and set aside. Toss together the remaining ingredients in a medium-sized bowl and spread them over the salmon, making sure all of the flesh is covered. Wrap tightly in plastic wrap and place in a shallow baking dish. Weight the salmon down with another baking dish or a plate, topped with about 3 one-pound cans; refrigerate for 48 hours. Unwrap salmon, brush off the spice mixture, and remove the skin using a thin sharp knife. Serve, thinly sliced, or rewrap the whole fillet in a fresh piece of plastic wrap and refrigerate for up to 1 week.

Nutrition information per 2-ounce serving—protein: 11.2 g; fat 3.6 g; carbohydrate: 1.6 g; fiber: 0; sodium: 824 mg; cholesterol: 31.2 mg; calories: 88.

DOUBLE-PESTO TERRINE

MAKES 8 SERVINGS

Pesto—a simple sauce made from fresh basil, garlic, pine nuts, Parmesan, and olive oil—was traditionally made using a mortar and pestle. New versions vary the herbs, which may be combined quickly in a food processor. Here, two types of pesto are layered between flavorful cheeses to create a colorful ribbon spread for crackers or bread.

BELL PEPPER PESTO:

1 yellow bell pepper, halved and seeded

2 cloves garlic, unpeeled

1 tablespoon extra-virgin olive oil

$1/4$ teaspoon salt

BASIL-SAGE PESTO:

1 cup fresh basil leaves

3 tablespoons pine nuts, toasted

2 tablespoons grated Parmesan cheese

2 tablespoons chopped fresh sage leaves

$1/8$ teaspoon salt

3 tablespoons extra-virgin olive oil

CHEESE FILLING:

1 8-ounce package cream cheese, softened

1 6-ounce log goat cheese, softened

1 tablespoon grated Parmesan cheese

$1/4$ teaspoon ground black pepper

$1/8$ teaspoon salt

Fresh basil leaves

Assorted crackers or slices of bread for serving

1 MAKE THE BELL PEPPER PESTO: Preheat oven to 425°F. Lightly coat a baking pan with vegetable oil cooking spray; add the bell pepper, cut side down, and the garlic. Roast in the oven, turning the pepper occasionally until charred on all sides—30 to 40 minutes. Place in a paper bag and let cool completely. Peel the charred skin off the pepper and remove the skin from the garlic. In a food processor fitted with the metal blade, process the pepper, garlic, oil, and salt until smooth. Transfer to a small bowl, cover, and refrigerate until ready to use.

2 MAKE THE BASIL-SAGE PESTO: In a food processor fitted with the metal blade, process the basil and pine nuts until well combined. Add the Parmesan, sage, and salt; process 30 seconds. With motor running, slowly add oil through the feed tube until smooth. Set aside.

3 MAKE THE CHEESE FILLING: In a medium bowl, stir together the cream cheese, goat cheese, Parmesan, pepper, and salt.

4 TO ASSEMBLE TERRINE: Sprinkle a 3- by 5-inch loaf pan with water. Line the pan completely with plastic wrap. Place the basil leaves to cover bottom of pan. Cover the basil leaves and bottom of the pan with $1/3$ of the cheese mixture. Spread the bell pepper pesto over the cheese mixture; top with $1/3$ layer of cheese mixture. Spread basil-sage pesto over cheese mixture and top with remaining $1/3$ cheese mixture. Cover tightly with plastic wrap and refrigerate several hours or overnight. To serve, invert pan onto a serving plate. Discard plastic wrap. Garnish with additional basil leaves.

Nutrition information per serving without crackers or bread—protein: 7 g; fat: 35 g; carbohydrate: 4 g; fiber: .8 g; sodium: 425 mg; cholesterol: 74 mg; calories: 354.

CHEESE CHOICES

What if you can't find the specific cheese called for in a recipe? Can you substitute another? Using a different cheese does alter the flavor of the finished dish, depending on what you substitute. For example, if a recipe calls for a melting cheese, such as mozzarella, the closest substitution would be another cheese whose melting quality is fairly similar, such as Fontina or Cheddar. If a recipe calls for an aged cheese, such as Gouda, use either Parmesan or Pecorino Romano. Aged Gouda is a slightly dry, complex cheese—very different in taste and texture than a young, creamy Gouda.

In the Fig and Brie Turnovers (see page 24) the possibilities abound-try a very different cheese, such as Maytag Blue or Stilton with great success, although the turnovers will have a bolder flavor than if made with Brie.

CUCUMBER CRUDITÉ DIP

Ready in minutes, this creamy dip is perfect for dunking sliced raw vegetables such as asparagus, carrot, endive, and jicama.

- 1 large seedless cucumber (about 20 ounces), peeled
- 1 teaspoon salt
- 1 8-ounce package cream cheese, softened
- 2 tablespoons sour cream
- 2 teaspoons chopped fresh thyme leaves plus sprigs (optional)
- 1 teaspoon grated lemon zest
- 1/4 teaspoon finely ground black pepper

MAKE THE DIP: In the bowl of a food processor fitted with a metal blade, combine the cucumber and salt. Process until the cucumber is pureed; strain the mixture through a fine strainer and set aside. In a small bowl, place the cream cheese, sour cream, thyme, zest, and pepper and stir until smooth. Add the pureed cucumber and stir to combine, cover, and refrigerate until ready to serve. Garnish with fresh thyme, if desired, and serve with fresh raw vegetables.

Nutrition information per tablespoon—protein: 1 g; fat: 3.6 g; carbohydrate: 1.5 g; fiber: .4 g; sodium: 359 mg; cholesterol: 10.9 mg; calories: 41.

FIG AND BRIE TURNOVERS

Great for eating out of hand, these flaky turnovers can also be made with your favorite kind of blue cheese.

- 1 tablespoon butter
- 2 medium onions, chopped (about 2 cups)
- 3/4 cup apple cider
- 1 tablespoon honey
- 3/4 cup dried figs, coarsely chopped
- 8 sheets phyllo dough, at room temperature
- 1/4 teaspoon ground black pepper
- 8 ounces Brie or blue cheese, cut into pieces

1 CARAMELIZE ONIONS: In a large nonstick skillet, melt the butter over medium heat. Add the onions and cook, stirring occasionally, until they are golden brown and caramelized—20 to 30 minutes. Set aside.

2 HYDRATE FIGS: In a small saucepan, combine cider and honey and bring to a boil. Remove pan from heat, add figs, and cover. Allow figs to hydrate until softened—about 1/2 hour. Drain and set aside.

3 MAKE THE TURNOVERS: Preheat oven to 350°F. Dampen a large dish towel. Remove phyllo from package and cover with dampened towel. Remove one sheet of dough, lay it on the work surface, and spray with cooking spray. Cover sprayed phyllo with a sheet of plastic wrap and press to allow the spray to penetrate the phyllo dough. Remove plastic wrap and lay another layer of phyllo over the sprayed piece. Repeat procedure using remaining 6 sheets of phyllo dough. Sprinkle dough evenly with black pepper. Cut the dough lengthwise (preferably with a pizza wheel) into 5 equal strips, then cut each strip in half horizontally. Place $1^{1}/2$ tablespoons cheese at the bottom of each strip, top with 2 teaspoons figs, then 1 tablespoon caramelized onion; fold each one into a triangle shape (as you would fold a flag). Repeat procedure with remaining phyllo strips. Transfer to a nonstick baking sheet and bake in the top third of the oven for 20 minutes or until top is lightly browned. Cool on a rack. Store in an airtight container until ready to serve.

Nutrition information per turnover—protein: 6.9 g; fat: 8.8 g; carbohydrate: 26 g; fiber: 2.4 g; sodium: 393 mg; cholesterol: 20 mg; calories: 207.

CHICKEN, DUCK, AND TURKEY

PRESERVED-LEMON CHICKEN > >

MAKES 4 SERVINGS

Salt, sugar, and slow cooking make lemons—rind and all—delicious in this dish as well as in other vegetable, meat, or fish dishes. Refrigerate unused preserved lemons for up to 2 months.

- 11 large lemons
- $1/2$ cup plus 2 tablespoons sea salt
- 1 tablespoon sugar
- $2/3$ cup plus 2 tablespoons fresh lemon juice
- 2 tablespoons olive oil
- $1/2$ teaspoon salt
- $1/4$ teaspoon ground black pepper
- 2 cloves garlic, minced
- $1/2$ teaspoon minced fresh oregano leaves
- $1/2$ teaspoon minced fresh thyme leaves
- 1 $3^{1}/2$-pound quartered chicken, rinsed, patted dry, and excess fat removed
- 15 cherry tomatoes
- 20 small green olives, such as picholine

1 MAKE THE PRESERVED LEMONS: Preheat oven to 300°F. Cut 9 lemons into 6 wedges each. In a medium-size oven-proof nonreactive baking dish, toss together lemon wedges, sea salt, sugar, and $2/3$ cup lemon juice. Cover the dish with foil and bake for $2^{1}/2$ hours. Remove from oven and cool completely. Reserve 12 wedges of preserved lemon. Store the remaining lemon wedges in the refrigerator for another use.

2 MAKE THE CHICKEN: Preheat oven to 450°F. Cut the reserved 12 preserved lemon wedges into $1/16$-inch-thick slices and set aside. Cut the 2 remaining fresh lemons into $1/2$-inch rounds. Coat a large ovenproof skillet with the olive oil and arrange the fresh lemon slices on the bottom of the skillet. Set aside. In a large bowl, mix together remaining lemon juice, salt, pepper, garlic, and herbs; add the chicken pieces and toss to coat well. Place the chicken pieces atop the lemon slices. Place the skillet on the middle shelf of the oven and roast for 30 minutes. Add the cherry tomatoes, green olives, and reserved preserved lemon wedges. Roast for 25 more minutes. Serve hot.

Nutrition information per serving—protein: 86.4 g; fat: 22 g; carbohydrate: 8.9 g; fiber: 2.2 g; sodium: 1,047 mg; cholesterol: 277 mg; calories: 588.

ROSEMARY-GARLIC CHICKEN

MAKES 6 MAIN-DISH SERVINGS

Olives, capers and rosemary add robust Mediterranean flavor to this easy one-dish, slow-cooked chicken-and-potato meal.

- 1 $5^{1}/2$-pound whole chicken, rinsed and patted dry
- $1^{1}/2$ teaspoons salt
- 1 teaspoon ground black pepper
- 20 cloves garlic, lightly crushed with the side of a knife
- 1 large yellow onion, cut into $1/2$-inch-thick rounds
- 1 pound small red potatoes (about 14), scrubbed and halved
- 1 tablespoon chopped fresh oregano leaves
- 1 teaspoon minced fresh rosemary leaves
- 1 cup small green olives, such as picholine, cracked
- $1/2$ cup fresh lemon juice

MAKE THE CHICKEN: Sprinkle the chicken skin and cavity with $1/2$ teaspoon salt and $1/2$ teaspoon pepper and place 10 garlic cloves inside. In a slow cooker, layer the onions and potatoes and sprinkle with the remaining salt, pepper, half of the oregano, and half of the rosemary. Place the chicken, breast-side down, on top of the potatoes and onions in the slow cooker. Sprinkle with the remaining rosemary and oregano. Add the olives, remaining garlic cloves, and lemon juice. Cover and cook on low for 6 hours. Pull meat from the bones and serve hot with the broth and vegetables.

Nutrition information per serving—protein: 92.5 g; fat: 18 g; carbohydrate: 19.4 g; fiber: 3 g; sodium: 1,766 mg; cholesterol: 291 mg; calories: 627.

COQ AU VIN BLANC

Traditionally, this classic French chicken recipe is made with red wine. We tried it with white wine with delicious results. Serve over rice or noodles, or with parslied new potatoes.

MARINADE:

3 cups dry white wine

1 medium onion, chopped (about 1 cup)

1 small carrot, sliced

1 stalk celery, sliced

3 cloves garlic, chopped

2 tablespoons olive oil

1–2 tablespoons loosely packed fresh
    flat-leaf parsley

8 whole black peppercorns

1/2 teaspoon salt

6 pounds assorted chicken pieces
    (thighs, breasts, drumsticks)

COQ AU VIN:

4 slices bacon, chopped

1 tablespoon olive oil

12 fresh or frozen small white onions,
    peeled

5 medium carrots, peeled and cut into
    1-inch chunks (about 2 cups)

2 stalks celery, sliced (about 1 cup)

3 cloves garlic, chopped

1 shallot, chopped

1/4 cup all-purpose flour

3 cups low-sodium chicken broth

1 tablespoon balsamic vinegar

1 bay leaf

1 teaspoon chopped fresh thyme leaves

1/2 teaspoon salt

1/4 teaspoon ground black pepper

1 pound small red potatoes, scrubbed

1 MARINATE THE CHICKEN: In a 3-quart saucepan, combine the white wine, onion, carrot, celery, garlic, oil, parsley, peppercorns, and salt. Bring to a boil over medium-high heat. Reduce heat to low and simmer 5 minutes. Remove pan from heat and let marinade cool to room temperature. In a large nonreactive container, arrange the chicken pieces and pour the cooled marinade over them. Cover and refrigerate at least 4 hours or overnight.

2 BROWN THE CHICKEN: Remove the chicken from the marinade and pat dry. Strain the marinade and reserve liquid; discard the vegetables. In a 6-quart heavy kettle or Dutch oven, cook the bacon over medium heat until crisp. Using a slotted spoon, transfer the bacon to paper towels. Brown the chicken parts in bacon drippings in the Dutch oven. Remove chicken from the Dutch oven and discard all but 1 tablespoon fat. Add the olive oil and white onions; sauté onions until lightly browned—8 to 10 minutes. Add the carrots, celery, garlic, and shallot; sauté 5 minutes longer.

3 BRAISE THE CHICKEN: In a medium bowl, combine the reserved marinade liquid and the flour. Add mixture to the Dutch oven along with the chicken broth, vinegar, bay leaf, thyme, salt, and pepper. Return the chicken to the Dutch oven and cook, covered, for 45 minutes. Add the potatoes and cook until fork-tender—about 20 minutes more. Divide the mixture evenly among six serving bowls. Garnish each serving with reserved chopped bacon.

Nutrition information per serving—protein: 61 g; fat: 24 g; carbohydrate: 41 g; fiber: 5 g; sodium: 1,096 mg; cholesterol: 176 mg; calories: 708.

CHICKEN POTPIE

MAKES 6 SERVINGS

To cook this one-pot meal, you can use any 9-inch ovenproof skillet or dish.

- 1 tablespoon vegetable oil
- 3/4 pound boneless, skinless chicken thighs, cut into 1 1/2-inch pieces
- 3/4 pound boneless, skinless chicken breasts, cut into 1 1/2-inch pieces
- 1 cup frozen pearl onions, thawed
- 1 cup thinly sliced carrots
- 1/3 cup thinly sliced celery
- 1 1/2 cups frozen peas
- 1 14 1/2-ounce can low-sodium chicken broth
- 3/4 cup milk
- 1/3 cup all-purpose flour
- 3/4 teaspoon salt
- 1/2 teaspoon poultry seasoning
- 1/4 teaspoon ground black pepper
- Flaky Piecrust (recipe follows) or 1/2 15-ounce package refrigerated piecrust

1 MAKE THE CHICKEN: In a large saucepan, heat the oil over medium heat. Add the chicken thighs and cook 2 minutes. Add the chicken breasts and pearl onions; sauté until chicken has cooked through and onions are lightly browned—5 to 7 minutes. Using a slotted spoon, transfer the chicken and onions to a plate and set the mixture aside. Heat the oven to 425°F

2 MAKE THE SAUCE: Add the carrots and the celery to saucepan; sauté vegetables until slightly softened—about 5 minutes. Stir in the peas and chicken broth. Bring mixture to a boil; reduce heat to low, cover, and simmer 5 minutes. In a 2-cup liquid measure, stir together milk, flour, salt, poultry seasoning, and pepper. Slowly whisk milk mixture into saucepan. Stir until thickened. (If mixture starts to seize, add a small amount of water.) Stir in the reserved chicken and onions.

3 MAKE THE PIE: Spoon chicken and vegetable mixture into 9-inch round baking dish or cast-iron skillet. Top with piecrust and cut slits to allow steam to escape. Bake until crust is golden and filling is bubbly—20 to 25 minutes. Let cool slightly and serve in dish.

Nutrition information per serving—protein: 31 g; fat: 17 g; carbohydrate: 32 g; fiber: 4 g; sodium: 769 mg; cholesterol: 87 mg; calories: 402.

FLAKY PIECRUST

MAKES 1 SINGLE 9-INCH CRUST

If you have the time to make piecrust from scratch, here's a recipe you may want to use for our Chicken Potpie as well as for any sweet filling.

- 1 1/2 cups unsifted all-purpose flour
- 1/2 teaspoon salt
- 1/2 cup vegetable shortening
- 4–5 tablespoons ice water

1 MAKE THE CRUST: In a medium bowl, combine the flour and salt. Using a pastry blender or 2 knives, cut the shortening into the dry ingredients until mixture resembles very coarse crumbs. Add cold water, 1 tablespoon at a time, mixing lightly with fork, until pastry is moist enough to hold together in a flattened ball. Wrap ball in waxed paper and refrigerate until chilled—about 30 minutes.

2 BAKE THE CRUST: Between 2 sheets of floured waxed paper, roll out the chilled pastry to an 11-inch round. Remove top sheet of waxed paper and invert crust over filling. Remove remaining sheet of waxed paper and trim excess pastry to fit baking dish. Bake as directed in Step 4 of Chicken Potpie recipe.

SPICY SOUTHERN-FRIED CHICKEN

< <

MAKES 8 SERVINGS

A buttermilk marinade tenderizes the chicken and helps create a crisp, flaky crust as it fries.

- 2 cups buttermilk
- 1 tablespoon Dijon mustard
- 1 teaspoon salt
- 1 teaspoon dry mustard
- 1 teaspoon ground red pepper
- 1 teaspoon cracked black pepper
- 1 3½-pound chicken, cut into 8 pieces
- 2 cups all-purpose flour
- 1 tablespoon baking powder
- 1 tablespoon garlic powder
- ½ teaspoon salt
- 5 cups vegetable shortening

1 MAKE THE BUTTERMILK MARINADE: In a gallon-size sealable plastic bag or a large bowl with a tight-fitting lid, combine the buttermilk, mustard, salt, dry mustard, red pepper, and black pepper. Add the chicken pieces and turn to coat. Seal and refrigerate for at least 2 hours or overnight.

2 MAKE THE CHICKEN: Preheat oven to 150°F. In a 13- by 9- by 2-inch pan, whisk together flour, baking powder, dry garlic, and salt. Add chicken pieces and turn to coat thickly. Let the chicken stand 10 minutes, turning occasionally to recoat with flour. Shake off excess flour before frying.

3 FRY THE CHICKEN: In a 10- by 12-inch heavy-gauge skillet with a deep-fry thermometer attached, heat the vegetable shortening over medium-high heat, bringing it to 375°F. In batches of four, fry the chicken pieces, turning once when the coating is sealed and begins to brown—3 to 4 minutes. Reduce the heat to medium to lower the temperature to 325°F. Maintain temperature and continue to fry, turning the pieces halfway through cooking time until chicken is golden brown and cooked through—about 20 more minutes. Transfer to a wire rack on a baking sheet and place in oven to keep warm. Repeat the procedure for the remaining batches. Serve warm or at room temperature.

Nutrition information per serving—protein: 39 g; fat: 19 g; carbohydrate: 14 g; fiber: 8 g; sodium: 597 mg; cholesterol: 119 mg; calories: 389.

CHICKEN-TOMATILLO CHILI

MAKES SIX 1-CUP SERVINGS

If you would like to make your own tortilla chips, simply brush either flour or corn tortillas lightly with olive oil, cut into strips or wedges, and bake on a nonstick baking sheet at 400°F for 5 to 7 minutes.

- 1 11-ounce can tomatillos, or 7 or 8 fresh tomatillos, husked and quartered
- 1 jalapeño pepper, halved and seeded
- 2 tablespoons vegetable oil
- 2 pounds boneless, skinless chicken thighs, cut into 1-inch pieces
- 1 medium onion, chopped (about 1 cup)
- 3 cloves garlic, minced
- 2 4½-ounce cans diced green chilies
- 2 teaspoons ground cumin
- 1 teaspoon ground coriander seeds
- 2 14½-ounce cans low-sodium chicken broth
- ½ cup chopped fresh cilantro leaves
- 1 teaspoon salt
- Tortilla chips or strips (optional)

1 MAKE THE FLAVOR PASTE: In a blender or food processor fitted with a metal blade, combine tomatillos and jalapeños. Blend until thick and smooth—about 1 minute. Set aside.

2 BROWN THE CHICKEN: In a large Dutch oven, add oil and heat over medium- high heat. Once oil is hot, add the chicken and cook until browned—3 to 4 minutes. Remove and set aside.

3 MAKE THE CHILI: Add onion to Dutch oven and sauté until translucent—about 3 minutes. Add garlic, sauté 1 minute, and then add the chicken, chilies, cumin, coriander, broth, and flavor paste. Bring to a boil and reduce heat to low. Simmer uncovered for 45 minutes.

4 TO SERVE: Stir in cilantro and salt. Serve hot with tortilla chips, if desired.

Nutrition information per serving without tortilla chips— protein: 32.2 g; fat: 17.3 g; carbohydrate: 9.6 g; fiber: 2.8 g; sodium: 541 mg; cholesterol: 105 mg; calories: 320.

CURRIED CHICKEN QUESADILLAS WITH PINEAPPLE SALSA AND PEANUT SAUCE

MAKES 8 SERVINGS

We used both jalapeño- and roasted-red-pepper-flavored tortillas, but feel free to substitute your favorite.

1 whole chicken breast (about 1 pound)

1 tablespoon olive oil

DRY RUB:

1/8 teaspoon ground black pepper

1/4 teaspoon salt

1 teaspoon curry powder

1/2 teaspoon ground cumin

MARINATED ONIONS:

1/4 cup thinly sliced red onion

1 tablespoon fresh lime juice

1/4 teaspoon salt

PINEAPPLE SALSA:

1 cup chopped fresh pineapple

1 small jalapeño pepper, seeded and minced

2 tablespoons chopped fresh cilantro leaves

1 shallot, minced

1 tablespoon fresh lime juice

1/4 teaspoon ground coriander seeds

1/4 teaspoon ground black pepper

1/4 teaspoon salt

PEANUT SAUCE:

1/2 cup coconut milk

1 teaspoon tomato paste

1/8 teaspoon hot pepper sauce

1/2 teaspoon garlic powder

1 teaspoon grated peeled fresh ginger

1/2 cup chunky peanut butter

1 tablespoon pure maple syrup

1 teaspoon soy sauce

1 teaspoon fresh lemon juice

4 8-inch flavored flour tortillas

1 COOK THE CHICKEN: Preheat oven to 375°F. Place chicken breast between sheets of waxed paper and pound to an even 1/2-inch thickness. Combine pepper, salt, curry powder, and cumin and rub into the breast. In a large saucepan, heat oil over medium-high heat and sauté chicken until golden—about 3 minutes; turn and cook the second side until golden. Transfer to a cutting board and shred with two forks.

2 MAKE THE ONIONS: In a small bowl, toss onion with lime juice and salt. Set aside.

3 MAKE THE PINEAPPLE SALSA: In a medium bowl, toss pineapple, jalapeño, cilantro, shallots, lime juice, coriander, pepper, and salt. Set aside.

4 MAKE THE PEANUT SAUCE: In a medium saucepan, combine coconut milk, tomato paste, hot pepper sauce, garlic powder, ginger, peanut butter, maple syrup, soy sauce, and lemon juice. Cook, stirring, until thick—about 10 minutes. Add water if too thick to spread.

5 ASSEMBLE AND BAKE QUESADILLAS: Arrange two tortillas on a baking sheet. Spread each with peanut sauce, then sprinkle with shredded chicken. Top each one with 2 tablespoons pineapple salsa and half the onions. Add second tortilla to cover and bake until lightly browned—about 5 minutes. Transfer to a cutting board and cut each into 4 wedges. Serve warm or at room temperature.

Nutrition information per serving—protein: 9.5 g; fat: 15 g; carbohydrate: 20 g; fiber: 2.3 g; sodium: 349 mg; cholesterol: 8.6 mg; calories: 244.

CHICKEN-MANCHEGO EMPANADAS

MAKES ABOUT 20 EMPANADAS

1½ cups plus 2 teaspoons all-purpose flour

¼ cup cornmeal

1 teaspoon salt

9 tablespoons cold butter, cut into small pieces

1 large boneless, skinless, chicken breast half (about ¾ pound)

1 tablespoon extra-virgin olive oil

½ teaspoon ground black pepper

1 cup finely shredded Manchego cheese (4 ounces)

1 4-ounce jar roasted red peppers, drained and diced

1 large egg, beaten

1 MAKE THE DOUGH: In a food processor fitted with the metal blade, combine the flour, cornmeal, and ½ teaspoon salt. Add the butter and pulse until the mixture resembles coarse meal. Add 1 tablespoon cold water and continue adding by the teaspoon until a rough dough forms. Shape the dough into a disk, wrap in plastic wrap, and refrigerate for 1 hour.

2 MAKE THE FILLING: Preheat grill to medium heat. Toss chicken, olive oil, remaining salt, and pepper together in a small bowl and grill chicken until cooked through—about 10 minutes per side. Transfer to a plate and let cool. Dice the chicken and place in a large bowl. Stir in the cheese and peppers and set aside.

3 MAKE THE EMPANADAS: Preheat oven to 375°F. Line a baking sheet with parchment paper and set aside. Combine the egg with 1 tablespoon water and set aside. On a lightly floured surface, roll the dough out to about ⅛-inch thickness and, using a 3½-inch round cutter, cut out rounds. Gather the scraps, reroll the dough, cut out rounds, and continue until all the dough is used. Fill each round with about 2 tablespoons of filling, fold in half, and crimp with the tines of a fork to seal. Transfer empanadas to the prepared baking sheet and brush with the prepared egg wash. Bake empanadas until golden brown—about 20 minutes. Serve warm.

Nutrition information per empanada—protein: 5.7 g; fat: 10.9 g; carbohydrate: 11.8 g; fiber: .6 g; sodium: 216 mg; cholesterol: 45.3 mg; calories: 170.

WALDORF CHICKEN SALAD SANDWICHES

MAKES 4 SANDWICHES

A little more than a century ago, Chef Oscar Tschirky, of New York City's Waldorf-Astoria Hotel, created a sensational salad using nothing more than apples, celery, and mayonnaise. We've updated his invention to include chicken and the intriguing flavor of tarragon.

1½ pounds boneless, skinless chicken breast halves

½ small onion

5 whole black peppercorns

¾ teaspoon salt

¼ cup mayonnaise

2 tablespoons extra-virgin olive oil

2 tablespoons tarragon vinegar

1 tablespoon Dijon mustard

2 teaspoons chopped fresh tarragon leaves

½ teaspoon ground black pepper

1 large apple, peeled, cored, and cut into ½-inch pieces

⅓ cup diced celery

⅓ cup chopped pecans, toasted

2 10-inch-long baguettes

4 large leaves red leaf lettuce

1 MAKE THE CHICKEN: In a 3-quart saucepan, combine chicken, onion, peppercorns, and ½ teaspoon salt with enough cold water to cover. Bring to a simmer over medium heat. Reduce heat to low and simmer until chicken has cooked through—15 to 18 minutes. Drain and set aside until chicken is cool enough to touch. Discard onion and peppercorns.

2 MAKE THE DRESSING: In a medium bowl, combine mayonnaise, olive oil, vinegar, mustard, tarragon, pepper, and the remaining ¼ teaspoon salt.

3 MAKE THE CHICKEN SALAD: Chop chicken into ½-inch pieces and toss with tarragon dressing. Add apple, celery, and pecans; toss to combine.

4 MAKE THE SANDWICHES: Slice baguettes lengthwise and place lettuce on bottom halves. Top with chicken salad, cover with baguette, and cut each baguette in half to make four sandwiches.

Nutrition information per sandwich—protein: 44 g; fat: 28 g; carbohydrate: 30 g; fiber: 3 g; sodium: 583 mg; cholesterol: 106 mg; calories: 551.

LOUISVILLE HOT BROWN

MAKES 6 SANDWICHES

Early versions of this open-face Kentucky original were made with country ham.

2 tablespoons butter

2 tablespoons all-purpose flour

1$\frac{1}{2}$ cups milk

1 cup shredded mild white Cheddar cheese (4 ounces)

$\frac{1}{4}$ cup grated Parmesan cheese

1$\frac{1}{2}$ tablespoons Dijon mustard

$\frac{1}{2}$ teaspoon hot pepper sauce

$\frac{1}{2}$ teaspoon salt

3 thick slices bacon

6 slices Italian ciabatta or other rustic bread, toasted

$\frac{1}{2}$ pound sliced roast turkey breast

1 large tomato, sliced

$\frac{1}{8}$ teaspoon ground black pepper

1 MAKE THE CHEESE SAUCE: In a 2-quart saucepan, melt the butter over medium heat. Add the flour and cook the mixture, stirring constantly, for 3 minutes. Add the milk and continue to stir. Increase heat to medium-high and bring the mixture to a boil. Cook for 1 more minute. Remove saucepan from the heat and whisk in the cheeses, mustard, hot pepper sauce, and salt. Cover and keep warm.

2 COOK THE BACON: In a large skillet, cook the bacon over high heat until crisp and browned—4 to 6 minutes. Transfer the bacon to a paper towel to drain. When bacon is cool, crumble or coarsely chop and set aside.

3 MAKE THE SANDWICHES: Preheat the oven broiler. In a large ovenproof dish, arrange the toasted bread slices and layer them with the turkey and tomato slices. Sprinkle with pepper and spoon the cheese sauce on top. Place the sandwiches under the broiler and cook until the sauce begins to brown lightly—2 to 3 minutes. Remove from oven, sprinkle with bacon, and serve immediately.

Nutrition information per sandwich—protein: 24.5 g; fat: 17 g; carbohydrate: 23.3 g; fiber: 1.1 g; sodium: 737 mg; cholesterol: 78.2 mg; calories: 347.

CLUBHOUSE SANDWICH > >

MAKES 4 SANDWICHES

Diced roast turkey or chopped fresh-cooked shrimp can easily be swapped for the chicken in this club sandwich variation.

6 stalks celery

2 medium onions

4 sprigs fresh parsley

1 teaspoon salt

$\frac{3}{4}$ teaspoon ground black pepper

2 pounds chicken pieces (breast and thighs)

1 cup mayonnaise

2 tablespoons thinly sliced green onion

1 tablespoon chopped fresh tarragon leaves

1 tablespoon fresh lemon juice

8 slices bacon

12 slices white bread, toasted

2 medium tomatoes, sliced

4 lettuce leaves

1 COOK THE CHICKEN: Cut 3 celery stalks and the onions into large pieces. In a 4-quart saucepan, combine 2 quarts water, celery pieces, onions, parsley, $\frac{1}{2}$ teaspoon salt, and $\frac{1}{2}$ teaspoon pepper and bring to a boil. Reduce heat to medium, add chicken, and simmer until chicken is cooked through—about 25 minutes. Remove chicken and allow to cool.

2 MAKE THE CHICKEN SALAD: Remove the chicken meat from the bones and discard the skin and bones. Chop or shred the chicken into bite-size pieces. Dice the remaining celery into $\frac{1}{4}$-inch pieces. In a medium bowl, combine chicken, mayonnaise, green onion, tarragon, diced celery, lemon juice, and remaining salt and pepper. Cover and refrigerate 4 hours or overnight.

3 COOK THE BACON: In a large skillet, cook the bacon over medium-high heat until crisp and brown—4 to 6 minutes. Transfer bacon to a paper towel to drain.

4 ASSEMBLE THE SANDWICHES: On a work surface, place 4 slices of toasted bread and spread $\frac{1}{2}$ cup of chicken salad on each. Add another slice of toast and place 2 slices bacon, 2 slices tomato, and a lettuce leaf on each sandwich. Place the remaining slices of toast on top of sandwiches, cut into quarters, and secure with a toothpick.

Nutrition information per sandwich—protein: 61.1 g; fat: 74.3 g; carbohydrate: 55.2 g; fiber: 4.8 g; sodium: 1,681 mg; cholesterol: 191 mg; calories: 1,134.

BLUEBERRY CHUTNEY-GLAZED DUCK BREAST

MAKES 4 SERVINGS

Slightly acidic blueberry chutney adds a tartness that complements the rich flavor of the duck.

- ½ teaspoon cracked black pepper
- ½ teaspoon salt
- 1 tablespoon dried thyme
- 4 6-ounce duck breast halves
- ½ cup Blueberry Chutney
  (recipe follows)

1 MAKE THE DUCK BREASTS: In a small bowl, combine pepper, salt, and thyme and rub evenly over duck breasts. Score duck breast's skin with a sharp knife in a crosshatch pattern.

2 COOK THE DUCK BREASTS: Heat a large, heavy skillet over high heat. When skillet is hot, place duck breasts skin side down and sear until deep golden brown—about 4 minutes. Reduce heat to medium low and cook 2 more minutes. Turn breasts over and spread 2 tablespoons of chutney on each breast. Cook breasts to medium rare (165˚F)—about 9 minutes. Place on a cutting board and let rest for 5 minutes. Slice breasts on an angle and fan onto warmed dinner plates. Serve with additional Blueberry Chutney.

Nutrition information per serving—protein: 34.4 g; fat: 7.5 g; carbohydrate: 11.4 g; fiber: 1.1 g; sodium: 436 mg; cholesterol: 131 mg; calories: 257.

BLUEBERRY CHUTNEY

MAKES 2 CUPS

Lightly spiced with tarragon, red pepper, and cardamom, this versatile chutney works well as a glaze on pork and poultry.

- ½ cup thinly sliced, shallots
- 1 clove garlic, mined
- ½ orange (including zest), cut into thin strips and seeded
- 4 cups fresh blueberries
- ½ cup balsamic vinegar
- ⅓ cup packed dark brown sugar
- 1 tablespoon chopped fresh or 1 teaspoon dried tarragon leaves
- ½ teaspoon crushed red pepper
- ½ teaspoon ground cardamom
- ½ teaspoon salt

MAKE THE CHUTNEY: In a large nonstick saucepan over high heat, cook shallots and garlic for 1 minute. Add orange, blueberries, vinegar, sugar, tarragon, red pepper, cardamom, and salt and bring to a boil. Reduce heat to medium low and simmer, stirring occasionally, until thickened—about 50 minutes. Pour chutney into a pint jar. Cover and store in the refrigerator for up to 1 month.

Nutrition information per 2-tablespoon serving—protein: .4 g; fat: .1 g; carbohydrate: 10.6 g; fiber: .9 g; sodium: 71.8 mg; cholesterol: 0; calories: 44.

BUTTER-BASTED ROAST TURKEY WITH MUSHROOM GRAVY

MAKES 8 SERVINGS

Wild mushrooms make a richer–tasting gravy than the domestic. Use any combination of cremini, oyster, and hen of the woods mushrooms, so long as you have $1/2$ pound in all.

2$1/2$ cups plus 2 tablespoons low-sodium chicken broth

1 cup (2 sticks) unsalted butter

2 teaspoons salt

1$1/4$ teaspoons ground black pepper

2 sprigs plus 1 teaspoon fresh thyme leaves

1 sprig fresh rosemary

1 bay leaf

1 12-pound fresh turkey, rinsed inside and out and patted dry

6 carrots, peeled and cut into 2-inch pieces

3 medium onions, peeled and quartered

$1/2$ cup dry red wine

$1/2$ pound assorted wild mushrooms (such as cremini, shitake, and oyster), sliced

1 teaspoon minced fresh sage leaves

1 tablespoon cornstarch

1 tablespoon fresh lemon juice

1 MAKE THE BASTING LIQUID: Combine 1 cup chicken broth, the butter, $1/2$ teaspoon salt, $1/2$ teaspoon pepper, thyme sprigs, rosemary, and bay leaf in a small saucepan over medium heat. Once the butter melts, reduce the heat to low and keep the mixture warm.

2 PREPARE THE TURKEY: Preheat oven to 325°F. Season the turkey cavity and skin with 1 teaspoon salt and $1/2$ teaspoon pepper. Truss the turkey and place breast side up in a roasting pan fitted with a wire rack. Arrange the carrots and onions around the bottom of the pan, place in the oven, and roast for 30 minutes. Baste the turkey with the basting liquid, covering all surfaces. Continue to roast, basting every 30 minutes, until a thermometer inserted into the thigh meat reads 175°F—about 3 hours. Remove the turkey from oven, reserve pan drippings, and let rest 30 minutes before carving.

3 MAKE THE GRAVY: Pour the drippings and solids from the roasting pan into a measuring cup. Skim off any fat, reserving 2 tablespoons. Return the drippings and the solids to the pan and place over medium-high heat. Stirring constantly, add the red wine and cook until any bits of vegetable or meat are loosened from the bottom of the pan—about 2 minutes. Strain, discard solids, and set aside. In a large saucepan, heat the reserved fat over medium-high heat and sauté the mushrooms until cooked through—about 8 minutes. Add the strained drippings, 1$1/2$ cups chicken broth, 1 teaspoon thyme, sage, and remaining salt and pepper. Cook over medium heat until slightly reduced—about 10 minutes. In a small bowl, combine the remaining chicken broth and cornstarch and stir until the cornstarch is dissolved. Stir the cornstarch mixture into the gravy and continue to cook until slightly thickened about 2 minutes. Stir in the fresh lemon juice and serve warm.

Nutrition information per serving—protein: 68.4 g; fat: 27 g; carbohydrate: 4.2 g; fiber: .8 g; sodium: 692 mg; cholesterol: 213 mg; calories: 554.

THE LANGUAGE OF POULTRY

Knowing what these terms mean will make you a better-informed consumer when selecting poultry.

> Fresh—A bird labeled "fresh" is refrigerated at a temperature above 26°F, so its flesh remains supple.

> Frozen—A frozen bird is kept at a temperature below 0°F and is rock solid.

> Free-range—Poultry must be allowed access to the outside to be labeled free-range.

> Natural—According to USDA standards, "natural poultry must be minimally processed with no artificial additives or preservatives."

> Organic—The USDA defines "organic meat" as meat from animals that are given no antibiotics or growth hormones and are fed organic feed.

> Kosher—Kosher poultry is salted, which seasons the meat and draws out the blood. It is then rinsed and processed. Koshering is done under strict rabbinical supervision.

MAPLE-GLAZED TURKEY DRUMSTICKS > >

MAKES 4 SERVINGS

Drumsticks roast in about a third of the time it takes to roast a whole turkey. The simple mix of maple syrup, hot mustard, and Worcestershire sauce used for basting creates a sensational sweet-hot glaze.

- 1/4 cup maple syrup
- 2 teaspoons prepared hot mustard
- 1 tablespoon Worcestershire sauce
- 1/2 teaspoon salt
- 1/8 teaspoon ground red pepper
- 2 1 1/4-pound turkey drumsticks, rinsed and patted dry
- 1/2 teaspoon ground black pepper
- 1 medium onion, cut into 1/4-inch-thick slices
- 2 tablespoons unsalted butter, cut into pieces

1 MAKE THE SAUCE: Preheat oven to 400°F. In a small bowl, combine maple syrup, mustard, Worcestershire sauce, 1/4 teaspoon salt, and ground red pepper. Set aside.

2 ROAST THE TURKEY: Season the turkey legs with remaining salt and the black pepper. Place the onions on the bottom of a roasting pan and put the turkey legs on top. Dot the turkey with butter and roast for 30 minutes. Brush turkey legs with the prepared sauce and reduce oven temperature to 325°F. Continue to roast, basting with the sauce every 20 minutes, until meat is very tender—about 90 more minutes. Serve hot or at room temperature.

Nutrition information per serving—protein: 39.8 g; fat: 19.6 g; carbohydrate: 7.7 g; fiber: .15 g; sodium: 371 mg; cholesterol: 143 mg; calories: 374.

CRANBERRY-PEAR WILD RICE STUFFING

MAKES 10 CUPS

Cooking the wild rice and storing it in the refrigerator (for up to 2 days) relieves you of this duty on the big day.

- 5 tablespoons butter
- 6 slices stale white bread, crumbled into small pieces
- 4 cups cooked wild rice
- 1 cup coarsely chopped hazelnuts
- 1 cup dried cranberries
- 1/2 cup finely chopped shallots
- 4 firm-ripe pears, peeled, cored, and cut into 3/4-inch pieces
- 2 teaspoons dried savory
- 1/2 cup finely chopped fresh parsley
- 1/2 teaspoon salt
- 1 teaspoon cracked black pepper
- 2 large eggs, beaten
- 1 cup apple cider

1 MAKE THE STUFFING: Preheat the oven to 350°F. Coat an 8 1/2- by 11-inch baking dish with 1 tablespoon butter. Combine the bread, wild rice, hazelnuts, and cranberries in a large bowl and toss to mix. In a large skillet, melt 4 tablespoons butter and sauté shallots and pears over medium heat until golden—about 10 minutes. Add savory, parsley, salt, and pepper and continue to cook—about 2 minutes. Pour the butter mixture over the bread mixture and toss well. Transfer the stuffing to the prepared pan and press down to compact.

2 BAKE THE STUFFING: Mix the eggs and apple cider together and pour over the stuffing mixture. Cover with foil and bake for 30 minutes. Remove the foil and continue to bake until brown—about 15 more minutes. Serve hot alongside roasted turkey and gravy.

Nutrition information per 1/2-cup serving—protein: 3.9 g; fat: 7.6 g; carbohydrate: 25.4 g; fiber: 2.6 g; sodium: 102 mg; cholesterol: 26.5 mg; calories: 176.

ROASTED APPLE TURKEY WITH APPLE BRANDY GRAVY

MAKES 8 SERVINGS

See our tips for roasting a turkey on the opposite page.

- 1 12- to 14-pound turkey
- 5 sweet medium apples, such as Rome Beauty or Jonathan (about 1$\frac{1}{2}$ pounds), peeled and quartered
- 3 medium onions, quartered
- $\frac{1}{2}$ bunch fresh parsley (about 20 sprigs)
- 2 bay leaves
- $\frac{1}{4}$ cup ($\frac{1}{2}$ stick) unsalted butter, melted
- 1 tablespoon ground black pepper
- 1 tablespoon all-purpose flour
- $\frac{1}{2}$ cup apple brandy
- $\frac{1}{2}$ cup low-sodium chicken broth

1 ROAST THE TURKEY: Preheat oven to 450°F. Stuff the turkey with 2 apples, 1 onion, 5 sprigs of parsley, and the bay leaves. Using kitchen twine, truss the turkey and place it breast side up in a roasting pan fitted with a wire rack. Arrange the remaining apples and onions around the bottom of the pan. In a small saucepan, melt 3 tablespoons butter. Stir in the pepper and brush the mixture over all surfaces of the turkey to ensure even browning. Place turkey in lower third of oven and roast for 30 minutes. Reduce heat to 325°F and continue to roast, basting with the pan drippings every 30 minutes, until a thermometer inserted into the thigh meat (do not touch bone) reads 175°F—about 1$\frac{1}{2}$ hours. Remove the turkey from the oven, reserving the pan drippings, apples, and onions, and let rest for 20 minutes before carving.

2 MAKE THE GRAVY: Separate the reserved roasted apples and onions from the turkey pan drippings and set aside. Skim the top fat layer from the turkey drippings and discard; measure 1 cup drippings and set aside. In a large saucepan, melt the remaining butter over medium-high heat. Stir in flour and continue to cook until slightly thickened—about 1 minute. Add the roasted apples and onions and cook for 1 more minute. Add the drippings, brandy, and broth and continue to cook until the liquids thicken slightly—3 to 4 minutes. Strain and keep warm. Serve with the turkey and Whipped Root Vegetables and Potatoes (see page 116).

Nutrition information per 8-ounce serving of turkey—protein: 63.7 g; fat: 20.6 g; carbohydrate: 0; fiber: 0; sodium: 163 mg; cholesterol: 186 mg; calories: 458.

Nutrition information per 1/4 cup serving of gravy—protein: 8 g; fat: 2.1 g; carbohydrate: 18 g; fiber: 2.4 g; sodium: 64 mg; cholesterol: 4.2 mg; calories: 118

SOURDOUGH MUSHROOM STUFFING

MAKES 11 CUPS

- 3 tablespoons unsalted butter
- 1 pound assorted wild mushrooms (such as cremini, shiitake, or oyster), sliced
- 3 cups chopped celery (about 9 stalks)
- 2 cups finely chopped onions (about 2 medium)
- $\frac{1}{2}$ cup chopped fresh flat-leaf parsley
- 1 tablespoon chopped fresh thyme leaves
- 1 tablespoon chopped fresh sage leaves
- 1 teaspoon chopped fresh rosemary leaves
- 2 teaspoons salt
- 1 teaspoon ground black pepper
- 1 1-pound loaf sourdough bread, cut into 1-inch cubes
- 1$\frac{1}{2}$ cups low-sodium chicken broth

MAKE THE STUFFING: Preheat oven to 350°F. Coat a 3-quart casserole dish with 1 tablespoon butter and set aside. In a large saucepan, melt remaining butter over medium-high heat. Add the mushrooms and sauté for 10 minutes. Add the celery and onion and sauté for 10 more minutes. Remove from heat, add the remaining ingredients, and toss to combine. Transfer the stuffing to the prepared baking dish and cover with aluminum foil. Bake, covered, for 45 minutes, remove the foil, and bake for 20 more minutes. Serve hot.

Nutrition information per 1-cup serving—protein: 5.7 g; fat: 5 g; carbohydrate: 27.9 g; fiber: 3 g; sodium: 687 mg; cholesterol: 9.2 mg; calories: 174.

CORNISH HENS WITH WILD RICE STUFFING

MAKES 4 SERVINGS

A prepackaged blend of rice that includes both brown and wild rice will work best for the stuffing. Chinese five-spice powder, which consists of equal parts of ground cinnamon, cloves, star anise, fennel, and peppercorns, is available in the spice section of most supermarkets.

3/4 cup wild-rice blend

2 tablespoons butter

1 tablespoon vegetable oil

1 medium onion, chopped

1/2 cup chopped fresh fennel
    (1/2 small bulb)

1/2 cup mixed dried fruit, diced

1/4 cup chopped pecans, toasted

5 tablespoons maple syrup
    (grade B, if available)

2 tablespoons chopped fresh parsley

2 tablespoons plus 2 teaspoons
    soy sauce

1 teaspoon grated orange zest

3/4 teaspoon salt

1/2 teaspoon ground cinnamon

1/4 teaspoon ground black pepper

1/4 teaspoon Chinese five-spice powder

4 1 1/4 pound Cornish hens

1 tablespoon orange juice

1 MAKE THE RICE: Cook rice according to package directions and set aside.

2 MAKE THE RICE STUFFING: In a large skillet, heat 1 tablespoon butter and the oil over medium heat. Add onion and fennel; sauté until softened and lightly browned—5 to 7 minutes. Stir in dried fruit, pecans, 2 tablespoons maple syrup, parsley, 2 teaspoons soy sauce, the orange zest, salt, cinnamon, black pepper, and five-spice powder. Cook until liquid has been absorbed—10 to 15 minutes. Remove from heat. Stir in rice mixture and let cool completely.

3 MAKE THE CORNISH HENS: Heat oven to 375°F. Remove giblets from Cornish hens; wash and pat dry. Stuff hens lightly with wild-rice mixture. Put any remaining mixture in a baking dish. Using kitchen twine, crisscross drumsticks and tie together, if desired. Place hens on a wire rack set in a roasting pan.

4 MAKE THE GLAZE: In a 1-quart saucepan, combine remaining 3 tablespoons maple syrup, 2 tablespoons soy sauce, 1 tablespoon butter, and the orange juice; cook over medium-high heat until butter melts and mixture thickens.

5 FINISH THE CORNISH HENS: Brush mixture onto hens and place in oven. Roast 1 hour. Place remaining wild-rice mixture in oven with hens. Cook until a meat thermometer inserted into thickest part of thigh registers 180°F and rice is heated through—about 30 minutes more. Let cool 10 minutes and serve.

Nutrition information per serving—protein: 70 g; fat: 24 g; carbohydrate: 41 g; fiber: 4 g; sodium: 698 mg; cholesterol: 234 mg; calories: 667.

ROAST TURKEY REVISITED

There are almost as many methods for roasting turkey as there are birds to be roasted. We recommend trussing a bird and roasting it breast-side up. This is the most straightforward roasting method. Some recipes call for turning the bird for even cooking, but this is not an easy task when roasting a large turkey. Trussing, skewering, or tying the wings and legs with kitchen twine prevents them from sticking out during cooking. And, creating a compact shape helps prevent the legs and wings from drying out before the breast meat is cooked. The neck opening and body cavity can be sewn closed to help to keep the stuffing inside, if you like. It is a good idea to use a rack because it lifts the bird off the bottom of the roasting pan, thereby promoting even roasting of the entire bird and guaranteeing crisp skin. Lastly, basting promotes even browning, thereby ensuring an impressive-looking bird.

CORNISH HENS BAKED IN SALT DOUGH   < <

When these little hens are baked, the crust seals the bird, keeping all the luscious juices inside and making the meat very flavorful. The crust is just for cooking and should be discarded, not eaten.

- 4²/₃ cups all-purpose flour
- 2¹/₄ cups fine sea salt
- 7 large eggs
- ²/₃ cup plus 2 tablespoons water
- 2 1¹/₂-pound Cornish hens
- 2 teaspoons olive oil
- ¹/₂ teaspoon ground black pepper
- 2 shallots, peeled and halved
- 2 sprigs fresh rosemary
- 8 bay leaves, preferably fresh
- Warm Pine Nut Vinaigrette (see recipe on page 166)

1 MAKE THE SALT DOUGH: In a large bowl, combine flour and salt. Using a wooden spoon, stir 6 eggs and ²/₃ cup water into the flour mixture until the dough forms a loose ball. If needed, add 1 to 2 tablespoons water. Turn the dough out onto a lightly floured surface and knead about 10 times. Wrap dough in plastic and let rest for 30 minutes at room temperature.

2 MAKE THE HENS: Preheat oven to 350°F. Rinse the hens and pat dry. Rub each hen with 1 teaspoon olive oil and ¹/₄ teaspoon black pepper. Stuff each hen with 2 shallot halves, 1 sprig rosemary, and 1 bay leaf. Tie the legs of each hen together with kitchen twine. Tuck the remaining bay leaves between each thigh and on top of the breast and set aside. Divide the dough in half and roll 1 half into a 12- by 23-inch rectangle ¹/₈-inch thick. Cut two 11-inch circles. Place a hen in the center of one circle and cover with the other circle. Trim the dough, leaving a 1- to 2-inch border all around, and crimp the edges to seal tightly. Repeat with second dough half for the second hen. Beat remaining egg and brush over both encased birds, being certain to cover the entire surface and rim. Transfer both to a baking pan and bake for 40 to 50 minutes. Transfer the hens to a wire rack and let rest for 10 minutes. Use a knife to break open the salt dough crust and remove the hens. Discard the crust. Serve hens with Warm Pine Nut Vinaigrette.

Nutrition information per serving—protein: 41.5 g; fat: 23 g; carbohydrate: .17 g; fiber: .07 g; sodium: 479 mg; cholesterol: 134 mg; calories: 384.

QUAIL WITH GOLDEN–CHERRY BBQ SAUCE

Tiny quail make the perfect-sized appetizer. We add ginger to the cherry sauce for a light touch of spice. For an entrée, use game hens or chicken breast in place of the quail.

- 4 teaspoons olive oil
- ¹/₄ cup chopped onion
- 1 tablespoon chopped peeled fresh ginger
- ³/₄ pound golden cherries, pitted and halved (about 2 cups)
- ¹/₄ cup low-sodium chicken broth
- 3 tablespoons orange juice
- 1 tablespoon fresh lemon juice
- 2 tablespoons honey
- 2 teaspoons cider vinegar
- 1 ¹/₄ teaspoons salt
- 4 5-ounce quail
- ¹/₂ teaspoon ground black pepper

1 MAKE THE SAUCE: In a medium nonstick saucepan, heat 1 teaspoon oil over medium heat. Add the onions and cook until soft and translucent—about 8 minutes. Add the ginger and cherries and sauté for 2 minutes. Add broth, orange juice, and lemon juice to the saucepan and cook for 20 minutes. Run cherry mixture through a food mill and return to saucepan. Add the honey, vinegar, and ¹/₄ teaspoon salt to saucepan and cook over low heat until thickened— about 20 minutes. Transfer to a small bowl and set aside or store refrigerated for up to 3 days.

2 GRILL THE QUAIL: Heat grill or grill pan over high heat. In a large bowl, combine quail, remaining oil, 1 teaspoon salt, and pepper and toss to coat quail completely. Transfer quail to hot grill and grill for 4 minutes per side. Brush quail with barbecue sauce and grill for about 1 minute more per side until cooked through. Serve quail hot with additional sauce on the side.

Nutrition information per serving—protein: 22.8 g; fat: 18.6 g; carbohydrate: 23.8 g; fiber: 1.6 g; sodium: 732 mg; cholesterol: 83.1 mg; calories: 347.

BEEF, PORK, AND LAMB

BEEF RIB ROAST WITH MUSHROOM SAUCE

MAKES 6 SERVINGS

This uses the best, most tender beef roast you can buy—the perfect choice for special occasions. To make the meat easier to roast and carve, ask the butcher to remove the chine, or backbone, separate the meat from the ribs, and tie it back onto the bones with string.

1 3-rib prime or choice beef roast (about 6 pounds), trimmed

2 teaspoons kosher salt

1½ teaspoons ground black pepper

3 tablespoons chopped fresh marjoram leaves

½ teaspoon chopped fresh rosemary leaves

1 tablespoon cornstarch

1 14½-ounce can low-sodium beef broth

⅓ cup minced shallots

1 pound assorted mushrooms, quartered

1 tablespoon fresh thyme leaves

⅓ cup port or Madeira wine

1 ROAST THE BEEF: Preheat oven to 425°F. In a roasting pan fitted with a rack, place the roast rib-side down and rub 1 teaspoon each salt and pepper, 1 tablespoon marjoram, and the rosemary into the meat. Roast for 15 minutes, reduce the temperature to 325°F, and continue to roast until a thermometer inserted into the center measures 125°F for rare, 135° to 145°F for medium, or 165°F for well done—2 to 3 hours. Remove the roast from the pan and let rest for at least 20 minutes. Reserve the pan drippings.

2 MAKE THE SAUCE: In a small bowl, dissolve the cornstarch in ¼ cup of the beef broth. Set aside. In a large skillet over high heat, heat 2 tablespoons of the reserved drippings. Add the shallots and sauté until the edges begin to brown. Add the mushrooms, thyme, and remaining marjoram and cook for 3 more minutes. Add the wine and remaining broth, salt and pepper and cook for 1 minute. Stir in the cornstarch mixture and cook until the sauce thickens—about 1 minute. Serve hot with the roast.

Nutrition information per serving—protein: 99.3 g; fat: 34.4 g; carbohydrate: 7.7 g; fiber: 1.4 g; sodium: 1,577 mg; cholesterol: 286 mg; calories: 774.

BARBECUE BEEF BRISKET SANDWICHES   > >

MAKES 8 SANDWICHES

The slow cooker makes preparing brisket so easy, you'll want to have these sandwiches often. You can also prepare it on the stovetop over a low flame, but unlike the slowcooker, you will have to tend to it during the 3 to 4 hours it needs to cook. A spicy–sweet sauce, made with honey and dark beer, keeps the meat nice and tender.

1 3-pound beef brisket, trimmed

1½ teaspoons kosher salt

¾ teaspoon ground black pepper

1 tablespoon vegetable oil

1 large onion, coarsely chopped

1½ tablespoons minced garlic

½ cup dark beer (such as porter or stout)

1 tablespoon Worcestershire sauce

2 tablespoons fresh lemon juice

3 tablespoons honey

½ cup ketchup

1 teaspoon paprika

6 kaiser or other sandwich rolls

COOK THE BRISKET: Season the brisket with salt and pepper. In a large skillet, heat oil over medium-high heat. Add the brisket, brown on all sides, and transfer to a slow cooker. Add the remaining ingredients to the slow cooker and stir well. Slow-cook, covered, until the meat is very tender—8 hours. Remove the meat, place it on a cutting board, and let it rest for 15 minutes. Reserve the sauce. Carve brisket into thin slices and divide it among kaiser rolls topped with reserved sauce. Serve warm.

Nutrition information per sandwich—protein: 55.8 g; fat: 32.6 g; carbohydrate: 47.9 g; fiber: .9 g; sodium: 1134 mg; cholesterol: 163 mg; calories: 726.

GLAZED BRISKET WITH ROOT VEGETABLES

MAKES 8 SERVINGS

This easy-to-prepare meal cooks slowly, yielding a very tender brisket.

BRISKET AND VEGETABLES:

2 tablespoons all-purpose flour

2 teaspoons salt

$1/2$ teaspoon ground black pepper

1 $4^1/2$- to 5-pound beef brisket, trimmed

2 tablespoons vegetable oil

1 large onion, chopped (about $1^1/2$ cups)

1 shallot, chopped

2 $14^1/2$-ounce cans beef broth

$1/4$ cup balsamic vinegar

$1/4$ cup maple syrup (grade B, if available)

10 whole black peppercorns

5 whole allspice berries

3 whole cloves

1 pound carrots (about 8 medium), peeled and cut into chunks

1 pound all-purpose potatoes (about 3 medium), peeled and cut into chunks

1 small rutabaga (about 1 pound), peeled and cut into large chunks

1 pound turnips (about 4 medium), peeled and cut into quarters

GLAZE:

1 $14^1/2$-ounce can beef broth

$1/2$ cup maple syrup (grade B, if available)

$1/4$ cup balsamic vinegar

1 teaspoon tomato paste

4 whole allspice berries

2 whole cloves

1 MAKE THE BRISKET AND VEGETABLES: Preheat oven to 350°F. On a large plate, combine the flour, 1 teaspoon salt, and ground black pepper. Rinse the brisket; pat dry with paper towels. Dredge in flour mixture, coating all sides. In an 8-quart Dutch oven, heat the oil over medium heat. Place the brisket in the Dutch oven and brown on all sides. Transfer to a large plate; set aside. Add the onion and shallot to the Dutch oven; sauté until softened and lightly browned—7 to 10 minutes. Stir in the beef broth, vinegar, maple syrup, peppercorns, allspice berries, cloves, and the remaining 1 teaspoon salt. Bring the broth mixture to a boil and remove from heat. Return brisket to the Dutch oven, cover, and place in oven; cook for $1^1/2$ hours. Add the carrots, potatoes, rutabaga, and turnips. Cover and cook until the vegetables are fork-tender—about 45 minutes.

2 MAKE THE GLAZE: In a 1-quart saucepan, combine the beef broth, maple syrup, vinegar, tomato paste, allspice berries, and cloves. Bring the mixture to a boil over high heat. Cook until the mixture thickens and reduces to $1/2$ cup—about 10 minutes. Discard the allspice berries and cloves.

3 GLAZE THE BRISKET: Remove Dutch oven from the oven. Place a wire rack on a large baking pan. Place the brisket on wire rack. Arrange the vegetables around brisket. Reserve the liquid in the Dutch oven. Brush the brisket and vegetables with some of the glaze. Increase oven temperature to 375°F. Place the baking pan in oven and cook, brushing occasionally with remaining glaze—15 to 20 minutes—until the meat and vegetables are glazed.

4 MAKE THE SAUCE: Cook the remaining liquid in Dutch oven over medium-high heat until thick enough to coat the back of a spoon—10 to 15 minutes. Strain the sauce and serve with the brisket and vegetables.

Nutrition information per serving—protein: 75 g; fat: 39 g; carbohydrate: 37 g; fiber: 5 g; sodium: 1,103 mg; cholesterol: 240 mg; calories: 807.

BEEF AND RED WINE STEW

This beef stew is slowly simmered in a hearty red wine until the meat is fork-tender and infused with flavor. Serve it over a bed of egg noodles or with a loaf of crusty French bread.

- 5 slices applewood-smoked bacon
- 4 pounds beef chuck, cut into 2-inch pieces
- 1/3 cup all-purpose flour
- 1–2 tablespoons olive oil
- 2 medium onions, chopped (about 2 cups)
- 1 tablespoon chopped garlic
- 3 cups dry red wine (such as cabernet sauvignon or pinot noir)
- 1 cup low-sodium beef broth
- 2 tablespoons red wine vinegar
- 1 28-ounce can chopped tomatoes
- 1 bay leaf
- 3/4 teaspoon salt
- 1 teaspoon coarsely ground black pepper

1 BROWN THE BEEF: Preheat oven to 325°F. In a large Dutch oven, cook bacon over medium-high heat until browned. Remove and place on a paper towel to drain. Pour off half the bacon fat and reserve. Toss the beef and flour together in a large bowl. Add 1 tablespoon oil to the Dutch oven, add the meat in batches, and brown on all sides. Add reserved bacon fat and 1 more tablespoon of oil, if needed. Transfer the beef to a plate.

2 FINISH THE STEW: Add the onions to the Dutch oven and sauté over medium-high heat until golden—about 5 minutes. Add the garlic and cook for 2 more minutes. Add the remaining ingredients, the browned beef, and the bacon and bring to a simmer. Cover and cook in the oven until the meat is very tender—about 2 1/4 hours. Serve the stew while it is hot.

Nutrition information per serving—protein: 52.7 g; fat: 15.3 g; carbohydrate: 9.3 g; fiber: 1.2 g; sodium: 393 mg; cholesterol: 155 mg; calories: 434.

LAVENDER AND PEPPER STEAK

Although lavender is most often associated with scented sachets, the herb is a relative of the mint family and has a sharp, fresh flavor. Often used in salads, it also makes a sensational spice rub for steaks.

- 1 tablespoon dried lavender buds
- 1 tablespoon whole black peppercorns
- 1/4 teaspoon whole green peppercorns
- 1/4 teaspoon whole pink peppercorns
- 1/4 teaspoon whole white peppercorns
- 4 whole allspice berries
- 1/4 teaspoon salt
- 4 12-ounce strip or shell steaks

MAKE THE STEAKS: Preheat grill to medium. Place lavender, all peppercorns, and allspice on a cutting board and, using the bottom of a small skillet, crush them until the herbs and spices are coarsely ground. Sprinkle salt on steaks and rub on the spice mixture. Grill to desired doneness—about 130°F for rare; 135°F for medium rare; 145°F for medium; and 155°F for medium well.

Nutrition information per serving—protein: 97.6 g; fat: 32.5 g; carbohydrate: 3.9 g; fiber: 2 g; sodium: 370 mg; cholesterol: 258 mg; calories: 725.

USING AN INSTANT-READ THERMOMETER FOR MEAT

Whether cooking a burger or roasting a beef tenderloin, always take the temperature of the thickest part of the meat, or if it is uniformly thick, in the center. If the meat you are cooking contains bone, make sure the thermometer does not touch it; bones conduct heat, so you will get a false reading. When cooking thinner cuts, such as steaks and chops, insert the thermometer into the middle of the meat, being sure not to go more than halfway in.

KOREAN-STYLE SHORT RIBS < <

MAKES 4 SERVINGS

As the beef simmers, the spicy braising liquid reduces to a rich sauce that you can spoon over white rice.

3½ pounds beef short ribs

½ teaspoon salt

½ teaspoon ground black pepper

3 tablespoons canola oil

3 cups low-sodium beef broth

2 cups water

½ cup medium-dark beer

¼ cup low-sodium soy sauce

5 large cloves garlic, sliced

1 tablespoon plus 1 teaspoon grated peeled fresh ginger

2 teaspoons chili or chili-garlic paste

¼ teaspoon ground dried chilies

3 carrots, peeled and cut into 2-inch chunks

½ pound onions (about 2 medium), cut into 1-inch wedges

3 green onions, sliced

MAKE THE RIBS: Preheat oven to 350°F. Season the ribs with salt and pepper. In a Dutch oven, heat the oil over high heat. Sear the ribs until browned on all sides. Remove the ribs from the skillet and discard fat. When the pan has cooled slightly, add the beef broth, water, beer, soy sauce, garlic, ginger, chili paste, ground chilies, and browned ribs. Cover and cook in the oven for 1 hour. Turn the ribs over and skim off any fat. Cover and cook for 1 more hour. Skim off any fat and add the carrots and onions. Cover and cook until the meat and vegetables are tender—about 30 more minutes. Garnish with green onions and serve immediately.

Nutrition information per serving—protein: 98.4 g; fat: 65.5 g; carbohydrate: 17 g; fiber: 2.8 g; sodium: 1,024 mg; cholesterol: 276 mg; calories: 1,079.

ALL-AMERICAN BURGER

MAKES FOUR 6-OUNCE BURGERS

This simple invention—a cooked ground–beef patty on a toasted bun—is viewed by many as genius. America's favorite sandwich might even be considered a national treasure.

1½ pounds ground chuck or sirloin

¼ teaspoon salt

¼ teaspoon ground black pepper

½ teaspoon Worcestershire sauce

1 large egg

4 slices Cheddar cheese (about 4 ounces)

1 large onion, sliced into rings

4 onion rolls, halved and toasted

1 large tomato, sliced

4 lettuce leaves

4 dill pickle chips

1 MAKE THE PATTIES: In a medium bowl, mix the ground beef, salt, pepper, Worcestershire sauce, and egg. Use your hands to form four equal-size patties.

2 COOK THE PATTIES AND ONIONS: In a large skillet, cook patties over high heat—about 4 minutes for medium or 5 minutes for well done—turning once midway through. Place one slice of cheese on top of each patty and cook for 1 more minute. Remove patties from skillet and place on a wire rack. Reduce heat to medium, add the onions, and cook, stirring occasionally, until golden brown—about 6 minutes. Remove skillet from heat.

3 ASSEMBLE THE BURGERS: On the bottom half of each roll, place one patty and top with tomato, lettuce, pickles, and onions. Cover with top of roll. Serve with ketchup.

Nutrition information per burger—protein: 55.9 g; fat: 46.1 g; carbohydrate: 32.9 g; fiber: 2.4 g; sodium: 823 mg; cholesterol: 227 mg; calories: 776.

COWBOY CHILI

This American classic was first concocted in the Lone Star State by—you guessed it—cowboys passing through on cattle drives. An ingredient you may not be familiar with, *masa harina de maíz*, is simply finely ground corn—similar to flour.

1 tablespoon vegetable oil

1 pound boneless chuck or rump roast, cut into ½-inch cubes

1 large onion, chopped (about 2 cups)

6 cloves garlic, minced

2 14½-ounce cans low-sodium beef broth

1 tablespoon chili powder

1 teaspoon ground cumin

1 14½-ounce can diced low-sodium tomatoes

2 dried ancho chilies

1 tablespoon *masa harina de maíz*

1 cup water

2 15½-ounce cans pinto beans, rinsed and drained

½ teaspoon salt

1 tablespoon cider vinegar

1 BROWN THE MEAT: In a large Dutch oven, add oil and heat over medium-high heat. When oil is hot but not smoking, add beef and cook until browned—about 5 minutes. Remove beef, set aside, and reduce heat to medium.

2 MAKE THE CHILI: Add onion to the Dutch oven and sauté until translucent—3 to 5 minutes. Add garlic and cook 1 more minute. Return the meat to the Dutch oven. Gradually add 1 can beef broth and deglaze by scraping up the brown bits from the bottom of the Dutch oven. Add chili powder, cumin, and tomatoes. Reduce heat to medium low, cover, and simmer for 1 hour.

3 PUREE THE CHILIES: In a small saucepan, bring the remaining can of beef broth to a boil over high heat. Add ancho chilies and let stand 15 minutes to hydrate. Remove and discard stems. Place chilies and broth in a blender or food processor fitted with the metal blade and blend until smooth—2 to 3 minutes.

4 FINISH THE CHILI: In a small bowl, whisk the *masa* and water together. Stir *masa* mixture into the chili. Add ancho chili mixture, pinto beans, salt, and vinegar. Simmer uncovered for 15 minutes. Serve hot.

Nutrition information per serving—protein: 37.7 g; fat: 11.1 g; carbohydrate: 31.6 g; fiber: 11.4 g; sodium: 489 mg; cholesterol: 76.3 mg; calories: 379.

T-BONE STEAKS WITH NORTH AFRICAN SPICES   > >

Serve with roasted eggplant and couscous to complete the Mediterranean theme.

2 1¼-pound T-bone beef steaks (about 1 inch thick)

½ teaspoon olive oil

½ teaspoon salt

2 teaspoons coriander seeds

1 teaspoon cumin seeds

1 teaspoon caraway seeds

2 teaspoons dried rosemary

½ teaspoon ground black pepper

¼ teaspoon ground cinnamon

¼ teaspoon ground turmeric

2 teaspoons canola oil

1 MAKE THE STEAKS: Preheat oven to 400°F. Fit a wire rack over a baking pan and set aside. Rub the steaks with olive oil, season with salt, and set aside. Coarsely grind the coriander, cumin, caraway, and rosemary using a mortar and pestle or an electric grinder. Transfer the ground spices to a bowl and mix in the black pepper, cinnamon, and turmeric. Rub each steak with 1 tablespoon spice mixture, making sure to cover both sides. Let the steaks sit at room temperature for 20 minutes.

2 COOK THE STEAKS: Heat a large skillet over high heat until very hot—about 3 minutes. Add the canola oil and sear the steaks until a brown crust forms. Turn and repeat on the other side. Transfer the steaks to the wire rack set over the prepared baking pan, place in oven, and cook to desired degree of doneness—about 9 minutes for rare, 11 for medium rare, 15 for medium, and 18 for well done.

Nutrition information per serving—protein: 120 g; fat: 50.6 g; carbohydrate: 3.4 g; fiber: 1.8 g; sodium: 815 mg; cholesterol: 339 mg; calories: 977.

CORNED BEEF HASH WITH BOSTON BROWN BREAD

MAKES 6 SERVINGS

While corned-beef hash is traditionally made from leftover brisket, we developed and tested this recipe using meat from the deli counter of the supermarket. To bake the egg right in the center of the hash, place the hash on a heatproof plate, make a well in the center, and crack a fresh egg in it; cook at 350˚F until the egg has set.

- 1 pound all-purpose potatoes, peeled and diced (2^1/$_2$ cups)
- 1 pound unsliced cooked corned beef
- 3 tablespoons vegetable oil
- 1 medium onion, chopped (about 1 cup)
- 2 cloves garlic, finely chopped
- ^{1}/$_4$ teaspoon salt
- ^{1}/$_4$ teaspoon ground black pepper
- 2 teaspoons coarse-grain mustard
- 2 tablespoons butter
- 6 fried or poached eggs (optional)
- Boston Brown Bread (see recipe on page 141)

1 MAKE THE POTATOES: Place potatoes in a 2-quart saucepan and cover with water. Bring to a gentle boil over high heat; cook until fork-tender—about 10 minutes. Drain.

2 In a food processor fitted with the metal blade, pulse corned beef until coarsely chopped. Alternatively, shred by hand.

3 MAKE THE HASH: In a large cast-iron or non-stick skillet, heat oil over medium heat. Add onions and garlic; sauté until softened—about 5 minutes. Add potatoes, salt, and pepper; cook until potatoes are soft. Reduce heat to low. Add the chopped corned beef, mustard, and butter. Cook, using a spatula to press mixture into bottom of skillet, until browned on one side. Turn mixture, in sections if necessary, and continue to cook until browned on the other side. Serve with cooked eggs, if desired, and Boston Brown Bread.

Nutrition information per serving without egg—protein: 23 g; fat: 22 g; carbohydrate: 22 g; fiber: 2 g; sodium: 910 mg; cholesterol: 75 mg; calories: 378.

BARBECUED COUNTRY RIBS WITH LEMON

MAKES 4 SERVINGS

Toasted cumin, mustard, and celery seeds plus lemon juice add some kick to a tomato-based barbecue sauce.

- 2 teaspoons cumin seeds
- 1^1/$_2$ teaspoons yellow mustard seeds
- ^{1}/$_2$ teaspoon celery seeds
- ^{1}/$_4$ cup (^{1}/$_2$ stick) unsalted butter
- 1 large onion, diced
- 1 teaspoon salt
- 1 14^1/$_2$-ounce can whole tomatoes, roughly chopped, juice reserved
- 1 cup ketchup
- ^{1}/$_4$ cup packed brown sugar
- 2 tablespoons Worcestershire sauce
- 2 tablespoons cider vinegar
- ^{3}/$_4$ teaspoon ground red pepper
- 4 pounds country-style pork ribs
- Freshly ground black pepper
- 3 tablespoons canola oil
- 1^1/$_2$ lemons, cut into ^{1}/$_8$–inch–thick slices

1 MAKE THE SAUCE: Preheat oven to 350˚F. In a small skillet, toast the cumin and yellow mustard and celery seeds over medium heat until fragrant. When cool, finely grind in a spice grinder or using a mortar and pestle. Set aside. In a large saucepan, melt the butter. Add the onions, season with ^{1}/$_2$ teaspoon salt, and cook until soft and brown—about 6 minutes. Add the tomatoes and their reserved juice, ketchup, brown sugar, Worcestershire sauce, vinegar, ground red pepper, and the toasted ground spices to the onions. Add 3 cups water, bring to a simmer, and set aside.

2 COOK THE RIBS: Season ribs with remaining salt and a few grindings of black pepper. In a large Dutch oven, heat oil over high heat. Add the ribs and brown on both sides. Discard the fat and pour the sauce over the ribs. Cover and braise in the oven for 2 hours. Remove the ribs from the oven, skim off any fat, turn the ribs over, and top with lemon slices. Return to the oven and continue to braise, covered, 45 more minutes. Serve immediately.

Nutrition information per serving—protein: 93.9 g; fat: 73.5 g; carbohydrate: 39.3 g; fiber: 3.2 g; sodium: 1,618 mg; cholesterol: 348 mg; calories: 1,198.

COUNTRY STYLE HAM WITH CRANBERRY GLAZE

MAKES ABOUT 25 SERVINGS

A whole smoked ham comes fully cooked but is cooked again so its glaze of cranberries, port wine, and the classic sugar and spice, can coat and permeate the meat.

1 10-pound bone-in smoked ham, fully cooked

$1^1/_2$ teaspoons whole cloves

1 teaspoon salt

$^1/_2$ teaspoon ground black pepper

1 bag fresh cranberries

1 cup dark brown sugar

2 tablespoons brown mustard

3 tablespoons port wine

GLAZE THE HAM: Preheat the oven to 350°F. In a small saucepan, place the cranberries, brown sugar, mustard, and $^1/_4$ cup water over medium heat. Bring to a boil, reduce heat, and simmer for 20 minutes. Strain the mixture, pushing all of the liquid from the berries. Discard the solids, and stir in the port. Trim the skin and fat off the ham leaving about $^1/_4$-inch of fat intact. Score the fat and stud the ham with the cloves. Season the ham with salt and pepper and transfer to a large roasting pan. Bake the ham for 20 minutes. Brush ham with half of the cranberry glaze and bake for 35 minutes. Baste with the remaining glaze and bake until heated through—about 35 more minutes.

Nutrition information per serving—protein: 39.3 g; fat: 30.6 g; carbohydrate: 7.5 g; fiber: .5 g; sodium: 2,170 mg; cholesterol: 112 mg; calories: 472.

BACON AND EGG HASH

MAKES 4 SERVINGS

The trick to making hash with a nice crispy crust is not to stir the potatoes.

$^1/_2$ pound slab bacon, cut into $^1/_2$-inch cubes

1 large onion, coarsely chopped

1 red bell pepper, coarsely chopped

$1^1/_2$ lbs. leftover potatoes, chopped

4 large eggs

MAKE THE HASH: In a large skillet, cook the bacon over medium-high heat until browned and crisp. Remove the bacon and set aside. Discard all but 2 tablespoons of the bacon fat, add the onions and peppers to the pan, and sauté for 3 minutes. Add the potatoes and bacon and cook until potatoes are heated through—about 5 minutes. Lower heat to medium low and gently crack the eggs onto the surface of the hash. Cover the pan and cook until the eggs are set—about 5 minutes. Serve immediately.

Nutrition information per serving—protein: 20.5 g; fat: 19.2 g; carbohydrate: 25.3 g; fiber: 3.8 g; sodium: 929 mg; cholesterol: 243 mg; calories: 359.

MAKING THE GRADE

The USDA grades beef, veal, lamb, and mutton. Pork is also graded but not at the retail level. Unlike the inspections the U.S. Department of Agriculture performs to guarantee that our meat is safe to eat, grading is strictly voluntary. The grade meat is given reflects how tender it is. Prime-and Choice-graded meat is marbled (has flecks of fat throughout the flesh) and any external fat is cream-colored. Prime beef is sold primarily to leading hotels and the best restaurants. Only a small amount ever reaches retail stores (usually the best butcher shops and specialty food shops). Select grade meat is of lesser quality and is therefore tougher. Meat graded Standard, Commercial, Utility, Cutter, and Canner are made into soaps, hot dogs, and dog food.

The USDA defines organic meat as meat that complies with National Organic Standards: it must come from animals that are given no antibiotics or growth hormones and are fed organic feed. Natural meat is minimally processed with no artificial additives or preservatives.

HERB-CRUSTED BONELESS PORK ROAST

MAKES 8 SERVINGS

Leftovers from this roast make terrific sandwiches.

- ¼ cup Dijon mustard
- 1 teaspoon grated orange zest
- 1 tablespoon fresh orange juice
- 1 3- to 3½-pound boneless pork loin
- 1½ teaspoons chopped fresh rosemary leaves
- 1 teaspoon chopped fresh sage leaves
- 1 clove garlic, minced
- 1 teaspoon salt
- ½ teaspoon ground black pepper

1 ROAST THE PORK: Preheat oven to 425°F. Lightly coat a rack with vegetable oil and place it in a roasting pan. In a small bowl, whisk mustard, orange zest, and juice. Spread over the surface of the pork loin and place it on the wire rack. Roast the pork on the middle rack of the oven for ½ hour.

2 MAKE THE CRUST: In a small bowl, toss rosemary, sage, garlic, salt, and pepper. Remove pork from the oven and pat the herb mixture onto the top and sides. Reduce temperature to 350°F and continue to roast until meat thermometer, inserted into the middle of the roast, registers 160°F—about 45 minutes longer.

3 TO SERVE: Remove pork from oven and allow to rest 15 minutes before serving. Slice and serve warm or at room temperature.

Nutrition information per serving—protein: 41 g; fat: 22 g; carbohydrate: 1.3 g; fiber: .15 g; sodium: 541 mg; cholesterol: 115 mg; calories: 379.

BLACKBERRY-GLAZED PORK TENDERLOIN

MAKES 8 SERVINGS

We've taken full advantage of summer's blackberry crop by using the fruit for both this recipe's marinade and its accompanying sauce.

- 2 14-ounce pork tenderloins
- 2½ cups fresh blackberries
- 2 tablespoons fresh rosemary leaves
- 4 tablespoons fresh thyme leaves
- 2 tablespoons white wine vinegar
- ⅔ cup water
- ½ teaspoon salt
- ½ teaspoon ground black pepper
- 2 cloves garlic, minced
- 1 tablespoon cornstarch
- ¼ cup cold water
- ⅔ cup blackberry liqueur

1 MARINATE THE MEAT: Place the tenderloins in a glass dish or zip-top bag. In a medium saucepan, bring 2 cups berries, rosemary, thyme, vinegar, water, salt, and pepper to a boil over medium high heat. Remove from heat and let cool. Pour the liquid over tenderloins, cover, and store in the refrigerator—8 hours to overnight. Turn tenderloins occasionally to ensure even marinating.

2 GRILL THE MEAT: Heat grill to medium high. Drain tenderloins and reserve the marinade. Grill the tenderloins on all sides, turning with tongs until cooked through (145°F-150°F)—25 to 30 minutes. Let rest for 5 minutes before slicing.

3 MAKE THE SAUCE: Strain the marinade through a fine strainer and reserve ½ cup of the liquid. In a medium skillet, bring the liquid to a boil over high heat. Add garlic and continue to cook until the liquid is reduced to ¼ cup. Dissolve cornstarch in the water and stir into the reduced liquid. Add blackberry liqueur and cook, stirring occasionally, until smooth, glossy, and thick—about 2 minutes. Toss in remaining ½ cup fresh berries.

4 SERVE: Thinly slice the tenderloins. Drizzle meat with 1 to 2 tablespoons sauce for each plate. Garnish with additional fresh blackberries, if desired.

Nutrition information per serving—protein: 21.9 g; fat: 5.6 g; carbohydrate: 5.5 g; fiber: 1.9 g; sodium: 178 mg; cholesterol: 54.6 mg; calories: 163.

WINE AND FRUIT-GLAZED PORK CHOPS

MAKES 4 SERVINGS

This main dish can be prepared in less than thirty minutes but will taste like you spent far more time putting it together.

4 6-ounce pork loin chops
    (about ³/₄ inch thick)

¹/₂ teaspoon salt

¹/₂ teaspoon ground black pepper

1 tablespoon olive oil

1 finely chopped shallot
    (about 2 tablespoons)

³/₄ cup chardonnay or riesling

¹/₂ cup cherry or seedless
    raspberry jam

¹/₄ teaspoon crushed red pepper

1 COOK THE PORK CHOPS: Sprinkle the pork chops with salt and pepper. In a large skillet, heat oil over medium-high heat, until very hot. Add pork chops and sauté for 7 minutes. Turn chops over and continue to cook for 5 more minutes. Add the shallots and cook until soft and pork chops are cooked through—about 2 minutes.

2 MAKE THE SAUCE: Remove the pork chops from the skillet, leaving the cooked shallots and pan juices. Add the wine and deglaze the skillet over medium-high heat, by stirring to loosen the browned particles. Cook until the liquid thickens slightly—about 2 minutes. Stir in the jam and crushed red pepper and cook until the sauce is thoroughly heated. Pour sauce over the pork chops and serve immediately.

Nutrition information per serving—protein: 36.9 g; fat: 13 g; carbohydrate: 29.3 g; fiber: .13 g; sodium: 362 mg; cholesterol: 100 mg; calories: 416.

PORK SHOULDER POT-AU-FEU

MAKES 8 SERVINGS

Pot-au-feu ("pot on fire"), the classic French boiled dinner, gets dressed up with the addition of two lesser-known root vegetables: kohlrabi and black radish. The black radish, with its sooty exterior and stark-white interior, has a bold, pronounced bite, while the green, bulbous kohlrabi's flavor falls somewhere between a turnip and a cabbage. If unavailable, substitute white turnip or daikon radish for the kohlrabi and rutabaga for the black radish.

3 bay leaves, preferably fresh

3 sprigs fresh thyme

2 cloves garlic, peeled and crushed with the side of a
    large knife

1 teaspoon whole allspice berries

1 teaspoon whole black peppercorns

1 whole clove

24 cups (6 quarts) water

2 tablespoons salt

1 6-pound pork shoulder, tied with kitchen twine

3 carrots, peeled and cut into 3-inch pieces

3 small kohlrabi, peeled and cut in half

2 parsnips, peeled and cut into 3-inch pieces

1 large black radish, scrubbed and cut into 6 wedges

1 small head savoy cabbage, cut into 6 wedges with
    stem end attached

1 COOK THE PORK: Place bay leaves, thyme, garlic, allspice, peppercorns, and clove in a square of cheesecloth and tie with kitchen twine to form a sachet. In a large stockpot, bring water and salt to a boil. Add the spice sachet and pork shoulder, making sure the water covers the meat. Simmer, with the cover slightly open, skimming the meat protein from the surface occasionally, until meat is very tender and easily pierced with a fork—about 3³/₄ hours. Transfer pork to a large plate and keep warm. Reserve the broth.

2 COOK THE VEGETABLES: Strain the broth through a cheesecloth-lined strainer and return to the stockpot. Add the carrots, kohlrabi, parsnips, and radish. Cook for 15 minutes. Add the cabbage and continue to cook until all vegetables are tender—about 15 more minutes. Lift vegetables from the liquid and keep warm alongside the pork. Arrange pork and vegetables on a deep serving platter. Serve with the broth, mustard, and coarse salt.

Nutrition information per serving—protein: 84 g; fat: 31.3 g; carbohydrate: 10.7 g; fiber: 3.2 g; sodium: 421 mg; cholesterol: 292 mg; calories: 678.

SWEET AND SPICY PORK CHILI

This chili goes well with an aromatic rice such as jasmine or basmati.

- 1 teaspoon vegetable oil
- 2 pounds boneless pork chops or tenderloin, cut into 1/2-inch cubes
- 2 shallots, coarsely chopped (about 1/3 cup)
- 2 cloves garlic, minced
- 2 teaspoons crushed red pepper
- 2 tablespoons chili powder
- 1 14 1/2-ounce can low-sodium beef broth
- 1 14-ounce can low-fat coconut milk
- 1 teaspoon peeled grated fresh ginger
- 3 medium carrots, peeled and sliced on the diagonal (about 1 cup)
- 3 tablespoons frozen orange juice concentrate
- 1 tablespoon low-sodium soy sauce
- 1/4 cup packed light brown sugar
- 6 cups hot cooked rice
- Chopped green onions (optional)

1 BROWN THE MEAT: In a large Dutch oven, heat oil over medium-high heat. Once oil is hot but not smoking, add pork; cook until lightly browned—6 to 8 minutes. Remove pork, set aside, and reduce heat to medium.

2 MAKE THE CHILI: Add shallots and sauté until translucent—about 2 minutes. Add garlic and cook 1 minute. Add crushed red pepper, chili powder, beef broth, coconut milk, and ginger. Reduce heat to low and simmer uncovered for 15 minutes. Add carrots and simmer for 10 more minutes.

3 FINISH THE CHILI: Add orange juice concentrate, soy sauce, and brown sugar. Simmer for 10 minutes. Serve warm over cooked rice and sprinkle with chopped green onions, if desired.

Nutrition information per serving—protein: 55.4 g; fat: 27 g; carbohydrate: 76.4 g; fiber: 3 g; sodium: 209 mg; cholesterol: 118 mg; calories: 779.

BUTTER BEAN AND SAUSAGE HOT POT

This hearty hotpot can stew in the slow cooker while you're at work or be prepared a day ahead—it will just get more flavorful.

- 1 pound smoked sausage (such as kielbasa)
- 1/4 pound sliced bacon
- 1 large bulb fennel, cut into 2-inch-long and 1/4-inch-wide matchsticks (3 cups)
- 1 cup thickly sliced celery
- 1 medium onion, diced (about 1 cup)
- 2 tablespoons coarsely chopped garlic (about 3 cloves)
- 1 pound dried butter beans
- 1 1/2 teaspoons chopped fresh rosemary leaves
- 1/4 teaspoon ground black pepper
- 1 bay leaf
- 2 14 1/2-ounce cans low-sodium chicken broth
- 5 cups water

MAKE THE HOT POT: In a large skillet, brown the sausage over medium-high heat. Remove and slice into 1/2-inch rounds. Set aside. Cook the bacon in the same skillet until crisp and golden brown; remove from skillet and set aside, reserving the bacon fat. Reduce heat to medium, add the fennel and celery to the bacon fat, and cook for 4 to 5 minutes. Add the onions and garlic and continue to cook until onions become translucent. Remove from heat. Place the browned sausage, cooked bacon, sautéed vegetables, and remaining ingredients in a slow cooker and cover. Cook on the low setting until beans are tender—6 to 8 hours. Serve hot.

Nutrition information per 1-cup serving—protein: 17 g; fat: 19 g; carbohydrate: 12.6 g; fiber: 4 g; sodium: 901 mg; cholesterol: 42.7 mg; calories: 290.

SAVORY BRAISED LAMB SHANKS

MAKES 4 SERVINGS

Long slow cooking makes the lamb fork-tender. Gremolata, a mixture of parsley, grated lemon zest, and garlic, is sprinkled over the finished dish for an extra burst of flavor.

- 2 cups dried Great Northern beans
- ¼ cup all-purpose flour
- 1 teaspoon paprika
- ½ teaspoon salt
- ¼ teaspoon ground black pepper
- 4 1 ¼-pound lamb shanks
- ¼ cup vegetable oil
- 2 medium onions, chopped (about 2 cups)
- 5 cloves garlic, chopped
- 3 cups beef broth
- 3 cups low-sodium chicken broth
- 1½ cups dry red wine
- 1 tablespoon tomato paste
- 2 bay leaves
- 1 tablespoon chopped fresh rosemary leaves
- 1 teaspoon chopped fresh sage leaves
- 2 large carrots, peeled and cut into ½-inch pieces (about 1 cup)
- 2 tablespoons chopped fresh flat-leaf parsley
- 2 tablespoons grated lemon zest

1 MAKE THE BEANS: In a 4-quart saucepan, place beans and cover with cold water. Set over high heat and bring to a boil. Remove pan from heat, cover, and allow to stand at room temperature for 1 hour. Drain and set beans aside.

2 In a shallow bowl, combine the flour, paprika, salt, and pepper. Dredge the lamb shanks in the flour mixture, shaking off excess.

3 MAKE THE LAMB: In an 8-quart Dutch oven, heat 2 tablespoons oil over medium heat. Brown lamb thoroughly on all sides. Remove from pan, cover, and set aside.

4 COOK THE LAMB: Pour off fat from saucepan and heat remaining 2 tablespoons vegetable oil. Add onion and sauté until softened and lightly browned—5 to 7 minutes. Add 3 cloves garlic, beef broth, chicken broth, 1 cup red wine, tomato paste, bay leaves, rosemary, and sage. Bring mixture to a boil over high heat. Reduce heat to low and simmer 5 minutes. Add reserved beans and lamb. Cover and cook for 1½ hours. Stir in the remaining ½ cup wine and the carrots. Cook until carrots are tender—about 30 minutes. In a small bowl combine remaining 2 cloves chopped garlic, parsley, and lemon zest.

5 SERVE THE LAMB: To serve, divide beans among 4 serving plates. Top with lamb; garnish with parsley-lemon mixture.

Nutrition information per serving—protein: 109 g; fat: 40 g; carbohydrate: 87 g; fiber: 6 g; sodium: 1,665 mg; cholesterol: 255 mg; calories: 1,214.

MINTED LAMB PATTIES   > >

MAKES 4 SERVINGS

Our grilled lamb burgers are spiced with fresh herbs, cinnamon, and pickled pepperoncini. Serve them in pita pockets with Tomato Relish and Lemon-Feta Dressing.

- 1 pound lean ground lamb
- ½ cup finely chopped fresh mint leaves (about 5 sprigs)
- ¼ cup finely chopped seeded pickled pepperoncini (6 or 7)
- 1 teaspoon salt
- ½ teaspoon coarsely ground black pepper
- ¼ teaspoon ground cinnamon
- 4 pita breads
- 1 small cucumber, thinly sliced
- Tomato Relish (see recipe on page 170)
- Lemon-Feta Dressing (see recipe on page 167)

1 GRILL THE LAMB PATTIES: Heat grill to high. Combine the lamb, mint, pepperoncini, salt, pepper, and cinnamon in a large bowl and form into 4 quarter-pound patties. Grill the lamb patties for 4 minutes on each side.

2 ASSEMBLE THE SANDWICHES: Place one lamb patty and ¼ cup Tomato Relish in the pocket of each pita. Divide the cucumber slices evenly among the sandwiches and place them inside the pita. Drizzle each sandwich with 1 tablespoon Lemon-Feta Dressing and serve immediately.

Nutrition information per serving—protein: 37.9 g; fat: 35 g; carbohydrate: 44.7 g; fiber: 3.8 g; sodium: 1,821 mg; cholesterol: 119 mg; calories: 650.

MOROCCAN LAMB KEBABS

Marinating meat in a mildly acidic liquid, such as buttermilk, not only tenderizes the meat but enhances its flavor.

- 1½ cups buttermilk
- 3 cloves garlic, chopped
- 2 tablespoons chopped fresh mint leaves
- 1 tablespoon chopped fresh flat-leaf parsley
- 1 teaspoon ground cumin
- ½ teaspoon salt
- ¼ teaspoon ground black pepper
- 1 pound boneless lamb shoulder
  (cut into 1½-inch chunks)
- 1 large red onion, cut into 6 wedges and halved
- 1 large red or yellow bell pepper, cut into 2-inch pieces
- 2 large lemons, halved, each half cut into thirds

1 MARINATE THE LAMB: In a large sealable plastic bag, combine buttermilk, garlic, mint, parsley, cumin, salt, and pepper. Mix well. Place lamb pieces inside bag and seal tightly. Refrigerate for 4 to 24 hours, turning occasionally.

2 ASSEMBLE AND GRILL THE KEBABS: Preheat grill for 15 minutes. On 12 skewers, alternate lamb, onion, pepper, and lemon; brush skewered meat with the reserved marinade. Grill each kebab for 8 minutes on each side. Serve hot on a bed of couscous or rice, if desired.

Nutrition information per kebab—protein: 14 g; fat: 3.7 g; carbohydrate: 3.7 g; fiber: .48 g; sodium: 184 mg; cholesterol: 42 mg; calories: 107.

RACK OF LAMB WITH MINT PESTO

A pesto rub made with fresh mint rather than basil, the classic ingredient in pesto, complements the lamb's flavor and also tenderizes the meat.

- 1 cup tightly packed fresh mint leaves,
  plus more for garnish (optional)
- ¼ cup chopped walnuts
- ¼ cup grated Parmesan cheese
- 2 cloves garlic, sliced
- ¼ teaspoon ground black pepper
- ¼ teaspoon salt
- 3 tablespoons olive oil
- 2 2½-pound racks of lamb, trimmed

1 MAKE THE MINT PESTO: In a food processor fitted with the metal blade, process the mint leaves and walnuts for 30 seconds. Add the Parmesan cheese, garlic, pepper, and salt; pulse until mixed. With motor running, slowly add oil through the feed tube until pesto mixture is smooth and well combined.

2 MAKE THE LAMB: Place the lamb in a large roasting pan. Rub the mint pesto over lamb. Cover and refrigerate 2 hours.

3 COOK THE LAMB: Preheat the oven to 350°F. Uncover the lamb and cook until a meat thermometer registers 145°F for rare, 160°F for medium, or 175°F for well done—55 to 65 minutes. Let rest 10 minutes.

4 SERVE THE LAMB: Transfer the lamb to a cutting board and cut each rack into 8 chops. Place the lamb chops on a serving platter and garnish with mint leaves, if desired.

Nutrition information per serving—protein: 62 g; fat: 34 g; carbohydrate: 1 g; fiber: 1 g; sodium: 300 mg; cholesterol: 201 mg; calories: 586.

MEAT SPEAK

A guide to commonly used cooking terms:

> **Braising:** Meat is cooked in liquid in a sealed container on the oven or stovetop. Beef chuck and round, lamb shanks, and pork shoulder are some cuts suited to braising.

> **Broiling:** A dry heat method, a direct flame usually below the oven of a gas or electric range. Good for lamb and veal chops, beef steaks, and kebabs.

> **Grilling:** Meat is cooked over a metal grate positioned over a very hot, direct heat source such as fire or coals. A thin crust-like layer forms and seals moisture inside. Thicker cuts of meat work best for grilling.

> **Sauteeing:** A very hot pan and a small amount of fat combine to quickly cook cuts such as filet mignon and pork or lamb chops.

> **Roasting:** Usually reserved for larger cuts or whole birds. Dry heat often started at a high temperature to crisp the exterior, then lowered to slowly cook the interior.

LAMB CHOPS MARINATED IN RED WINE

The chops must be marinated for at least four hours (or as long as overnight) so they absorb all of the flavor from the herbs and spices. Put the accompanying vegetables in a grill basket before setting them on the grill.

1/2 cup dry red wine

1/4 cup olive oil

2 tablespoons red wine vinegar

1 tablespoon fresh lemon juice

zest of 1 lemon cut into strips

3 large cloves garlic, minced

4 sprigs fresh thyme plus 2 teaspoons leaves

2 teaspoons chopped fresh mint leaves

3/4 teaspoon ground black pepper

8 4-ounce lamb rib chops

1 green bell pepper, cut lengthwise into eighths

1 red bell pepper, cut lengthwise into eighths

3 small onions, peeled and quartered

8 cherry tomatoes

1 teaspoon salt

1 MAKE THE MARINADE: In a baking dish, combine red wine, 3 tablespoons olive oil, vinegar, lemon juice, lemon peel, garlic, 2 teaspoons thyme, mint, and 1/2 teaspoon pepper. Reserve 1/4 cup of the marinade and set aside. Add lamb chops to the remaining marinade, cover, and refrigerate for 4 hours, turning meat over halfway through to be sure it is thoroughly marinated.

2 GRILL THE CHOPS: Heat grill or grill pan over high heat until very hot. Remove chops from marinade, pat dry, and set aside. In a large bowl, combine the peppers, onions, tomatoes, remaining olive oil, reserved marinade, salt, remaining pepper, and thyme sprigs and toss to coat. Grill the vegetables until just softened—5 to 6 minutes per side. Remove from heat and keep warm. Grill the chops—about 4 minutes per side for medium rare. Divide evenly among 4 plates and serve immediately with grilled vegetables.

Nutrition information per serving—protein: 61.4 g; fat: 28.1 g; carbohydrate: 11.1 g; fiber: 2.5 g; sodium: 712 mg; cholesterol: 189 mg; calories: 563.

PRIZED FAMILY MEAT LOAF

1 1/4 cups ketchup

1/4 cup Worcestershire sauce

1/4 cup packed light brown sugar

4 teaspoons low-sodium soy sauce

2 cups very coarse fresh bread crumbs

1/2 cup milk

1 cup minced onion (about 1 large)

2/3 cup minced celery (about 2 ribs)

1 tablespoon minced garlic (about 2 cloves)

1/4 cup minced fresh parsley

1 tablespoon dry mustard

2 teaspoons fresh thyme leaves, plus 8 sprigs

3 large eggs

2 teaspoons kosher salt

1 teaspoon coarsely ground black pepper

1 1/2 pounds ground beef

1 pound ground pork

1/2 pound ground veal

1 medium onion, sliced into rings

6 slices bacon

1 MAKE THE KETCHUP GLAZE: In a medium bowl, combine the ketchup, Worcestershire sauce, brown sugar, and soy sauce and stir until combined. Set aside.

2 MAKE THE MEAT LOAF: Preheat oven to 400°F. Combine the bread and the milk in a small bowl and let sit 5 minutes. In a large bowl, combine the minced onion, celery, garlic, parsley, mustard, thyme, eggs, salt, and pepper. Add the bread, meat, and 1/3 cup of the ketchup glaze and toss gently with your hands. Be careful not to overmix—it should be soft but hold its shape.

3 BAKE THE MEAT LOAF: Line a baking sheet with parchment paper. Transfer the meat mixture to the pan, form into a 16- by 5-inch loaf, and coat with 1/3 cup of the ketchup glaze. In a small bowl, combine the onion rings with 2 tablespoons of glaze. Spread the coated onions over the top of the meat loaf. Place the thyme sprigs over the onions and twist the bacon slices in diagonals over the thyme. Place on center rack of oven and bake for 15 minutes. Reduce temperature to 350°F and bake until an internal temperature of 160°F is reached—about 50 more minutes. Remove from oven and allow to rest 15 minutes. Serve with remaining glaze.

Nutrition information per serving—protein: 24.8 g; fat: 17.9 g; carbohydrate: 15.4 g; fiber: .9 g; sodium: 734 mg; cholesterol: 118 mg; calories: 325.

SEAFOOD

STEWED MONKFISH

‹ ‹

This French-style stew is made with monkfish, which has a delicate, sweet flavor similar to that of lobster.

- 4 tablespoons olive oil
- 3 tablespoons chopped garlic
- 3 tablespoons chopped shallots
- 6 7-ounce monkfish fillets
- 6 cups diced plum tomatoes (about 15 tomatoes)
- 2 tablespoons tomato paste
- 1/2 teaspoon salt
- 1/2 teaspoon ground black pepper
- 1/8 teaspoon saffron
- 1/3 cup Cognac or brandy
- 1/4 cup heavy cream
- 1 tablespoon finely chopped fresh parsley

MAKE THE STEW: In a pressure cooker, heat 2 tablespoons olive oil over high heat. Sauté the garlic and shallots, remove from the pot, and set aside. Wipe the pot with a paper towel and heat the remaining olive oil. Sauté the monkfish in batches until lightly browned and remove. Wipe the pot clean again and add the tomatoes, tomato paste, salt, pepper, and saffron to the pressure cooker; stir until well blended. Add the Cognac and return the garlic, shallots, and monkfish to the pressure cooker. Seal the pressure-cooker lid and bring the cooker to high pressure. Reduce the heat just enough to maintain high pressure and cook for 13 minutes. Turn off the heat, quick-release the pressure, and carefully unlock the lid. Gently stir in the cream and parsley. Serve immediately.

Nutrition information per serving—protein: 40.2 g; fat: 17.2 g; carbohydrate: 15 g; fiber: 2.5 g; sodium: 664 mg; cholesterol: 77 mg; calories: 402.

HERB-STUFFED GRILLED TROUT

› ›

Thyme and red onion lend delicate flavors to fresh trout cooked over an open fire.

- 4 1-pound whole trout, gutted and rinsed, with heads and tails left on
- 24 sprigs fresh thyme
- 1 medium red onion, sliced into 1/4-inch-thick rounds
- 1 teaspoon salt
- 1/2 teaspoon ground black pepper
- 2 tablespoons olive oil

1 PREPARE THE FISH: Preheat grill to medium high. Place the trout on a clean work surface. Evenly divide the thyme, red onion, salt, and pepper among the 4 trout and place in the cavity of each. Rub the outside of each trout with the oil and set aside. Cut twelve 10-inch lengths of kitchen twine; tie 3 around the body of each trout to secure the herb stuffing.

2 COOK THE TROUT: Place the trout in a large grill basket and cook directly on the grill rack for about 7 minutes. Flip the grill basket over and continue cooking until the fish is opaque in the center—about 7 more minutes. Remove twine and serve immediately.

Nutrition information per serving—protein: 18.3 g; fat: 21.2 g; carbohydrate: 4 g; fiber: .8 g; sodium: 674 mg; cholesterol: 0; calories: 447.

CRISPY CITRUS AND SESAME FISH FILLETS « <

A crispy coating of black and white sesame seeds keeps this fish tender and moist.

6 ¼-pound fish fillets
(such as bass or halibut)

2 large egg whites

2 tablespoons cornstarch

2 tablespoons white wine vinegar

1 teaspoon kosher salt

¼ cup fresh lime juice

Zest of ½ lime

¼ cup honey

2 tablespoons fresh lemon thyme leaves

⅓ cup white sesame seeds

¼ cup black sesame seeds

¼ cups canola oil

2 cups mâche or mixed baby greens

1 MAKE THE FISH: Cut the fish fillets into 3–inch pieces and transfer to a shallow dish. In a small bowl, stir the egg whites, cornstarch, vinegar, and ½ teaspoon salt together. Pour the mixture over the fish, being certain to coat both sides of each fillet. Cover the dish with plastic wrap and chill for 10 to 15 minutes.

2 MAKE THE CITRUS SAUCE: In a small saucepan, combine fresh lime juice, zest, honey, lemon thyme, and remaining salt over high heat. Boil until it thickens slightly—about 3 minutes—and set aside.

3 FRY THE FISH: Place the sesame seeds in a shallow dish and dip each fillet into the dish to coat each side lightly with the seeds. In a large skillet, heat 2 tablespoons of oil over medium-high heat until very hot. Place the fish, a few fillets at a time, in skillet and fry until cooked through and the white seeds are golden brown—about 4 minutes on each side. Drain fillets, adding more oil as necessary. Place the mâche or greens on a serving platter and place the fish on top. Drizzle the fish and greens with the citrus sauce and serve immediately.

Nutrition information per serving—protein: 25.3 g; fat: 15.1 g; carbohydrate: 18.9 g; fiber: 1.6 g; sodium: 559 mg; cholesterol: 58.6 mg; calories: 301.

CILANTRO-AND-MINT-CRUSTED SEA BASS

We used sea bass, but feel free to substitute other firm-flesh fish such as halibut, cod, or haddock. Choose toasted sesame oil for the richest flavor.

DIPPING SAUCE:

½ cup low-sodium soy sauce

2 tablespoons toasted (dark) sesame oil

2 cloves garlic, finely chopped

2 tablespoons honey

1 tablespoon grated peeled fresh ginger

FISH FILLETS:

⅔ cup finely chopped fresh cilantro leaves

½ cup finely chopped fresh mint leaves

8 6-ounce sea bass fillets

3 cups thinly sliced napa cabbage

1 cup snow peas, cut in half on the diagonal

1 large carrot, cut on the diagonal into thin slices

1 small yellow bell pepper, cut into thin strips

2 green onions, cut on the diagonal into thin slices

Sesame seeds (optional)

1 MAKE THE DIPPING SAUCE: In a small bowl, stir together soy sauce, sesame oil, garlic, honey, and ginger. Cover and set aside.

2 MAKE THE FISH: In a large shallow dish, combine cilantro and mint. Brush 2 tablespoons dipping sauce on the fillets. Dredge them in the herb mixture, patting to coat all sides.

3 COOK THE FISH: Heat oven to 200°F. Heat a large nonstick skillet over medium-high heat. Brush skillet with vegetable oil. Place several fish fillets in skillet and cook until lightly browned—3 to 4 minutes. Turn fillets over and cook just until cooked through—3 to 4 minutes more. Transfer fillets to baking dish and keep warm in the oven. Repeat process with remaining fillets.

4 MAKE THE VEGETABLES: In the same skillet, heat 1 tablespoon dipping sauce over medium heat. Add cabbage, snow peas, carrot, bell pepper, and green onions. Stir-fry until vegetables soften—about 2 minutes. Transfer fillets to plates. Divide vegetables among them and serve with dipping sauce. Sprinkle vegetables with sesame seeds if desired.

Nutrition information per serving—protein: 36 g; fat: 6 g; carbohydrate: 10 g; fiber: 2 g; sodium: 723 mg; cholesterol: 63 mg; calories: 250.

HONEY GINGER-GLAZED SALMON

This just might become your favorite "quick and easy" way to prepare salmon.

- 3 tablespoons honey
- 3 tablespoons dry sherry
- 3 tablespoons soy sauce
- 2 tablespoons fresh lime juice
- 1 tablespoon peeled fresh grated ginger
- 1 tablespoon Dijon mustard
- 4 6-ounce salmon fillets (about 1 inch thick)
- 4 cups hot cooked short-grain rice
- Green onions, for garnish

1 MARINATE THE SALMON: In a shallow glass dish, combine the honey, sherry, soy sauce, lime juice, ginger, and mustard. Place the salmon in a single layer in the dish and turn to coat all sides. Marinate, covered, about 20 minutes, turning from time to time.

2 COOK THE SALMON: Heat the broiler or grill. Lightly coat the broiler pan or grill rack with vegetable oil and arrange salmon fillets, sides not touching. Cook 4 inches from the heat source until the salmon is cooked to desired doneness— 8 to 10 minutes. Use a wide spatula to carefully turn the fish only once halfway through the cooking.

3 TO SERVE: Place salmon fillets on warm dinner plates. Serve with rice and garnish with sliced scallions.

Nutrition information per serving—protein: 40 g; fat: 66 g; carbohydrate: 75 g; fiber: 1.3 g; sodium: 982 mg; cholesterol: 89 mg; calories: 535.

MAPLE-MARINATED ROASTED SALMON

The marinade recipe can be halved and used with several salmon steaks.

- 3/4 cup maple syrup (grade B, if available)
- 2 tablespoons grated peeled fresh ginger
- 2 tablespoons fresh lemon or lime juice
- 2 tablespoons low-sodium soy sauce
- 1/2 teaspoon ground black pepper
- 1/4 teaspoon salt
- 1 2 1/4-pound salmon fillet, skin on

1 MARINATE THE SALMON: Preheat the oven to 400°F. In a large baking dish, combine the maple syrup, ginger, lemon juice, soy sauce, pepper, and salt. Place the salmon, skin-side up, in dish. Cover, refrigerate, and marinate 15 minutes. Turn; marinate 15 minutes more.

2 ROAST THE SALMON: Line a large baking pan with parchment paper. Place the salmon on parchment, skin-side down. Brush the salmon with marinade and place in oven. Roast the salmon 10 minutes; brush with remaining marinade and continue roasting until flesh flakes when tested with a fork—10 to 15 minutes more. Serve.

Nutrition information per serving—protein: 34 g; fat: 11 g; carbohydrate: 27 g; fiber: 0; sodium: 369 mg; cholesterol: 94 mg; calories: 347.

SALMON AND GOAT CHEESE FRITTATA

MAKES 6 SERVINGS (ONE 10-INCH FRITTATA)

This one-dish meal makes a fine entreé for an early-autumn brunch or dinner alfresco. Serve it with a side dish of roasted beets, whose rich, mellow flavor pairs well with the tang of goat cheese.

- 2 tablespoons vegetable oil
- 2 cups shredded potatoes (about 1½ large)
- 4 large egg whites
- 4 large eggs
- 4 ounces smoked salmon, cut into ½-inch pieces
- 1 tablespoon chopped fresh dill
- ½ teaspoon ground black pepper
- ¼ teaspoon salt
- 6-ounce log mild goat cheese, crumbled

1 COOK THE POTATOES: Preheat oven to 500°F. In a 10-inch nonstick, ovenproof skillet, heat oil over medium-high heat. Sauté potatoes until golden brown—about 10 minutes.

2 COOK THE FRITTATA: In a large bowl, combine the egg whites, eggs, salmon, dill, pepper, and salt. Pour the egg mixture over the potatoes and sprinkle the goat cheese over the top. Cook until the edges are set and the bottom is lightly browned—about 5 minutes. Place the pan in the oven and bake until the center of the frittata is set and the top is golden brown—about 3 minutes. Cut into 6 slices and serve immediately or keep warm in the oven.

Nutrition information per serving—protein: 15.9 g; fat: 14.7 g; carbohydrate: 7.8 g; fiber: .7 g; sodium: 421 mg; cholesterol: 159 mg; calories: 229.

GRILLED LOBSTER WITH LIME-BAY BUTTER

MAKES 6 SERVINGS

These lobsters are first parboiled, then finished on the grill, for a no-fuss but special treat.

- 3 1½-pound fresh lobsters
- ½ cup (1 stick) butter
- ¼ cup fresh lime juice
- ½ teaspoon crushed bay leaf
- ¼ teaspoon ground black pepper
- ¼ teaspoon salt
- Lime wedges (optional)
- Bay leaves (optional)

1 BOIL THE LOBSTERS: In an 8-quart saucepan, bring 3 inches of water to boiling over high heat. Add the lobsters to the pan, cover, and cook 10 minutes. Remove lobsters from saucepan and let cool.

2 MAKE THE LIME-BAY BUTTER: In a 1-quart saucepan, heat the butter, lime juice, bay leaf, black pepper, and salt over low heat for 10 minutes.

3 GRILL THE LOBSTERS: Heat grill to medium. When lobsters are cool to the touch, cut in half lengthwise and brush cut side with lime-bay butter. Place lobsters, cut-side down, on the grill about 4 inches from heat source. Cook 5 minutes. Carefully turn lobsters over, brush with butter, and continue grilling until lobster meat is cooked through—about 5 minutes longer.

4 TO SERVE: Transfer lobsters to a serving plate and garnish with lime wedges and bay leaves, if desired. Serve ½ lobster per person.

Nutrition information per serving—protein: 32 g; fat: 17 g; carbohydrate: 2 g; fiber: 0; sodium: 728 mg; cholesterol: 203 mg; calories: 291.

JOHNNYCAKES WITH NANTUCKET BAY SCALLOPS AND HORSERADISH CREAM

MAKES ABOUT 2 DOZEN JOHNNYCAKES

Scallops and fresh corn update our johnny-cakes—traditional cornmeal griddlecakes from New England.

1 cup yellow cornmeal

1 tablespoon all-purpose flour

1 teaspoon baking powder

1/2 teaspoon baking soda

1/2 teaspoon ground black pepper

1/2 teaspoon salt

1/2 pound bay scallops, quartered

3/4 cup fresh or frozen whole
    corn kernels

1 cup buttermilk

1 large egg

1 tablespoon maple syrup

1 tablespoon minced roasted red pepper

1/2 cup crème fraîche or sour cream

1 tablespoon prepared horseradish

1/8 teaspoon ground white pepper

1/3 cup vegetable oil

Chopped fresh chives (optional)

1 MAKE THE SCALLOPS: In a large bowl, mix together the cornmeal, flour, baking powder, baking soda, black pepper, and salt. Add the scallops and corn kernels.

2 MAKE THE JOHNNYCAKES: In a medium bowl, whisk together the buttermilk, egg, and maple syrup. Fold in the red pepper. Pour the buttermilk mixture into the cornmeal mixture and stir just until combined. Set aside.

3 MAKE THE HORSERADISH CREAM: In a small bowl, whisk together the crème fraîche, horseradish, and white pepper. Cover and refrigerate until ready to serve.

4 PREPARE THE JOHNNYCAKES: Heat oven to 225°F. In a large nonstick skillet, heat 1 tablespoon oil over medium high. Drop heaping tablespoons of the batter onto the hot skillet and cook until edges of johnnycakes begin to brown—2 to 3 minutes. Do not let johnnycakes touch. Turn the johnnycakes over and continue cooking until cooked through—2 to 3 minutes longer. Transfer the johnnycakes to a serving platter that can be kept warm in a preheated oven. Repeat the process to cook all the johnnycakes.

5 SERVE THE JOHNNYCAKES: Serve with horseradish cream, and chives, if desired.

Nutrition information per johnnycake—protein: 3 g; fat: 5 g; carbohydrate: 7 g; fiber: .6 g; sodium: 108 mg; cholesterol: 14 mg; calories: 81.

CHOOSING/STORING SEAFOOD

Fish is highly perishable, so it's best to seek out a reliable source for good-quality, fresh fish. When shopping for food, purchase fish that last and get it into your refrigerator as soon as possible. Fish should not smell fishy, sour, or of ammonia. The eyes should be bright and clear—not cloudy or sunken. If buying prepackaged fish, sniff closely, as off-odors can penetrate the plastic. Poke the flesh with your finger. It should be firm and resilient and spring back. Whole fish should have tight, shiny scales and not feel slippery or slimy. The gills should be clean red—never brownish or sticky. The flesh of a fish steak or fillet should look moist and slightly translucent and not contain any gaps.

SEA SCALLOPS AND PASTA WITH GARDEN HERB PESTO < <

A blend of fresh herbs offers a pungent counter-point to succulent scallops. We chose perciatelli, a tubular kind of spaghetti, but you could substitute linguini, rigatoni, or farfalle.

HERB PESTO:

3/4 cup loosely packed fresh basil leaves

3/4 cup loosely packed fresh mint leaves

1/3 cup loosely packed fresh flat-leaf parsley

1/4 cup loosely packed fresh sage leaves

1/3 cup grated Parmesan cheese

1/4 cup walnuts

1/2 teaspoon salt

1/4 teaspoon ground black pepper

6 tablespoons extra-virgin olive oil

ROASTED TOMATOES:

2 pints cherry tomatoes, stemmed and halved

1/4 teaspoon salt

1/8 teaspoon ground black pepper

2 tablespoons extra-virgin olive oil

SCALLOPS:

1 16-ounce package perciatelli or other strand pasta

1 pound sea scallops

2 tablespoons chopped fresh dill

1 tablespoon vegetable oil

1 MAKE THE HERB PESTO: In a food processor fitted with the metal blade, pulse together the basil, mint, parsley, and sage. Add the Parmesan, walnuts, salt, and pepper; process to combine. With the motor running, slowly add the olive oil through the feed tube until mixture forms a paste.

2 PREPARE ROASTED TOMATOES: Preheat the oven to 425°F. In a medium bowl, toss the tomatoes, salt, pepper, and olive oil. Place the tomato halves cut-side down on a nonstick baking pan. Roast the tomatoes until they are softened and the edges are lightly browned—15 to 25 minutes.

3 Prepare the pasta according to package directions; drain well.

4 PREPARE SCALLOPS: In a shallow bowl, combine the scallops and 1 tablespoon dill. In a large skillet, heat the vegetable oil over medium-high heat. When the oil is hot, add the scallops; cook 2 minutes. Turn the scallops over and cook until they are just cooked through—2 to 3 minutes more. Be careful not to overcook them.

5 ASSEMBLE THE DISH: Return the pasta to the cooking pot. Stir the pesto into the hot pasta. Stir in the roasted tomatoes, scallops, and remaining 1 tablespoon dill. Transfer to warm rimmed soup bowls and serve immediately.

Nutrition information per serving—protein: 28 g; fat: 27 g; carbohydrate: 65 g; fiber: 6 g; sodium: 531 mg; cholesterol: 30 mg; calories: 611.

SEAFOOD PAELLA

MAKES 18 SERVINGS

This rustic peasant dish, traditionally cooked outdoors over a wood fire, can be prepared in your backyard over a grill or on your kitchen stove. This dish is named for the pan it is made and served in—a two handled, broad, but shallow dish that is usually made of hammered steal.

- 8 1-pound lobsters
- 3 pounds medium shrimp
- ¼ cup extra-virgin olive oil
- 4 medium Spanish onions, chopped (about 4 cups)
- 2 pounds chorizo, cut into ½-inch-thick slices
- 12 cloves garlic, chopped
- 3 pounds plum tomatoes, chopped
- ½ cup dry white wine
- ¼ cup fresh lemon juice
- 3 cups chopped fresh flat-leaf parsley
- 1 teaspoon ground black pepper
- 1 teaspoon salt
- 4 cups short- or medium-grain white rice (32 ounces)
- 1 tablespoon crushed saffron threads
- 8 cups low-sodium chicken broth
- 48 littleneck clams (about 3 pounds), scrubbed
- 48 mussels (about 3 ½ pounds), scrubbed and beards removed
- 3 cups fresh or frozen green peas

1 MAKE THE LOBSTERS AND SHRIMP: In an 8-quart stockpot, bring 6 quarts of water to a rolling boil over high heat. Plunge the lobsters into boiling water, one or two at a time, and cook until they're bright red—6 to 8 minutes. With tongs, transfer the lobsters to a large platter to cool. In the same stockpot, add the shrimp and cook until pink—1 to 3 minutes. With a slotted spoon, remove the shrimp to a bowl and let cool.

2 When shrimp are cool enough to handle, peel shells and add the shells to the stockpot of boiling water. Place the peeled shrimp in a bowl, cover, and refrigerate.

3 Remove tails and claws from the lobsters. Cut the lobster tails in half lengthwise and then crosswise with kitchen shears. Place the claws and tail pieces in a bowl, cover, and refrigerate.

4 MAKE THE STOCK: Reduce heat to low and simmer the shrimp-shell mixture to make stock for the paella, adding water as needed to maintain 4 quarts of liquid—30 to 40 minutes. Strain and reserve the liquid.

5 MAKE THE PAELLA: In a 26-inch paella pan, warm the olive oil over medium heat. Add the onion, chorizo, and garlic to the pan and sauté until the onion is translucent—5 to 7 minutes. Add the tomatoes, white wine, lemon juice, parsley, pepper, and salt; cook 1 minute. Stir in the rice, saffron, chicken broth, and 3 quarts shrimp stock. Heat to boiling, reduce heat (move to a cool side of the grill), and simmer, stirring occasionally, until liquid is absorbed—20 to 30 minutes. Add the remaining 1 quart shrimp stock, clams, mussels, lobster, shrimp, and peas. Cook, stirring occasionally, until the clams and mussels open and are cooked through—5 to 7 minutes. Discard any unopened clams or mussels. Serve immediately.

Nutrition information per serving—protein: 53 g; fat: 28 g; carbohydrate: 48 g; fiber: 4 g; sodium: 1,783 mg; cholesterol: 254 mg; calories: 674.

TUNA-EGG ROLL-UP

MAKES 4 SERVINGS

The tuna salad in this recipe can easily be doubled for extra wraps, or can be served alone on a bed of lettuce.

- 1 12-ounce can white albacore tuna packed in water, drained and flaked
- 2 hard-cooked large eggs, chopped
- 1 tablespoon chopped fresh parsley
- 1/4 teaspoon salt
- 1/4 teaspoon ground black pepper
- 1/4 cup Curry-Dijon Mayonnaise (recipe follows)
- 4 10-inch sandwich wraps (such as flour tortillas or lavash)
- 1 cup diced tomato
- 8 large leaves Bibb lettuce

1 MAKE THE SALAD: In a large bowl, combine the tuna, egg, parsley, salt, and pepper. Add the Curry-Dijon Mayonnaise and stir until mayonnaise is evenly distributed. Refrigerate in an airtight container until ready to use.

2 ASSEMBLE THE SANDWICHES: On a clean work surface, place 4 wraps and spread about 1/2 cup tuna salad on each. Sprinkle 1/4 cup of the chopped tomatoes over each wrap and top with 2 lettuce leaves. Fold the wrap into a sandwich and serve immediately.

Nutrition information per sandwich—protein: 31.7 g; fat: 20 g; carbohydrate: 35.4 g; fiber: 2 g; sodium: 916 mg; cholesterol: 150 mg; calories: 455.

CURRY-DIJON MAYONNAISE

MAKES ABOUT 3/4 CUP

- 3/4 cup mayonnaise
- 2 tablespoons Dijon mustard
- 2 tablespoons fresh lemon juice
- 1 1/2 teaspoons curry powder

MAKE THE DRESSING: In a small bowl, combine all ingredients. Store refrigerated in an airtight container until ready to use.

Nutrition information per tablespoon—protein: .3 g; fat: 11 g; carbohydrate: .9 g; fiber: .1 g; sodium: 142 mg; cholesterol: 8.1 mg; calories: 103.

OREGON HOT CRAB

MAKES 4 SERVINGS

Produced for more than 100 years in its namesake Oregon county, Tillamook Cheddar comes from fresh milk whose natural enzymes are key to making quality Cheddar cheese. On this open-face crab-salad sandwich it's the icing on the cake.

CHEESE SAUCE:
- 2 tablespoons butter
- 2 tablespoons all-purpose flour
- 1 cup milk
- 1 1/2 cups shredded Tillamook or other mild Cheddar cheese (about 6 ounces)
- 1 teaspoon dry mustard
- 1/2 teaspoon Worcestershire sauce
- 1/4 teaspoon salt
- 1/8 teaspoon ground red pepper

SANDWICH FILLING:
- 3/4 pound fresh crabmeat, picked over and shell pieces discarded
- 1/4 cup chopped green onions
- 2 tablespoons mayonnaise
- 1/2 teaspoon hot pepper sauce
- 1 teaspoon fresh lemon juice
- 1/8 teaspoon ground black pepper

SANDWICH BASE:
- 8 slices sourdough bread

1 MAKE THE CHEESE SAUCE: In a 2-quart saucepan, melt the butter over medium heat. Add the flour and cook mixture, whisking constantly—about 1 minute. Add the milk and continue to whisk. Increase heat to medium-high and bring the mixture to a boil. Cook 1 more minute. Remove from heat and whisk in the cheese, mustard, Worcestershire sauce, salt, and red pepper. Cover and keep warm.

2 ASSEMBLE THE SANDWICHES: Preheat broiler. In a medium bowl, mix together the crabmeat, green onions, mayonnaise, hot pepper sauce, lemon juice, and black pepper. On a sheet pan, place the bread slices and top each with 1/2 cup of the crab salad. Pour 1/4 cup cheese sauce over each sandwich and place under broiler until lightly browned—about 2 minutes. Serve immediately.

Nutrition information per serving—protein: 35 g; fat: 30 g; carbohydrate: 33.2 g; fiber: 1.7 g; sodium: 1,065 mg; cholesterol: 148 mg; calories: 547.

SEAFOOD GUMBO > >

MAKES EIGHTEEN 1 1/2-CUP SERVINGS

Gumbo filé powder, the ground leaves of the sassafras tree, can be ordered.

1 cup all-purpose flour

1 cup vegetable oil

6 stalks celery, diced (about 3 cups)

3 medium onions, diced (about 3 cups)

3 large green bell peppers, diced (about 3 cups)

7 cups low-sodium chicken broth

1½ pounds okra, cut into ½-inch-thick slices (about 3 cups)

1 pound smoked ham, diced

½ pound crabmeat, picked over and shell pieces discarded

2 28-ounce cans crushed tomatoes, drained, juice reserved

½ cup chopped fresh flat-leaf parsley

1 tablespoon fresh lemon juice

1 tablespoon sugar

1 teaspoon dried oregano

½ teaspoon dried thyme

½ teaspoon Old Bay seasoning

½ teaspoon salt

¼ teaspoon ground black pepper

¼ teaspoon ground red pepper

2 pounds fresh or frozen medium shrimp, peeled and deveined

½ teaspoon gumbo filé powder

9 cups hot cooked rice

Hot-pepper sauce to taste

1 In a 12-quart heavy kettle or Dutch oven, heat the flour and oil over medium-low heat. Cook, stirring frequently, until the flour browns to a dark mahogany color, being careful not to let it burn—40 to 50 minutes. Stir in the celery, onion, and bell pepper. Cook, stirring occasionally, until the vegetables are soft—about 30 minutes.

2 Add the chicken stock, okra, ham, and crabmeat; cook 40 minutes more. Stir in the tomatoes and juice, parsley, lemon juice, sugar, oregano, thyme, Old Bay seasoning, salt, black pepper, and red pepper. Cook 30 minutes. Stir in the shrimp and filé powder; cook until the shrimp have cooked through—about 15 minutes. Serve warm over rice with hot-pepper sauce or freeze for up to 2 months.

Nutrition information per serving (with ½ cup rice)—protein: 39 g; fat: 20 g; carbohydrate: 42 g; fiber: 3 g; sodium: 788 mg; cholesterol: 156 mg; calories: 512.

SEAFOOD SUBSTITUTIONS

To help cooks who do not find their first choice at the seafood market, here is a list of suggested substitutions for some of the seafood in this chapter.

> You can usually substitute any variety of fresh or salt-water trout (brook, brown, rainbow or salmon) in any recipe that calls for trout.

> In many salmon recipes, Chinook (King), Atlantic Coho, and sockeye, can be used interchangeably.

> Instead of turbot, any mild-flavored white fish, such as flounder, fluke, or sole, can be substituted.

> In recipes calling for (saltwater) sea bass, (freshwater) white bass, snapper, grouper or black cod can be used.

> The only real substitute for lobster is its cousin the spiny lobster, which has no claws and lives in warmer waters.

PASTA AND GRAINS

FRESH HERB PASTA > >

This dish was designed to showcase fresh veggies from the spring farmers' markets. It's also wonderful made with sweet sugar snap peas or slivered baby carrots in place of the asparagus.

1/2 cup plus 2 tablespoons olive oil

1 cup fresh flat-leaf parsley

2 sprigs fresh mint

1 tablespoon fresh marjoram leaves

1 tablespoon fresh thyme leaves

2 tablespoons fresh lemon juice

1 large clove garlic, coarsely chopped

1 tablespoon grated lemon zest

1 tablespoon plus 1 teaspoon salt

1/4 teaspoon ground black pepper

1/2 pound asparagus, trimmed and cut into 2-inch pieces

1 16-ounce package bowtie pasta

2 cups baby Roma and yellow pear tomatoes, halved

8 ounces goat's milk Gouda (Arina) or ricotta salata, crumbled into 1/2-inch pieces

1 MAKE THE HERB SAUCE: In a food processor fitted with the metal blade, place the olive oil, herbs, lemon juice, garlic, zest, 1 teaspoon salt, and pepper. Pulse until the herbs are coarsely chopped. Remove the sauce and set aside.

2 BLANCH THE ASPARAGUS: In a medium saucepan, bring 1 quart of water to a boil. Add the asparagus and cook until just tender—2 to 3 minutes. Drain and immediately transfer to a bowl of ice water to cool. Drain and set aside.

3 COOK THE PASTA: In a large saucepan, bring 2 quarts of water to a boil over high heat. Add the remaining salt, stir in the pasta, and cook for 10 minutes. Drain and set aside.

4 FINISH THE PASTA: In a large bowl, combine the pasta, asparagus, herb sauce, tomatoes, and half of the goat cheese. Toss well to coat and top with the remaining cheese. Serve at room temperature or chilled.

Nutrition information per serving—protein: 16.4 g; fat: 36.7 g; carbohydrate: 26.7 g; fiber: 2.5 g; sodium: 497 mg; cholesterol: 39.7 mg; calories: 497.

PUMPKIN RAVIOLI IN SAGE BUTTER SAUCE

Using *Gyoza* wrappers, round Japanese dumpling skins, speeds up making the "ravioli." Gyoza wrappers are available in Asian markets and in some supermarkets.

1/4 cup plus 1 tablespoon pepita (pumpkin) seeds

1 cup canned unsweetened pumpkin puree

1 teaspoon fresh lemon juice

4 ounces Asiago cheese, cut into cubes

2 cups loosely packed arugula, coarsely chopped

1 teaspoon freshly ground pink peppercorns

1 3/4 teaspoons salt

1 tablespoon cornstarch

48 Gyoza wrappers

6 tablespoons butter

6 tablespoons chopped fresh sage leaves

1/2 teaspoon ground black pepper

Shaved Asiago cheese (optional)

1 MAKE THE PUMPKIN FILLING: In a large skillet, toast the pepitas over medium-high heat—about 3 minutes. In a food processor fitted with the metal blade, combine 1/4 cup toasted pepitas, pumpkin puree, lemon juice, cubed cheese, chopped arugula, peppercorns, and 1/4 teaspoon of the salt; blend until smooth.

2 ASSEMBLE THE RAVIOLI: Dissolve cornstarch in 1 cup water. Place 1 tablespoon filling in the center of one Gyoza wrapper. Wet the wrapper edges with cornstarch mixture and fold in half. Repeat the process with the rest of the filling. Place the finished ravioli on a parchment-lined baking sheet that has been lightly sprinkled with cornstarch.

3 COOK AND SERVE: In a large pot, bring 2 quarts water to a boil. Boil the ravioli until they rise to the surface — about 3 minutes. Drain and set aside. In a small skillet, melt butter over medium heat until golden brown. Remove from heat and stir in the sage, the remaining salt, and pepper. Drizzle over the ravioli. Garnish with the remaining toasted pepitas and shaved Asiago cheese, if desired. Serve immediately.

Nutrition information per serving—protein: 9.7 g; fat: 14 g; carbohydrate: 33 g; fiber: 1.3 g; sodium: 782 mg; cholesterol: 41 mg; calories: 292.

GRANDDAD'S SPECIAL LASAGNA

MAKES 8 SERVINGS

This vegetarian lasagna tastes even better when made ahead. Doing so allows time for the flavors to marry.

MARINARA SAUCE:

1 tablespoon olive oil

2 medium onions, chopped
   (about 2 cups)

4 cloves garlic, chopped

1 bay leaf

2 28-ounce cans crushed tomatoes

1 6-ounce can tomato paste

2 teaspoons salt

1/4 teaspoon ground black pepper

1 teaspoon dried Italian seasoning

BÉCHAMEL SAUCE:

4 tablespoons butter

4 tablespoons all-purpose flour

3 cups milk

1 bay leaf

10 whole black peppercorns

1/4 teaspoon ground nutmeg

LASAGNA:

3 cups ricotta cheese

2/3 cup grated Parmesan cheese

3 tablespoons chopped fresh parsley

2 large eggs

2 8-ounce packages oven-ready
   lasagna noodles

1 pound shredded mozzarella
   cheese

1 MAKE MARINARA SAUCE: In a 6-quart saucepan, heat the olive oil and sauté the onions and garlic until lightly browned—about 10 minutes. Add the bay leaf, crushed tomatoes, tomato paste, salt, pepper, and Italian seasoning and bring to a boil. Lower the heat and simmer 20 minutes. Remove from heat, discard the bay leaf, and set aside.

2 MAKE BÉCHAMEL SAUCE: In a 2-quart saucepan, melt the butter over medium heat. Whisk in the flour and cook 1 minute. Add the milk, bay leaf, and peppercorns and bring the mixture to a boil, stirring constantly until the sauce thickens. Remove from heat and stir in the nutmeg; strain into a small mixing bowl and set aside.

3 MAKE CHEESE FILLING: In a medium bowl, combine the ricotta, Parmesan, parsley, and eggs and set aside.

4 ASSEMBLE THE LASAGNA: Preheat the oven to 350˚F. In a 10- by 14-inch pan, spread a thin layer of marinara sauce. Place a layer of lasagna noodles over the sauce. Spread a layer of béchamel sauce over the noodles and top with another layer of noodles. Spread this with a layer of marinara sauce and top with another layer of noodles. Spread the cheese filling over noodles. Sprinkle with half the shredded mozzarella cheese. Top this with another layer of noodles and more marinara sauce; sprinkle with the remaining mozzarella cheese. Bake the lasagna until it is bubbly and the top is lightly browned—about 50 minutes.

5 TO SERVE: Allow the lasagna to stand at room temperature 1/2 hour before serving. Cut into squares. Serve the remaining marinara sauce on the side.

Nutrition information per serving—protein: 19 g; fat: 20 g; carbohydrate: 26.5 g; fiber: 3.4 g; sodium: 709 mg; cholesterol: 89 mg; calories: 356.

PERCIATELLI CARBONARA

MAKES 8 SERVINGS

There is little secret to what makes this creamy pasta dish so heavenly—sharp Pecorino Romano cheese, rich egg yolks, and the full, smoky flavor of applewood–smoked bacon.

2 large egg yolks, beaten

$1^1/2$ cups half-and-half

$1/2$ pound sliced applewood-smoked bacon, cooled and crumbled

1 medium onion, chopped (about 1 cup)

2 tablespoons minced garlic

$1/2$ cup grated Pecorino Romano cheese

$1/2$ cup chopped fresh parsley

1 teaspoon salt

$1/2$ teaspoon ground black pepper

1 16-ounce package perciatelli pasta, cooked according to package directions

MAKE THE CARBONARA SAUCE: In a medium bowl, lightly beat the egg yolks and half-and-half and set aside. In a large skillet over medium-high heat, cook bacon until crisp. Remove bacon; set aside to drain on paper towels. Reserve 1 tablespoon bacon fat and cook the onions over medium heat until translucent—about 5 minutes. Add the garlic and continue to cook 2 more minutes. Reduce heat to low and add the egg mixture and the bacon. Stirring constantly, cook until the sauce begins to thicken slightly—about 5 minutes. Stir in $1/4$ cup of the cheese, parsley, salt, and pepper and remove from heat. Pour the sauce over the cooked pasta, toss until well coated, and sprinkle with the remaining cheese. Serve immediately.

Nutrition information per serving—protein: 18.8 g; fat: 23.4 g; carbohydrate: 36.6 g; fiber: 2.2 g; sodium: 918 mg; cholesterol: 101.3 mg; calories: 426.

CURRIED BUTTERNUT SQUASH AND RICE CASSEROLE

MAKES 6 SERVINGS

This baked rice dish makes a satisfying meal.

2 tablespoons vegetable oil

1 medium onion, chopped (about 1 cup)

1 shallot, chopped

1 tablespoon curry powder

1 teaspoon salt

$1/2$ teaspoon ground coriander

$1/4$ teaspoon ground black pepper

2 cups low-sodium chicken or vegetable broth

1 14-ounce can reduced-fat coconut milk

$1^1/2$ pounds butternut squash, peeled and cut into $1/2$-inch chunks (about $2^1/2$ cups)

$1^1/2$ cups basmati rice

$1/4$ cup sliced almonds

$1/4$ cup golden raisins

MAKE THE CASSEROLE: Preheat oven to 375°F. In a 4-quart shallow Dutch oven, heat the oil over medium heat. Add the onions, shallots, curry powder, salt, coriander, and pepper. Sauté until onion has softened—5 to 7 minutes. Stir in the broth and the coconut milk. Bring the mixture to a boil over high heat. Cook 1 minute. Remove the pan from heat and stir in the squash, rice, almonds, and raisins. Cover tightly and place in oven. Bake 20 minutes. Carefully remove the cover and bake 10 minutes longer. Serve immediately.

Nutrition information per serving—protein: 6 g; fat: 7 g; carbohydrate: 57 g; fiber: 5 g; sodium: 567 mg; cholesterol: 4 mg; calories: 310.

GORGONZOLA-BUTTERMILK PASTA WITH ARUGULA < <

Gorgonzola—Italian blue cheese—blends well with peppery arugula and buttermilk in this easy pasta dish.

- 1 tablespoon plus $1/4$ teaspoon salt
- 8 ounces penne pasta
- 4 ounces Gorgonzola, crumbled
- $1/2$ cup buttermilk
- 2 tablespoons chopped fresh flat-leaf parsley
- $1/4$ teaspoon coarsely ground black pepper
- 2 cups loosely packed fresh arugula, rinsed, dried, and torn
- 2 tablespoons pine nuts, toasted

1 MAKE THE PASTA: In a large pot, bring 4 quarts water to a boil over high heat. Add 1 tablespoon of the salt and stir in the pasta until water boils again. Continue to cook 10 to 12 minutes, until done. Remove from heat and drain. Place in a large pasta bowl and set aside.

2 DRESS THE PASTA: In a small bowl, stir together the Gorgonzola, buttermilk, parsley, remaining salt, and pepper. Pour over hot cooked pasta and toss to coat evenly.

3 SERVE THE PASTA: Add the arugula to the pasta, toss well, top with pine nuts, and serve immediately.

Nutrition information per serving—protein: 14 g; fat: 11 g; carbohydrate: 28.6 g; fiber: 4.4 g; sodium: 656 g; cholesterol: 26 g; calories: 261.

PORCINI-PANCETTA RISOTTO

This creamy rice dish is pure comfort food—Italian style. Serve it as a first course with grilled meats, or as a main dish with a salad on the side. If your supermarket doesn't carry pancetta, the quintessential Italian cured bacon, look for it in a gourmet food or butcher shop. Or substitute thinly sliced smoked bacon.

- $1^1/2$ ounces dried porcini mushrooms
- 6 ounces pancetta, chopped
- 1 medium onion, chopped (about 1 cup)
- 2 tablespoons finely chopped garlic
- $1^1/2$ cups arborio rice
- $1/2$ cup Marsala wine
- $2^1/2$ cups low-sodium chicken broth
- $1/2$ teaspoon finely chopped fresh rosemary leaves
- 1 teaspoon salt
- $1/2$ teaspoon ground black pepper
- $1/2$ cup grated Asiago cheese
- 2 teaspoons grated lemon zest
- 1 teaspoon finely chopped fresh parsley

1 REHYDRATE THE MUSHROOMS: Place the mushrooms in a medium bowl, add $1^1/2$ cups boiling water, and steep until soft—about 15 minutes. Use a slotted spoon to remove the mushrooms, reserving the broth. Roughly chop the mushrooms and set aside. Pour the mushroom liquid through a very fine strainer or cheesecloth and reserve.

2 MAKE THE RISOTTO: In a pressure cooker, cook the pancetta over medium-high heat until lightly browned. Add the onions and garlic and cook until soft. Stir in the rice, add the Marsala, and continue to cook until most of the liquid has been absorbed—about 2 minutes. Add the mushrooms, reserved mushroom broth, chicken broth, rosemary, salt, and pepper. Seal the pressure-cooker lid and bring the cooker to high pressure. Reduce the heat just enough to maintain high pressure and cook for 7 minutes. Turn off the heat, quick-release the pressure, and carefully remove the lid. Over medium-high heat, stir the rice constantly until it becomes creamy and thick—1 to 2 minutes. Remove from heat and stir in the Asiago and lemon zest. Garnish with parsley and serve immediately.

Nutrition information per serving—protein: 14.8 g; fat: 8.9 g; carbohydrate: 45.8 g; fiber: 2.7 g; sodium: 821 mg; cholesterol: 24.8 mg; calories: 336.

SAGE BAKED MACARONI AND CHEESE

Our zesty version of macaroni and cheese combines two rich Italian cheeses and fresh sage with a generous sprinkling of salt-cured ham. Little tube pasta (ditalini) replaces elbow macaroni.

1 16-ounce package ditalini pasta

$1^3/_4$ cups half-and-half

$^3/_4$ cup whole milk

1 8-ounce package cream cheese

3 tablespoons unsalted butter

2 cups grated provolone cheese (about 10 ounces)

$1^3/_4$ cups coarsely grated Parmesan cheese (about 5 ounces)

2 ounces prosciutto, coarsely chopped (about $^1/_2$ cup)

1 tablespoon minced fresh sage leaves

1 teaspoon ground black pepper

$^1/_2$ teaspoon salt

1 MAKE THE SAUCE: Preheat the oven to 350°F. Cook the pasta following package directions. Strain the pasta, rinse with cold water to cool, drain well, and transfer to a large bowl. Set aside. In a medium saucepan, combine the half-and-half, milk, cream cheese, and butter. Cook over medium heat, stirring occasionally, until the butter and cream cheese have melted—about 10 minutes.

2 ASSEMBLE THE MACARONI AND CHEESE: Toss the provolone, $1^1/_2$ cups Parmesan, prosciutto, sage, pepper, and salt with the reserved pasta. Add the hot milk mixture and stir until well combined. Evenly divide the macaroni mixture among eight 4-ounce ramekins. Place the filled cups on a baking sheet and sprinkle the remaining $^1/_4$ cup Parmesan cheese evenly over the tops. Bake until the macaroni is set and the tops are golden brown—about 25 minutes. Serve hot in ramekins.

Nutrition information per serving—protein: 23 g; fat: 34.5 g; carbohydrate: 21.7 g; fiber: .8 g; sodium: 882 mg; cholesterol: 102 mg; calories: 489.

HERBED RICE-STUFFED SWISS CHARD

This Asian–inspired side dish, gently spiced with cilantro, mint, peanuts, and ginger, makes a wonderful appetizer. Serve it with Asian beer or iced tea.

8 large leaves fresh Swiss chard

1 cup cooked long-grain white rice

2 carrots, coarsely grated (about $^1/_2$ cup)

$^1/_2$ cup chopped fresh mint leaves

$^1/_4$ cup coarsely grated peeled, seeded cucumber

2 green onions, chopped

3 tablespoons low-sodium soy sauce

2 teaspoons grated peeled fresh ginger

1 teaspoon honey

$^1/_2$ teaspoon salt

$^1/_4$ teaspoon ground black pepper

$^1/_3$ cup rice vinegar

3 tablespoons sugar

2 teaspoons toasted (dark) sesame oil

1 teaspoon crushed red pepper

1 PREPARE SWISS CHARD: Fill a large bowl with ice water and set aside. Fill a large saucepan with water and bring to a boil over high heat. Blanch chard leaves by submerging in the boiling water until the rib is softened and the leaves become limp—about 1 minute. Transfer to the prepared ice bath, drain cooled leaves and stack between sheets of paper towel until dry. Cut out the rib on each leaf and set leaves aside.

2 MAKE THE ROLLS: In a large bowl, combine the rice, carrot, mint, cucumber, $^1/_2$ the onion, 1 tablespoon soy sauce, ginger, honey, salt, and pepper. Place about $^1/_4$ cup of filling in the center of a chard leaf and roll into a cigar shape. Keep chilled until ready to serve.

3 MAKE THE DIPPING SAUCE: In a small bowl, mix the rice vinegar, sugar, remaining soy sauce, remaining onion, sesame oil, and red pepper until combined. Serve alongside rolls.

Nutrition information per roll with sauce—protein: 5.9 g; fat: 1.7 g; carbohydrate: 23.9 g; fiber: 5.5 g; sodium: 345 mg; cholesterol: 0; calories: 135.

BUTTERCUP-BARLEY STEW

MAKES 4 SERVINGS

This autumn recipe calls for buttercup squash, which has a flavor reminiscent of sweet potato. You can also substitute delicata, sweet dumpling, or acorn squash.

- 2 teaspoons cumin seeds
- 1 tablespoon vegetable oil
- 1 large onion, chopped (about 1 $^1/_2$ cups)
- $^1/_3$ cup barley
- 1 teaspoon sugar
- 2 large cloves garlic, finely chopped
- 2 tablespoons all-purpose flour
- 1 tablespoon chili powder
- $^1/_2$ teaspoon salt
- 2 pounds buttercup or other winter squash, peeled and cut into 1-inch pieces (about 5$^1/_2$ cups)
- 2 cups water
- 1 14$^1/_2$-ounce can vegetable or low-sodium chicken broth
- $^1/_2$ cup chopped red bell pepper
- $^1/_4$ cup minced fresh cilantro leaves

MAKE THE STEW: In a large saucepan, place the cumin and toast over medium heat until fragrant—about 1 minute. Remove the cumin from the pan and set aside. Add the oil to the saucepan and heat until hot. Add the onion, barley, sugar, and 1 teaspoon toasted cumin seeds and sauté until the onions are lightly browned—about 5 minutes. Stir in the garlic, flour, chili powder, and salt. Add the squash, water, and broth and bring to a boil. Reduce the heat to medium low, cover the saucepan, and simmer for 10 minutes. Remove the cover and continue to simmer until the squash is very tender and the stew thickens—about 10 more minutes. Stir in the remaining cumin seeds, bell pepper, and cilantro. Serve immediately.

Nutrition information per 1$^1/_2$-cup serving—protein: 6.3 g; fat: 6 g; carbohydrate: 46 g; fiber: 10.8 g; sodium: 1,255 mg; cholesterol: 0; calories: 243.

CRANBERRY-WALNUT COUSCOUS

MAKES 6 SERVINGS (5 CUPS)

Here's the perfect sidekick for roast chicken or even Thanksgiving turkey. Toasting the walnuts make them crunchier. Simply place the nuts on a sheet pan and set in a 350°-400°F oven until lightly brown and crispy, watching them carefully and shaking the pan occasionally to avoid burning.

- $^1/_2$ cup dried cranberries
- 2$^1/_2$ cups low-sodium chicken broth
- 1 tablespoon olive oil
- $^1/_2$ cup chopped onion
- 1 tablespoon minced garlic
- 1 teaspoon kosher salt
- $^1/_4$ teaspoon ground black pepper
- 1$^1/_4$ cups couscous
- $^1/_2$ cup chopped walnuts, toasted
- 1/4 cup chopped fresh mint leaves

1 REHYDRATE THE CRANBERRIES: In a small saucepan, bring the cranberries and $^1/_2$ cup chicken broth to a boil over medium-high heat. Remove from heat and allow to steep until the cranberries are plump—about 10 minutes. Set aside.

2 MAKE THE COUSCOUS: In a medium saucepan, heat the oil over medium-high heat. Add the onions and cook until translucent—about 5 minutes. Add the garlic and cook until golden—about 2 minutes. Add the remaining broth, salt, and pepper and bring to a boil. Immediately stir in the couscous, cover, and remove from heat. Let the couscous stand 5 minutes. Remove cover and use a fork to separate and fluff the couscous grains. Stir in the walnuts, plumped cranberries, and mint. Serve warm or at room temperature.

Nutrition information per serving—protein: 5.3 g; fat: 9.5 g; carbohydrate: 28 g; fiber: 3 g; sodium: 413 mg; cholesterol: 2.3 mg; calories: 192.

OREGANO-LEMON COUSCOUS SALAD

MAKES 8 SERVINGS

Mild couscous provides a welcome home for aromatic oregano-lemon dressing. For ease, make this summer salad ahead of time to have on hand for light meals.

LEMON-OREGANO DRESSING:

¼ cup fresh lemon juice

¼ cup extra-virgin olive oil

1 clove garlic, finely chopped

1 tablespoon chopped fresh oregano leaves

½ teaspoon ground black pepper

¼ teaspoon salt

COUSCOUS SALAD:

2 cups water

1 tablespoon butter

¼ teaspoon salt

1 10-ounce package plain couscous

½ small red onion, thinly sliced

½ cup pitted kalamata olives, halved

⅓ cup crumbled feta cheese (2 ounces)

⅓ cup golden raisins

¼ cup fresh flat-leaf parsley leaves

¼ cup pine nuts, toasted

Thin strips lemon zest (optional)

1 MAKE THE OREGANO-LEMON DRESSING: In a small bowl, whisk together the lemon juice, olive oil, garlic, oregano, pepper, and salt. Cover and set aside.

2 MAKE THE COUSCOUS SALAD: In a 2-quart saucepan, heat the water, butter, and salt to boiling over high heat. Stir in the couscous and red onion. Cover and remove from heat. Let stand 5 minutes. Fluff with a fork.

3 In a large serving bowl, combine the couscous, olives, feta, raisins, parsley, and pine nuts. Stir in the dressing and toss. Garnish with strips of lemon zest if desired.

Nutrition information per serving—protein: 7 g; fat: 14 g; carbohydrate: 34 g; fiber: 3 g; sodium: 569 mg; cholesterol: 10 mg; calories: 278.

RICE VARIETIES

In the past, serving rice meant a side-dish of white rice, brown rice, or wild rice. Today's cook has a tempting array of rice to choose from, including black rice, sticky rice, and red rice. Here is a guide to some of the more popular rices now available.

> Arborio: The grains of this super-starchy white rice are short and oval. It is most often used for risotto. Other varieties of Italian rice used for risotto are Carnaroli and Vialone Nano. These rices absorb up to five times their weight in liquid, which results in a creamy textured risotto.

> Aromatic rice: The most famous aromatic rice is basmati, a long-grain rice commonly used in Indian cooking. It has a nutty fragrance and almost buttery texture.

> Jasmine: A long-grain white rice from Thailand similar in flavor to basmati.

> Glutinous (or sticky) rice : This rice can be long- or short-grained and has a soft, sticky texture. In Southeast Asia, sticky rice is used in many savory and sweet dishes, including New Year's sticky rice cakes.

CHEESE GRITS AND CORN PUDDING

For anyone who grew up eating grits, this pudding will be a revelation. It's light, airy, and deliciously flavored with corn—yet still has that familiar grits taste.

1¹/₂ cups milk

1 teaspoon kosher salt

¹/₄ cup grits

³/₄ cup shredded aged Cheddar cheese

2 large egg yolks

³/₄ cup pureed canned or frozen whole corn kernels

¹/₄ teaspoon ground black pepper

3 large egg whites

1 MAKE THE GRITS: Preheat the oven to 375°F. In a small saucepan, bring the milk to a simmer over medium heat. Add ¹/₂ teaspoon salt and slowly add the grits in a steady stream while stirring constantly. Continue stirring over medium heat until thickened—about 25 minutes. Transfer the grits to a large mixing bowl and let cool slightly.

2 MAKE THE PUDDING: Add the cheese, egg yolks, and corn to the grits; stir to combine, and set aside. Transfer the mixture to a large bowl and add the pepper and remaining salt and toss. With an electric mixer on high speed, beat the egg whites until they form stiff peaks. Fold the egg-white mixture into the corn mixture in thirds. Fill eight 1-cup capacity ramekins ³/₄ full and place on a baking sheet. Bake until the tops are brown and the soufflés have puffed—40–45 minutes. Serve immediately.

Nutrition information per serving—protein: 7.1 g; fat: 6.4 g; carbohydrate: 10 g; fiber: .9 g; sodium: 378 mg; cholesterol: 70.6 mg; calories: 123.

CORNMEAL FRITTERS WITH SPICY BUTTERMILK DIPPING SAUCE

Somewhat akin to hush puppies, these crispy fritters have the added zest of fresh herbs and a piquant sauce for dipping as an appetizer.

4 cups canola oil

³/₄ cup buttermilk

¹/₃ cup finely chopped onion

¹/₄ cup heavy cream

¹/₂ cup plus 3 tablespoons sour cream

2 large eggs

4 teaspoons chopped fresh parsley

4 teaspoons chopped fresh chives

1 teaspoon chopped fresh thyme leaves

1 cup cornmeal

¹/₂ cup all-purpose flour

1 teaspoon baking powder

¹/₄ teaspoon baking soda

1¹/₄ teaspoons salt

¹/₈ teaspoon ground black pepper

¹/₂ teaspoon hot pepper sauce

1 MAKE THE BATTER: In a large saucepan, heat the oil over medium-high heat to 385°F. Whisk together ¹/₂ cup buttermilk, onions, cream, 3 tablespoons sour cream, eggs, and herbs in a large bowl and set aside. In a medium bowl, combine the cornmeal, flour, baking powder, baking soda, and ¹/₂ teaspoon salt. Add the flour mixture to the buttermilk mixture and stir to combine.

2 MAKE THE SAUCE: Stir together the remaining sour cream, buttermilk, ¹/₄ teaspoon salt, black pepper, and hot sauce in a small bowl. Chill until ready to serve.

3 FRY THE FRITTERS: Drop the batter by 2-teaspoon spoonfuls into the hot oil and fry until dark brown—3–5 minutes. Transfer the fritters to paper towels to drain, sprinkle with remaining salt and serve hot alongside dip.

Nutrition information per serving—protein: 3.5 g; fat: 23.6 g; carbohydrate: 16.5 g; fiber: 1.2 g; sodium: 372 mg; cholesterol: 58.4 mg; calories: 288.

GRILLED VEGETABLES WITH ROSEMARY GOAT CHEESE POLENTA

MAKES 6 SERVINGS

Goat cheese adds a tangy creaminess to this side dish. We serve it with grilled vegetables, but it also is an ideal partner for grilled meats.

- 1 tablespoon unsalted butter
- $1/2$ cup finely chopped onion
- $3/4$ cup polenta or stone-ground yellow cornmeal
- 1 14-ounce can low-sodium chicken broth
- $1^1/2$ teaspoons kosher salt
- $1^1/2$ teaspoons ground black pepper
- $1/4$ teaspoon ground red pepper
- 1 cup water
- 3 tablespoons mild goat cheese
- 2 tablespoons fresh rosemary leaves, roughly chopped
- $1/2$ cup plus 2 tablespoons extra-virgin olive oil
- 6 pounds mixed vegetables (such as Japanese eggplant, baby squash, red potatoes, or bell peppers), halved or quartered

1 MAKE THE POLENTA: Line a baking sheet with plastic wrap and set aside. In a large heavy saucepan, melt the butter over medium heat, then sauté the onion until golden—about 10 minutes. Stir in the polenta, broth, $1/2$ teaspoon salt, $1/2$ teaspoon black pepper, and red pepper and bring the mixture to a boil. Lower heat and cook until polenta thickens—10 to 15 minutes. Stir in 1 cup water, cheese and chopped rosemary. Transfer polenta to prepared pan, spread evenly, and cool completely.

2 GRILL THE POLENTA: Heat a grill until very hot. Invert the polenta pan onto a clean surface. Cut the polenta into 3-inch triangles, brush each with olive oil, and place on grill. Cook until polenta is heated through and golden—about 10 minutes. Place the grilled polenta triangles on a platter and keep warm.

3 GRILL THE VEGETABLES: In a large bowl, place the vegetables, add the remaining olive oil, salt, and pepper, and toss to coat. Grill the vegetables until they just begin to soften. Place the grilled vegetables over the polenta and serve immediately.

Nutrition information per serving—protein: 7.3 g; fat: 19 g; carbohydrate: 32.3 g; fiber: 6 g; sodium: 435 mg; cholesterol: 10 mg; calories: 313.

CORN
From Flour to Meal to Polenta

Corn flour, cornmeal, and corn grits differ only in the size of the corn particles. *Corn flour* is almost as fine as wheat flour and can be used in cakes and cookies (it should not be confused with the thickening agent cornstarch). *Cornmeal* is more coarsely ground than corn flour, so it is a more granular. Polenta is Italian cornmeal and the name of the classic cornmeal mush it is traditionally used to make. Polenta is made from ground flint corn, while American cornmeal is made from flour corn. *Corn grits* is also made from flour corn and is the coarsest grind of corn. Grits is used for making a mush that is a beloved breakfast food in the South.

VEGETABLES

BRAISED BELGIAN ENDIVE WITH WALNUTS

In this simple and elegant side dish, endive slowly cooks in a bath of dry white wine. Try it with roasted chicken or veal stew.

- 3 tablespoons butter
- 4 large heads Belgian endive, quartered lengthwise
- 1 tablespoon chopped fresh basil leaves
- $1/4$ teaspoon ground white pepper
- 1 cup dry white wine
- 2 tablespoons chopped walnuts, toasted

BRAISE THE ENDIVE: In a large skillet, melt the butter over medium heat. Add the endive pieces, basil, and pepper and cook until the endive is lightly browned—about 2 minutes on each side. Add $3/4$ cup wine, reduce heat to medium low, and simmer, turning the endive periodically, for 20 minutes. Add the remaining wine and continue to cook until the endive is lightly browned and tender and the liquid has reduced—5 to 10 more minutes. Arrange the endive on a platter and garnish with the walnuts. Serve immediately.

Nutrition information per serving—protein: 2.2 g; fat: 11 g; carbohydrate: 5 g; fiber: 2.6 g; sodium: 29 mg; cholesterol: 23 mg; calories: 160.

HOT COLLARD SLAW   > >

- $1/4$ cup olive oil
- 2 tablespoons cider vinegar
- 2 tablespoons coarse-grain mustard
- $1/2$ teaspoon salt
- $1/2$ teaspoon ground black pepper
- $1/2$ teaspoon sugar
- 1 clove garlic, crushed with the side of a large knife
- 2 pounds collard greens, washed, dried, and cut horizontally into $3/4$-inch-wide strips (about 16 cups)
- $1/2$ pound thick-sliced bacon, cut into $1/2$-inch-wide strips and cooked crisp

MAKE THE SLAW: In a small bowl, combine 3 tablespoons olive oil, vinegar, mustard, salt, pepper, and sugar and set aside. In a large saucepan, heat the remaining olive oil over medium-high heat. Add the garlic clove and the greens and sauté until tender—5 to 6 minutes. Add the vinegar mixture and toss to distribute evenly. Transfer to a serving dish, top with bacon pieces, and serve immediately.

Nutrition information per serving—protein: 8.4 g; fat: 25.5 g; carbohydrate: 12.1 g; fiber: 5.6 g; sodium: 1,102 mg; cholesterol: 28.4 mg; calories: 317.

SOUTHERN VEGETABLE SAUTÉ

< <

In this update on a traditional Southern dish, we combined black-eyed peas with greens and added carrots for color and sweetness. Also new—the vegetables are cooked just until tender rather than spending hours on the stovetop.

- 6 slices bacon, cut into ½-inch-wide strips
- 2 tablespoons unsalted butter
- 1 large onion, chopped (about 1 ½ cups)
- 1 cup chopped celery
- 1 cup chopped carrots
- 2 teaspoons kosher salt
- ¼ teaspoon ground black pepper
- 2 cloves garlic, minced
- ½ pound chopped collard greens, (about 4 cups)
- 3½ cups black-eyed peas (8 ounces dried)

COOK THE VEGETABLES: In a large saucepan, cook the bacon over medium-high heat until browned. Transfer the bacon to paper towels to drain and pour off all but 1 tablespoon of the bacon fat. Add 1 tablespoon butter to the saucepan. When the butter has melted, add the onion, celery, and carrots, 1 teaspoon salt, and ⅛ teaspoon pepper and cook until the vegetables are just tender—about 10 minutes. Set aside. In another large saucepan, place 1 tablespoon butter and the garlic over medium-high heat. When the garlic has cooked through, add the collard greens and cook until they are just tender—about 5 minutes. Stir in the peas, bacon, and vegetables and warm through. Season with remaining salt and pepper and serve immediately.

Nutrition information per serving—protein: 9 g; fat: 5.7 g; carbohydrate: 22.8 g; fiber: 4.7 g; sodium: 635 mg; cholesterol: 11.8 mg; calories: 173.

BAYOU-STYLE GREENS

Greens, long a staple of the Southern table, are almost always cooked with smoked or salted meat in a lot of water. The resulting broth, called "pot likker" in the South, is considered a delicacy when ladled over the greens and splashed with a touch of pepper sauce.

- 2 smoked turkey wings (about 1¾ pounds)
- 12 cups water
- 3 bunches collard greens, washed, stems removed, leaves cut in half (about 8 cups)
- 3 bunches turnip greens, washed, stems removed, leaves cut in half (about 8 cups)
- 3 bunches mustard greens, washed, stems removed, leaves cut in half (about 8 cups)
- ½ teaspoon salt
- 1 teaspoon ground black pepper

1 PREPARE AND COOK THE GREENS: In a large stockpot, place the turkey wings and cover with the water; bring to a boil. Reduce to a simmer and begin adding the greens one bunch at a time, starting with the collard greens. Stir and allow the greens to wilt before adding the next bunch. Cook the greens until tender—about 1 hour.

2 TO SERVE: Remove and discard the turkey wings; do not drain the liquid. Add salt and pepper. Serve the greens in a bowl or crock with the "pot likker."

Nutrition information per serving—protein: 2 g; fat: 9 g; carbohydrate: 5.8 g; fiber: 2.6 g; sodium: 155 mg; cholesterol: 51 mg; calories: 185.

SAUTÉED BRUSSELS SPROUTS

MAKES 8 SERVINGS

Cutting Brussels sprouts into shreds before sautéing them brings out a bittersweet caramelized flavor that seems to transform them into a new vegetable. It only takes a few minutes to shave, or "chiffonade," them.

 2 pints Brussels sprouts

 2 tablespoons butter

 ½ teaspoon salt

 ½ teaspoon coarsely ground
     black pepper

 2 tablespoons minced red onion

 1 cup chicken broth

 1 teaspoon grated lemon zest

 1 tablespoon fresh lemon juice

 ½ cup hazelnuts, toasted and chopped

PREPARE THE BRUSSELS SPROUTS: Trim the bases off the Brussels sprouts and discard. Cut the sprouts in half. Lay a sprout half on a cutting board flat side down. Using a sharp knife and beginning at the base, cut the sprout half into very thin strips. Repeat for the remaining sprout halves. In a large skillet, heat the butter over medium heat. Add the sprouts, salt, pepper, and red onion. Cook until the sprouts are tender, stirring frequently, for 10 minutes. Add chicken broth and simmer for 7 minutes more. Stir in the zest, lemon juice, and hazelnuts. Serve immediately.

Nutrition information per serving—protein: 2.9 g; fat: 7.5 g; carbohydrate: 5.7 g; fiber: 2.9 g; sodium: 215 mg; cholesterol: 7.8 mg; calories: 93.7.

LEMON-DRESSED STEAMED ASPARAGUS

MAKES 8 SERVINGS

The best way to steam asparagus is to use either a metal or bamboo steamer basket placed in a five-quart saucepan filled with a half-inch of boiling water.

 ⅓ cup olive oil

 ¼ teaspoon grated lemon zest

 ¼ cup fresh lemon juice

 1 teaspoon sugar

 ½ teaspoon dry mustard

 ¼ teaspoon salt

 3 pounds large fresh asparagus spears,
     woody ends trimmed

1 MAKE THE DRESSING: In a small jar with a tight-fitting lid, combine the olive oil, lemon zest and juice, sugar, mustard, and salt. Seal the jar and shake well, mixing the dressing.

2 MAKE THE ASPARAGUS: Steam the asparagus just until tender—5 to 10 minutes. Transfer to a serving platter and serve the dressing on the side.

Nutrition information per serving—protein: 5 g; fat: 9 g; carbohydrate: 7 g; fiber: 3 g; sodium: 69 mg; cholesterol: 0; calories: 121.

PARSLEY AND LEMON CHICKPEAS

- 1 tablespoon vegetable oil
- ³/4 cup finely chopped onion
- ¹/2 cup finely chopped celery
- 1 cup dried chickpeas, rinsed and drained
- 2 14¹/2-ounce cans low-sodium chicken broth
- 1 small clove garlic, finely minced
- 3 tablespoons finely chopped fresh parsley
- ¹/4 cup fresh lemon juice
- 2 tablespoons olive oil
- ¹/2 teaspoon salt
- ¹/8 teaspoon ground black pepper

MAKE THE CHICKPEAS: In a pressure cooker, heat the vegetable oil over high heat. Add the onion and celery and sauté until translucent. Add the chickpeas and chicken broth. Seal the pressure-cooker lid, bring the cooker to high pressure, and cook for 40 minutes. Strain the chickpeas, transfer them to a large bowl, and toss with the garlic, parsley, lemon juice, olive oil, salt, and pepper. Serve warm.

Nutrition information per serving—protein: 12.8 g; fat: 18.4 g; carbohydrate: 36 g; fiber: 7.4 g; sodium: 387 mg; cholesterol: 4.2 mg; calories: 345.

SAUTÉED SUMMER SQUASH WITH PISTACHIO PESTO

This tantalizing mix of pale yellow squash ribbons and bright green pesto looks like summer on a plate. Served it with grilled chops or chicken.

- 1 bunch fresh basil (1¹/4 cups tightly packed leaves)
- 4 cloves garlic
- ¹/2 cup grated Parmesan
- zest and juice of ¹/2 lemon
- ¹/2 cup pistachio nuts
- ³/4 cup plus 3 tablespoons extra-virgin olive oil
- ¹/2 teaspoon kosher salt
- 1 teaspoon ground black pepper
- ¹/4 cup minced shallots
- 6 medium-small yellow summer squash
- 2 teaspoons fresh lemon thyme
- ¹/2 teaspoon fine salt

1 MAKE THE PESTO: In a food processor fitted with the metal blade, place the basil, garlic, cheese, zest, pistachio nuts, ³/4 cup olive oil, kosher salt, and ¹/2 teaspoon pepper. Pulse to make a coarse puree. Transfer to a small bowl and drizzle the top with 1 tablespoon of olive oil to prevent darkening.

2 COOK THE SQUASH: Using a mandoline or a potato peeler, cut the squashes into long, thin ribbons. Heat a 12-inch skillet over medium-high heat, then add remaining oil. Sauté the shallots until golden, then add the squashes, lemon thyme, fine salt, and remaining pepper. Sauté just until the squashes are tender, 5 to 8 minutes. Toss with the pesto and transfer to a large platter. Garnish with lemon thyme sprigs and pistachios, and serve.

Nutrition information per serving—protein: 6.1 g; fat: 34.8 g; carbohydrate: 4.5 g; fiber: 1.5 g; sodium: 334 mg; cholesterol: 6.6 mg; calories: 345.

FRIED TOMATOES WITH GINGER PARSLEY CRUST > >

Using panko, the Japanese breadcrumbs which are large and quite different to Western-style breadcrumbs, gives these fried tomatoes a deliciously crispy crust. If you need to add more oil and butter to the skillet between batches, be sure to let it heat up before frying the tomatoes.

2/3 cup all-purpose flour

1 1/2 teaspoons sugar

1 teaspoon kosher salt

3/4 teaspoon ground red pepper

2 large eggs

1 tablespoon milk

3 cups panko (Japanese
    bread crumbs)

2 tablespoons chopped
    fresh parsley

2 teaspoons grated peeled fresh ginger

2 teaspoons grated garlic

1 1/2 pounds large firm tomatoes
    (about 3), cut into 1-inch-thick
    wedges

1/4 cup (1/2 stick) unsalted butter

4 tablespoons vegetable oil

1 COAT THE TOMATOES: Preheat the oven to 375°F. Line a baking sheet with waxed paper and set aside. In a shallow bowl, combine flour, sugar, salt, and ground red pepper and set aside. Whisk eggs and milk together in a small bowl and set aside. Combine bread crumbs, parsley, ginger, and garlic in a shallow bowl and set aside. Dredge a tomato wedge in the flour mixture and shake off the excess. Dip tomato in the egg and roll in bread crumb mixture to coat. Transfer coated wedges to the prepared baking sheet.

2 FRY THE TOMATOES: In a large skillet, heat 1 tablespoon butter and 1 tablespoon oil over medium–high heat until the mixture begins to foam. Fry tomatoes in small batches until golden—about 3 minutes per side. Continue with the remaining tomatoes, adding more butter and oil as needed. Transfer fried tomatoes to a baking sheet and keep warm until all tomatoes are fried. Serve hot.

Nutrition information per serving—protein: 11 g; fat: 13.4 g; carbohydrate: 54 g; fiber: 3.9 g; sodium: 821 mg; cholesterol: 81.7 mg; calories: 379.

STORING VEGETABLES

What Goes Into the Refrigerator and What Doesn't?

> Avocados—To ripen, leave at room temperature on the counter. A ripe avocado can be refrigerated for a few days before use (not in a bag).

> Carrots—Remove any greens and store in a sealed plastic bag in the crisper drawer.

> Bell peppers—Store unwashed in a resealable plastic bag in the crisper drawer.

> Lettuce—Wrap head lettuce in damp paper towels and store in a plastic bag in the crisper drawer.

> Mesclun—Should be stored in an unsealed plastic bag in the crisper drawer.

> Onions—Whole onions should be stored in a dry, cool place with good ventilation. Do not store them near potatoes. The gas that potatoes give off causes onions to spoil. Scallions should be stored in the crisper drawer.

> Potatoes—Store in a dark, cool place (a brown paper bag is ideal) but not in the refrigerator. Storing potatoes at temperatures lower than 45°F causes them to darken and develop a high-sugar content, which gives them a sweet taste.

> Tomatoes—Should be stored at room temperature. Refrigeration ruins their flavor and imparts a mealy texture.

MAQUE CHOUX

Pronounced "mock shoe," this Cajun dish is a little spicy. If you prefer less heat, reduce the amount of red pepper.

12 ears fresh corn, husked and silked (or 9 cups frozen corn kernels)

4 slices bacon

1 large onion, diced (about 1½ cups)

¾ cup diced red bell pepper

¾ cup diced green bell pepper

2 teaspoons ground black pepper

¼ teaspoon ground red pepper

2 teaspoons salt

1 PREPARE THE CORN: Hold an ear of corn firmly, with the bottom end on a cutting board or in a large bowl to keep the kernels from splattering. With a sharp knife, cut straight down the cob, cutting off only 2 or 3 rows at a time until all the kernels are removed. Then, using the back of the knife blade, scrape down the cob to remove the corn "milk." Add this milk to the corn kernels in a large bowl. Repeat the procedure with each of the remaining ears of corn. Set aside.

2 COOK THE MAQUE CHOUX: In a large stockpot, cook the bacon until crisp. Save the bacon strips for another use. Leave the bacon fat in the bottom of the stockpot. Cook onions and the red and green bell peppers in the bacon fat until soft—about 5 minutes. Add the corn kernels and corn milk, ground black pepper, red pepper, and salt. Cook over medium-low heat for 20 to 25 minutes, stirring occasionally to keep the corn from sticking. Cover the pot, lower the heat, and simmer 5-10 minutes. Serve warm.

Nutrition information per serving—protein: 7.2 g; fat: 2 g; carbohydrate: 42 g; fiber: 5.4 g; sodium: 594 mg; cholesterol: 2.7 mg; calories: 187.

HONEY-ROASTED BEETS < <

We used an assortment of golden, purple, and crimson beets, turning an ordinary dish into a bounty of flavor and color.

3½ pounds assorted fresh medium beets, trimmed

⅓ cup honey

¼ cup sherry vinegar

2 tablespoons unsalted butter, softened

2 tablespoons water

1 teaspoon grated orange zest

1 teaspoon minced fresh thyme leaves

¼ teaspoon salt

⅛ teaspoon ground black pepper

1 PRECOOK THE BEETS: Pierce the beets with fork tines. Arrange the beets and 3 cups water in a microwave-safe dish. Seal airtight with a double layer of plastic wrap. Microwave on high (100 percent) until crisp-tender—8 to 10 minutes. Drain the beets and set aside until cool to the touch. Peel off and discard skins. Randomly cut the beets into quarters and crosswise slices and place in a large bowl.

2 PREPARE FOR ROASTING: Preheat oven to 425°F. Lightly coat a large nonstick baking pan with vegetable oil. In a small bowl, combine the honey, vinegar, butter, water, orange zest, thyme, salt, and black pepper; pour over the beets and toss.

3 ROAST BEETS: Transfer the coated beets to the prepared baking pan; roast, turning occasionally, until the juices thicken to a glaze and the beets are cooked through—15 to 20 minutes.

4 To serve, transfer the beets to a bowl and serve warm or at room temperature.

Nutrition information per serving—protein: 3.6 g; fat: 3.3 g; carbohydrate: 33 g; fiber: 5 g; sodium: 222 mg; cholesterol: 7.8 mg; calories: 167.

CREAMED PEARL ONIONS > >

MAKES 8 SERVINGS

2 pounds white pearl onions,
    peeled

1¹/₂ cups low-sodium chicken broth

4 sprigs thyme plus
    ¹/₂ teaspoon minced

¹/₂ cup heavy cream

¹/₂ teaspoon salt

¹/₂ teaspoon ground black pepper

CREAM THE ONIONS: In a medium saucepan, bring the onions, chicken broth, and 1¹/₂ cups water to a boil over medium-high heat. Reduce heat to a simmer, add the thyme sprigs, cover the saucepan, and cook until the onions are tender—about 15 minutes. Using a slotted spoon, remove the onions, place in a small bowl, and set aside. Over medium-high heat, reduce the cooking liquid by half—about 15 minutes. Stir in the cream, salt, minced thyme, and pepper. Cook until slightly thickened—about 2 minutes. Return the onions to the pan and cook until heated through, about 5 minutes. Serve warm.

Nutrition information per serving—protein: 2.3 g; fat: 6.1 g; carbohydrate: 11.5 g; fiber: 1.8 g; sodium: 408 mg; cholesterol: 21.3 mg; calories: 103.

ALL ABOUT ONIONS

Onions are enjoyed cooked and raw in an immense variety of dishes. Many cooks start dinner every night by chopping onions, but few are aware of the tremendous range of onions and the differences in their tastes and textures.

> The most common onions are bronze-skinned yellow onions also known as common or storage onions. Their pungent flavor is mellowed by cooking. They are available year-round, as are similarly textured red and white onions.

> Mild (Sweet) onions are grown primarily from fall to spring in warm-weather states, such as Texas and Georgia. Varieties include Vidalia, Maui, Texas Sweet, and Walla Walla. They are juicy, have soft flesh, and are mild or sweet-tasting.

> Small onions such as pearl onions (both white and purple), and boilers, taste pretty much alike and can be cooked whole in stews or ragouts, or roasted, boiled, sautéed, and pickled.

> Shallots are small and mild tasting. They are a staple of both French and Southeast Asian cooking and are used cooked, in sauces and reductions, or raw, chopped in fresh salad dressings.

ROASTED FENNEL AND APPLE

MAKES 8 SERVINGS

Your oven does most of the work here, caramelizing the fennel and apples so that they're sweet and tender. Serve it with roast pork or chicken.

2 bulbs fennel, trimmed and cut into
   1/4-inch-thick wedges

2 Rome Beauty apples
   (about 1 1/2 pounds), cut into
   1-inch-thick wedges

1/4 cup olive oil

1 tablespoon honey

1/2 teaspoon salt

1/4 teaspoon ground black pepper

ROAST THE FENNEL AND APPLES: Preheat the oven to 400°F. In a large bowl, place all the ingredients and toss to combine. Arrange in a single layer on a baking sheet and place in the lower third of the oven. Roast for 20 minutes, turn fennel and apple pieces over, and roast until golden and cooked through—about 20 more minutes. Serve warm.

Nutrition information per serving—protein: .9 g; fat: 7.2 g; carbohydrate: 19.5 g; fiber: 4.1 g; sodium: 97.3 mg; cholesterol: 0; calories: 136.

OVEN-BAKED SWEET POTATO FRIES

MAKES 4 SERVINGS

1/2 teaspoon ground cumin

1/2 teaspoon salt

1/4 teaspoon ground red pepper

1 tablespoon vegetable oil

2 12-ounce sweet potatoes

1 PREPARE THE SWEET POTATOES: In a small bowl, combine the cumin, salt, and pepper. Set aside. Preheat the oven to 400°F. Peel the potatoes, cut each in half lengthwise, and cut each half into 6 wedges. In a large bowl, combine the oil, cut potatoes, and spice mixture. Toss until potatoes are evenly coated.

2 BAKE THE FRIES: On a baking sheet, arrange the potatoes in a single layer and place on the middle shelf of the oven. Bake until the edges are crisp and the potatoes are cooked through—about 30 minutes. Serve immediately.

Nutrition information per serving—protein: 1.73 g; fat: 3.78 g; carbohydrate: 24.1 g; fiber: 0; sodium: 295 mg; cholesterol: 0; calories: 136.

GOLDEN MASHED POTATOES

MAKES EIGHT 1/2-CUP SERVINGS

2 pounds Yukon Gold potatoes (about 5),
   peeled and cut into eighths

2 teaspoons salt

1 cup heavy cream

1/2 cup (1 stick) unsalted butter

1/2 teaspoon ground white pepper

MAKE THE MASHED POTATOES: In a large saucepan, bring the potatoes, 1 teaspoon salt, and enough water to cover to a boil. Cook the potatoes until just tender—about 20 minutes. Drain the potatoes, return them to the saucepan, and use a potato masher or a fork to mash the potatoes until smooth. Stir in the cream, butter, remaining salt, and pepper and serve immediately.

Nutrition information per serving—protein: 2 g; fat: 22.6 g; carbohydrate: 14.4 g; fiber: .9 g; sodium: 549 mg; cholesterol: 71.8 mg; calories: 263.

CANDIED YAMS WITH APPLES

MAKES 8 SIDE-DISH SERVINGS

This fabulous combination is traditionally "candied" with brown sugar. We used honey for its distinct flavor.

- 3 pounds yams, peeled and cut into 1-inch pieces
- 1 pound Granny Smith apples (about 2), peeled and chopped
- 2 medium onions, cut in 1-inch-thick wedges
- ¼ cup (½ stick) unsalted butter
- ¼ cup honey
- 1 teaspoon salt
- ¼ teaspoon ground nutmeg
- ¼ teaspoon ground red pepper

ROAST THE YAMS: Preheat oven to 350°F. In a large bowl, toss all the ingredients until well combined. Transfer to a large shallow baking dish and bake, stirring occasionally, until potatoes are tender—about 60 minutes. Increase the oven temperature to 500°F and broil until the cooking liquid has evaporated and the potatoes are browned—10-15 minutes. Serve immediately.

Nutrition information per serving—protein: 4.2 g; fat: 8.1 g; carbohydrate: 73.9 g; fiber: 7.8 g; sodium: 380 mg; cholesterol: 20.7 mg; calories: 372.

POTATO LATKES WITH APPLE-APRICOT COMPOTE

MAKES 6 SERVINGS
(TWELVE 3-INCH PANCAKES)

Our crisp potato pancakes are topped with warm compote, an update on the traditional applesauce.

- 3 firm, sweet apples (such as Gala or Fuji), peeled, cored, and chopped
- ¼ cup packed light brown sugar
- 2 tablespoons fresh lemon juice
- 1 teaspoon grated peeled fresh ginger
- ¼ teaspoon dry mustard
- ⅓ cup dried apricots, cut into ¼-inch-thick strips
- ¼ cup golden raisins
- 2 pounds Yukon Gold potatoes, peeled and grated
- 1 medium onion, grated
- 1 large egg
- 3 tablespoons matzo meal
- 1 teaspoon salt
- ½ teaspoon ground black pepper
- Vegetable oil for frying

1 MAKE THE APPLE-APRICOT COMPOTE: In a small saucepan, combine the apples, brown sugar, lemon juice, ginger, and mustard; cook over medium-low heat, stirring occasionally, for 10 minutes. Add the apricots, raisins, and ¼ cup water, cover, and cook for 10 more minutes. Lightly mash the compote with the back of a wooden spoon, cover, and cook for 5 more minutes. Transfer to a bowl and set aside.

2 MAKE THE LATKES: Place small batches of grated potatoes in the center of a dish towel, gather up the sides of the towel, and wring all excess liquid from the potatoes. Transfer the potatoes to a large bowl and repeat with the remaining potatoes. Add the remaining ingredients to the potatoes, mix well, and set aside. In a 12-inch skillet, heat ¼ inch vegetable oil over medium-high heat. Add the potato mixture by the ¼ cupful to the hot oil, lightly flatten pancakes with a spatula, and cook latkes until golden—about 5 minutes. Turn over and cook until heated through and golden brown—about 5 more minutes. Serve warm.

Nutrition information per serving—protein: 5.4 g; fat: 13.3 g; carbohydrate: 57.6 g; fiber: 4.8 g; sodium: 379 mg; cholesterol: 35.5 mg; calories: 358.

ROSEMARY-ROASTED POTATOES

Remember when potatoes were either boilers or bakers? Today we can choose from dozens of varieties, including yellow-fleshed Yukon Golds, purple Peruvians, and delicate fingerlings. Combined, they provide visual interest and varied texture. Aromatic rosemary makes this simple side dish sing.

- 3 pounds assorted potatoes
- 1 head of garlic, root end trimmed
- 1 teaspoon salt
- 1/4 teaspoon fresh-milled black pepper
- 3 tablespoons extra-virgin olive oil
- 1 tablespoon chopped fresh rosemary leaves

1 ROAST THE POTATOES: Heat the oven to 400°F. Cut the potatoes into uniform pieces for even cooking. Place the potatoes and garlic on a large baking pan. Sprinkle with salt and pepper and coat with olive oil. Roast just until the garlic starts to soften and the potatoes begin to brown—about 30 minutes. Sprinkle the potatoes with rosemary and continue roasting until the garlic has completely softened and the potatoes are fork-tender—10 to 15 minutes more. Transfer the potatoes and garlic to a serving platter. Squeeze the roasted garlic cloves out of their skins and serve with the potatoes.

Nutrition information per serving—protein: 4 g; fat: 5 g; carbohydrate: 45 g; fiber: 4 g; sodium: 281 mg; cholesterol: 0; calories: 237.

ROASTED ONIONS WITH PARSNIP PUREE > >

- 1 tablespoon butter
- 2 pounds parsnips, peeled and cut into 1/2-inch-thick slices
- 1/2 teaspoon kosher salt
- 1/4 teaspoon ground black pepper
- 1 cup chicken broth
- 4 large onions (about 8-ounces each)
- 1/2 tablespoon olive oil
- 1/2 cup crumbled Roquefort
- 1/4 cup chopped walnuts, toasted

1 PUREE THE PARSNIPS: Preheat the oven to 425°F. In a medium saucepan, melt the butter. Over medium-low heat, add the parsnips, salt, and pepper and cook for 5 minutes. Add the broth, cover, and continue to cook until the parsnips are very tender—about 15 minutes. Let the parsnips cool for 10 minutes. Transfer the parsnips and broth to a food processor fitted with the metal blade and puree until smooth. Set aside.

2 ROAST THE ONIONS: Line a baking pan with foil and set aside. Cut a thin slice from the root end of each onion so it won't roll. Cut 3/4-inch from the top of each onion and use a small knife to cut out the center, leaving at least a 3/4-inch wall. Finely chop the onion centers and stir into the parsnip puree. Fill each onion with parsnip puree. Rub the onion skins with the olive oil and arrange on a baking pan. Bake for 1 1/2 hours. Remove and top each with Roquefort cheese and walnuts. Serve immediately.

Nutrition information per serving—protein: 11.4 g; fat: 16.6 g; carbohydrate: 69.6 g; fiber: 16.7 g; sodium: 855 mg; cholesterol: 24.3 mg; calories: 450.

WHICH POTATO?

Not all potatoes are created equal. Not only do they vary in size and skin color, but different varieties are best suited to different cooking methods.

> Low-starch, high-moisture "waxy" potatoes are best for boiling or steaming, as they remain firm-textured when sliced and diced. Use them for stews, salads, soups, and other dishes where you want the potato to retain its shape. Red potatoes, fingerlings, and new potatoes fall into this category.

> Medium-starch potatoes, such as long whites, round whites, and yellow-flesh potatoes have a dense, creamy texture. They can be used in most dishes.

> Hi-starch potatoes, such as russets are available year-round. They have drier flesh and turn fluffy when baked or mashed. They tend to fall apart in stews. Russets make fabulous french fries and are good for roasting.

WHIPPED ROOT VEGETABLES AND POTATOES

6 medium baking potatoes, peeled and
    cut into large pieces

2 teaspoons salt

1/2 cup milk

1/4 cup (1/2 stick) salted butter

1 teaspoon ground black pepper

1 medium parsnip, peeled and cut into
    large pieces

2 medium carrots, peeled and cut into
    large pieces

2 medium sweet potatoes, peeled and
    cut into large pieces

2 cups chicken broth

1 COOK THE POTATOES: In a large pot, place the potatoes and enough water to cover them. Add 1 teaspoon salt and boil until potatoes are just tender—20 to 30 minutes. Drain in a colander. In a large bowl, mash the potatoes, adding 1/4 cup milk and 2 tablespoons butter. Add 1/2 teaspoon salt and 1/2 teaspoon pepper. Using a mixer, whip the potatoes until fluffy—about 2 minutes.

2 COOK THE ROOT VEGETABLES: In another pot, cover the parsnip, carrots, and sweet potatoes with chicken broth and boil over medium-high heat until tender—about 35 minutes. Drain, mash, and add the remaining milk, butter, salt, and pepper. Using a mixer, whip the vegetables until fluffy—about 5 minutes. Spoon the whipped potatoes and vegetables side by side into a serving bowl. Serve immediately.

Nutrition information per serving—protein: 7.9 g; fat: 6.9 g; carbohydrate: 48.8 g; fiber: 6.8 g; sodium: 707 mg; cholesterol: 17.6 mg; calories: 291.

ROASTED GARDEN VEGETABLES

Cipollini, which look, smell, and taste like onions, are members of the lily family, the same group that other onions belong to. Look for them in the produce section of your market or substitute small white onions.

3 tablespoons extra-virgin olive oil

1 pound cipollini onions, peeled

1 1/2 pounds small red potatoes, scrubbed
    and quartered

1 large bulb fennel, trimmed and cut
    lengthwise into 1/2-inch-thick wedges

1 pint Brussels sprouts

2 large red bell peppers, cut into
    thick strips

1 large yellow bell pepper, cut into
    thick strips

1 large orange bell pepper, cut into
    thick strips

3/4 cup balsamic vinegar

2 teaspoons sugar

3 cloves garlic, minced

1 1/2 teaspoons salt

1/2 teaspoon ground black pepper

1 ROAST THE VEGETABLES: Preheat the oven to 425°F. In a large bowl, combine the olive oil, cipollini, and potatoes and toss to coat on all sides. Place in a roasting pan and roast 10 minutes. Add the fennel and Brussels sprouts to the cipollini and potatoes and roast 10 more minutes. Add the red, yellow, and orange peppers and continue to roast, stirring occasionally, until all the vegetables are tender—about 20 more minutes.

2 MAKE THE DRESSING: In a small saucepan, combine the vinegar and sugar and bring to a boil. Continue to cook until the mixture is reduced to 3 tablespoons. Add the garlic, salt, and pepper to the balsamic mixture and drizzle over the vegetables. Toss to coat; serve warm or at room temperature.

Nutrition information per serving—protein: 7.9 g; fat: 5.7 g; carbohydrate: 64.7 g; fiber: 10.7 g; sodium: 457 mg; cholesterol: 0; calories: 324.

CHIPOTLE-VEGETABLE CHILI

By roasting the vegetables and combining them with chipotle peppers, you will add a rich, smoky sweetness to this vegetarian chili.

- 1 red bell pepper, diced
- 1 small eggplant, cubed
- 1 medium onion, cut into eight wedges
- 2 medium zucchini, cubed
- 1/2 teaspoon salt
- 2 tablespoons olive oil
- 2 cloves garlic, minced
- 1 pound white mushrooms, quartered
- 1 bay leaf
- 1 teaspoon chili powder
- 1 dried chipotle pepper, stemmed and diced
- 1 19-ounce can white cannellini beans, rinsed and drained
- 1 14 1/2-ounce can low-sodium vegetable broth
- 1 14 1/2-ounce can low-sodium diced tomatoes
- 2 tablespoons chopped fresh flat-leaf parsley

1 ROAST THE VEGETABLES: Preheat the oven to 400°F. Lightly coat a large baking sheet with vegetable oil. In a medium bowl, combine the bell pepper, eggplant, onion, zucchini, and salt with the olive oil. Arrange the vegetables in a single layer on the prepared baking sheet. Roast the vegetables, turning occasionally, until just softened—25 to 30 minutes.

2 MAKE THE CHILI: In a large Dutch oven, heat the oil over medium-high heat. Once the remaining oil is hot but not smoking, add the garlic and mushrooms. Sauté until the mushrooms soften—about 5 minutes. Add the bay leaf, chili powder, chipotle pepper, beans, broth, tomatoes, and roasted vegetables. Bring to a boil and reduce heat to low. Simmer uncovered for 20 minutes.

3 TO SERVE: Stir in the parsley and serve hot.

Nutrition information per serving—protein: 7.8 g; fat: 6.1 g; carbohydrate: 29.7 g; fiber: 8.4 g; sodium: 957 mg; cholesterol: 0; calories: 191.

FARM STAND SUCCOTASH

We gave the classic American sweet corn dish a dash of vibrant color by replacing the lima beans with edamame—the bright green Japanese soy beans.

- 6 slices bacon, chopped
- 2 tablespoons extra-virgin olive oil
- 1 large sweet onion, chopped (about 1 1/4 cups)
- 4 ears corn, husked, silked and kernels cut from cobs (about 2 cups)
- 1/2 red bell pepper, chopped (about 1/2 cup)
- 1 cup low-sodium chicken broth
- 1 1/2 teaspoons salt
- 1/2 teaspoon sugar
- 1/2 teaspoon ground black pepper
- 1 cup cooked edamame (green soybeans)
- 1/4 cup fresh basil leaves, coarsely chopped

MAKE THE SUCCOTASH: In a large skillet, cook the bacon over medium heat until crisp. Remove bacon from pan and set aside. Add olive oil and onion to the skillet and cook until translucent—about 5 minutes. Add the corn and cook for 5 minutes. Stir in the bell pepper, broth, salt, sugar, and pepper and cook for 10 minutes. Add the edamame and cook for 5 more minutes. Stir in the reserved bacon and basil, transfer to bowls, and serve warm.

Nutrition information per serving—protein: 3.7 g; fat: 6.5 g; carbohydrate: 11.1 g; fiber: 2.1 g; sodium: 496 mg; cholesterol: 4.7 mg; calories: 109.

BALSAMIC-GRILLED SUMMER VEGETABLES

MAKES 8 SERVINGS

Although balsamic vinegar is more expensive than other types, we recommend it in this recipe for the intense, sweet flavor it imparts. Besides, a little goes a long way, so it's worth the extra expense.

- 3 small white eggplants (about 1 pound), quartered lengthwise
- 3 small purple eggplants (about 1 pound), quartered lengthwise1
- 4 small yellow squash (about 1 pound), halved lengthwise
- 4 small green zucchini (about 1 pound), halved lengthwise
- 1/2 pound green beans, trimmed
- 1/4 cup extra-virgin olive oil
- 2 tablespoons aged balsamic vinegar
- 1/2 teaspoon salt
- 1/2 teaspoon ground black pepper

GRILL THE VEGETABLES: In a large bowl, combine the white and purple eggplant, squash, zucchini, and green beans. Add the oil, vinegar, salt, and pepper and toss to coat thoroughly. On a hot grill, place the vegetables cut side down, and cook until dark grill marks are apparent—3 to 5 minutes. Turn and continue to grill until the vegetables are tender—3 to 5 more minutes. Serve hot or at room temperature. Store covered in the refrigerator for up to 3 days.

Nutrition information per serving—protein: 2.7 g; fat: 7 g; carbohydrate: 13.9 g; fiber: 5.5 g; sodium: 140 mg; cholesterol: 0; calories: 121.

BAKED STUFFED PUMPKIN < <

MAKES 4 SERVINGS

Use miniature pumpkins such as 'Jack Be Little,' 'Little Boo,'or 'Small Sugar' for this dramatic dish.

- 4 ounces sweet Italian sausage links, casings removed
- 1/2 cup chopped onion
- 1 1 1/2-pound pumpkin, peeled, seeded, and cut into 3/4-inch chunks (about 2 cups)
- 1 small Granny Smith apple, chopped (about 1/2 cup)
- 1/4 cup white dry wine
- 1 cup Israeli couscous, cooked according to package directions
- 1/4 cup dried cranberries
- 1 tablespoon extra-virgin olive oil
- 1 teaspoon fresh thyme leaves
- 1 teaspoon fresh oregano leaves, chopped
- 1/2 teaspoon salt
- 1/4 teaspoon ground black pepper
- 4 1-pound pumpkins, tops cut off and seeded

1 MAKE THE STUFFING: Preheat the oven to 350°F. Crumble the sausage meat and place it in a large saucepan over medium-low heat. Cook the sausage until it is almost done—about 8 minutes. Remove the sausage from the pan, increase heat to medium, and add the onion and 2 cups of the chopped pumpkin. Sauté until the pumpkin begins to soften—5 to 7 minutes. Add the apples and sausage and sauté for 3 minutes. Add the wine, cook for 2 minutes, remove from heat, and set aside. In a large bowl, combine the couscous, dried cranberries, olive oil, thyme, oregano, salt, and pepper. Add the meat mixture to the bowl and toss to combine.

2 BAKE THE PUMPKINS: Evenly fill the hollowed-out small pumpkins with the stuffing mixture and place them in a shallow baking dish. Cover the dish with aluminum foil, bake for 25 minutes, remove the foil, and bake for 10 more minutes. Serve immediately.

Nutrition information per serving—protein: 7.8 g; fat: 12.6 g; carbohydrate: 33.3 g; fiber: 4 g; sodium: 480 mg; cholesterol: 21.5 mg; calories: 281.

SALAD

GRILLED CHICKEN, MUSHROOM, AND FIG SALAD > >

Here's a wonderfully easy first course to make on a hot summer night. Lightly grill the chicken, mushrooms, figs and prosciutto, then simply toss with a lemony herbed dressing. For a main dish, double the recipe.

1/4 cup fresh lemon juice

1/4 cup olive oil

1 tablespoon chopped fresh oregano leaves

1 clove garlic, chopped

1/2 teaspoon salt

1/4 teaspoon ground black pepper

3/4 pound boneless, skinless chicken breast halves (about 2)

2 cups mixed wild mushrooms (such as shiitake, cremini, and portabello)

4 figs, quartered

4 slices prosciutto

1 MARINATE THE INGREDIENTS: In a shallow dish, combine the lemon juice, oil, oregano, garlic, salt, and pepper. Add the chicken, mushrooms, figs, and prosciutto, and let sit for 20 minutes.

2 GRILL THE INGREDIENTS: Heat a grill until very hot. Grill chicken until cooked through—about 5 minutes on each side. Remove chicken from grill, slice into 1-inch-thick pieces, and set aside. Grill the mushrooms, turning occasionally, until browned and softened—about 6 minutes. Remove mushrooms from grill, halve or quarter each, and set aside. Place prosciutto on the grill, cook for 30 seconds per side, and slice into 1-inch pieces.

3 TO SERVE: Divide the grilled ingredients 4 plates and serve immediately.

Nutrition information per serving—protein: 22.4 g; fat: 11.8 g; carbohydrate: 12.3 g; fiber: 2.1 g; sodium: 435 mg; cholesterol: 53.6 mg; calories: 241.

GRILLED FLANK STEAK WITH CUCUMBER-NOODLE SALAD

1/2 cup low-sodium soy sauce

1/4 cup orange juice

2 medium cloves garlic, coarsely chopped (about 1 tablespoon)

3 tablespoons grated peeled fresh ginger

1 1/2 pounds flank steak

7 ounces rice sticks (rice-flour noodles) or angel hair pasta

1 tablespoon toasted (dark) sesame oil

2 tablespoons chili oil

2 tablespoons rice wine vinegar

1 teaspoon packed brown sugar

1 tablespoon fresh lemon juice

1 teaspoon salt

3 green onions, thinly sliced

1 seedless cucumber, chopped

1 red bell pepper, cut into 1/2-inch-thick rings

1/2 cup salted roasted peanuts, chopped

1 MAKE THE MARINADE: In a shallow dish, stir 1/4 cup soy sauce, orange juice, garlic, and 1 tablespoon ginger together. Place the steak in the dish, turn to coat, and let marinate for 30 minutes, turning occasionally.

2 MAKE THE NOODLES: Bring a large pot of water to a boil and cook the rice noodles until tender—about 3 minutes. Strain the noodles and rinse them with cold water. Transfer to a large bowl and toss with sesame oil. Set aside. In a small bowl, combine remaining soy sauce and ginger, chili oil, vinegar, sugar, lemon juice, and salt. Toss the dressing, green onions, and cucumber with the noodles. Heat a grill to high heat and grill the red pepper until just cooked through—about 5 minutes. Dice the pepper into 1/2-inch pieces and add it and the peanuts to the salad. Set aside.

3 GRILL THE STEAK: Grill the meat for 8 minutes on each side; transfer to a cutting board. Let rest for 5 minutes. Thinly slice and serve with the salad.

Nutrition information per serving—protein: 37.2 g; fat: 20 g; carbohydrate: 26 g; fiber: 1.9 g; sodium: 949 mg; cholesterol: 76.3 mg; calories: 434.

BUTTER LETTUCE SALAD WITH CHERRY VINAIGRETTE

Salt and sweet are a superb flavor combination. Here we combined pungent Roquefort cheese and sweet cherries for a tantalizing salad. Serve it with a simple roasted chicken or grilled pork chops.

1 pound sweet cherries (2 cups), pitted and halved

1 tablespoon fresh lemon juice

2 teaspoons sugar

5 tablespoons olive oil

1/4 cup red wine vinegar

1/4 teaspoon salt

1/4 teaspoon ground black pepper

3 heads butter lettuce

3/4 cup dried cherries (recipe follows)

1/2 cup crumbled Roquefort

1 MAKE THE VINAIGRETTE: In a large saucepan, place the sweet cherries, 1/4 cup water, lemon juice, and sugar over medium–high heat, stir to combine, and cook until cherries soften—about 10 minutes. Run the cherries and any liquid through a food mill, strain the mixture, discard the solids, and return the liquid to the saucepan. Cook over low heat until reduced to 1/3 cup—about 20 minutes. Cool completely. Whisk the reduced cherry liquid, olive oil, vinegar, salt, and pepper together in a small bowl and set aside.

2 ASSEMBLE THE SALAD: In a large bowl, toss together the lettuce, dried cherries, and Roquefort cheese. Drizzle with dressing and serve immediately.

Nutrition information per serving—protein: 4 g; fat: 15.3 g; carbohydrate: 13.2 g; fiber: 1.9 g; sodium: 296 mg; cholesterol: 10.2 mg; calories: 196.

DRIED CHERRIES

2 cups cold water

1500 milligrams vitamin C, crushed

1/2 pound cherries (about 25), pitted

DRY THE CHERRIES: Preheat the oven to 175°F. Combine the water and vitamin C in a large bowl. Add the cherries and let soak for 5 minutes. Pat cherries dry, place on a wire rack set over a baking sheet, and bake until dry—about 4 hours. While baking, place the handle of a wooden spoon in the oven door to let moisture escape. Cool cherries completely on the wire rack and store in an airtight container for up to 2 weeks.

THE SECRET TO GREAT VINAIGRETTES
Extra-Virgin Olive Oil

Extra-virgin olive oil is from the first pressing of the olives, without heat or added chemicals. The oil from this initial pressing is considered the highest quality. Extra-virgin oil cannot have more than 1% oleic acid and its color can range from gold to deep green, depending on the origin and type of olives used. This oil is best used within a year of pressing. Keep at cool room temperature (below 70°F), away from direct heat and light.

FIRE-ROASTED RED PEPPER SALAD

MAKES 8 SERVINGS

Roasted peppers make a colorful accompaniment to cheese boards, or serve them as a simple side dish with pasta.

4 large red bell peppers

2 tablespoons extra-virgin olive oil

1/2 teaspoon salt

1/2 teaspoon ground black pepper

8 cups mesclun (mixed salad greens)

Pesto Vinaigrette (recipe follows)

1 head Belgian endive, quartered lengthwise (optional)

1 ROAST THE PEPPERS: Heat a grill until very hot. Rub the peppers with olive oil and place them directly on the grill. Using tongs, turn the peppers to char skin on all sides. In a large heatproof bowl, place the blackened peppers and cover tightly with plastic wrap. Set aside to cool for 10 to 15 minutes. Rub or peel the charred skins from the peppers; cut each pepper in half and remove stem, seeds, and membrane. (If desired, roasted peppers can be refrigerated in an airtight container for up to 5 days.)

2 ASSEMBLE THE SALAD: Cut the peppers into strips and season with salt and pepper. Divide the greens among 8 chilled salad plates. Drizzle each salad with 2 tablespoons Pesto Vinaigrette. Place the pepper strips alongside the greens and serve. Garnish with Belgian endive, if desired.

Nutrition information per serving—protein: 1 g; fat: 3.6 g; carbohydrate: 1.9 g; fiber: 1 g; sodium: 148 mg; cholesterol: 0; calories: 40.

PESTO VINAIGRETTE

MAKES 1 1/2 CUPS

Drizzle this versatile dressing over a plate of sliced, ripe tomatoes for a simple and delicious summer salad.

1/4 cup walnuts

1/2 cup loosely packed fresh basil leaves

2 cloves garlic

1/4 cup white wine vinegar

1/2 cup extra-virgin olive oil

1/3 cup grated Parmesan cheese

1/2 teaspoon salt

1/2 teaspoon ground black pepper

1 TOAST THE WALNUTS: In a small skillet, toast the walnuts over medium-high heat—shaking skillet occasionally to prevent walnuts from burning—about 3 minutes.

2 MAKE THE PESTO: In a food processor fitted with the metal blade, place the basil, garlic, and vinegar and pulse until well combined—about 30 seconds. Add the toasted walnuts and, with processor running, add olive oil in a thin stream until the basil mixture thickens and emulsifies. Add the cheese, salt, and pepper and process for 30 more seconds. Serve with Fire-Roasted Red Pepper Salad. Refrigerate, covered, for up to 2 days.

Nutrition information per serving—protein: 1.6 g; fat: 11.4 g; carbohydrate: 1.2 g; fiber: .19 g; sodium: 140 mg; cholesterol: 2.2 mg; calories: 111.

TOMATO, WATERMELON, AND CUCUMBER SALAD « «

Chunks of juicy summer fruits and vegetables create a crunchy and refreshing salad. A zesty red wine vinaigrette and fragrant fresh basil add bold flavors which complement the crisp textures.

- 2 large tomatoes, cut into 1-inch-thick wedges (about 2 cups)
- 2 pounds watermelon, cut into 2 1/2- by 1/2-inch-thick wedges
- 1 cucumber, peeled, halved, seeded and cut into 1/2-inch-thick slices
- 1/2 small red onion, thinly sliced (about 1/4 cup)
- 3 tablespoons red wine vinegar
- 2 tablespoons extra-virgin olive oil
- 1 teaspoon salt
- 1/4 teaspoon ground black pepper
- 1/4 cup loosely packed fresh basil leaves, thinly sliced

MAKE THE SALAD: In a large bowl, gently toss tomatoes, watermelon, cucumber, and onion together and set aside. Combine vinegar, oil, salt, and pepper in a small bowl. Pour vinaigrette over the watermelon mixture and toss to combine. on a platter. Cover and refrigerate for up to 2 hours. Sprinkle with basil and serve.

Nutrition information per serving—protein: 1.7 g; fat: 5.3 g; carbohydrate: 13.8 g; fiber: 1.5 g; sodium: 364 mg; cholesterol: 0; calories: 100.

TOMATO FLOWERS

MAKES 4 SERVINGS

DRESSING:

- 2 ripe kiwis, peeled and chopped
- 1 clove garlic, minced
- 1/8 teaspoon grated peeled fresh gingerroot
- 1 teaspoon Dijon mustard
- 2 tablespoons cider vinegar
- 1/2 cup vegetable oil
- 1/4 teaspoon salt
- Ground black pepper

COMPOSED SALAD:

- 4 medium tomatoes
- 4 ounces fresh mozzarella, diced
- 1 ripe avocado, halved, pitted, peeled, and diced
- 5 ounces mesclun (mixed salad greens)

1 MAKE THE DRESSING: In a blender or food processor fitted with the metal blade, puree the dressing ingredients. Set aside.

2 PREPARE THE TOMATOES: Slice a thin cap from the top (stem end) of each tomato. Cut each tomato into 4 to 6 partial wedges by cutting each wedge almost to the bottom of the tomato but not all the way through. Fan the wedges open into a "flower."

3 In a bowl, combine the mozzarella and avocado for the filling.

4 SERVE THE TOMATO FLOWERS: Place greens on individual plates. Place a tomato flower in the center. Mound the tomato with filling and drizzle 2 to 3 tablespoons dressing on top.

Nutrition information per serving—protein: 10.2 g; fat: 41.8 g; carbohydrate: 19.6 g; fiber: 5.3 g; sodium: 364 mg; cholesterol: 16 mg; calories: 473.

HAZELNUT-CRUSTED GOAT CHEESE SALAD WITH BLUEBERRY VINAIGRETTE

MAKES 6 SERVINGS

We reduced our Blueberry-Bay Vinegar to a thick syrup. The resulting extra intensity adds a slightly sweet touch to classic vinaigrette.

- 1/2 cup Blueberry-Bay Vinegar (see recipe on page 167)
- 2 tablespoons sugar
- 1 teaspoon chopped fresh tarragon leaves or 1/2 teaspoon dried
- 1/2 teaspoon Dijon mustard
- 1/4 teaspoon salt
- 1/4 teaspoon ground black pepper
- 1/8 teaspoon ground red pepper
- 1/2 cup extra-virgin olive oil
- 1/4 cup fresh blueberries
- 6 cups mesclun (mixed salad greens)
- 1 6-ounce log mild goat cheese, cut into 6 rounds
- 1/2 cup chopped hazelnuts, toasted

1 REDUCE THE VINEGAR: In a small saucepan, bring Blueberry-Bay Vinegar and sugar to a boil. Cook until the liquid is reduced to 2 tablespoons. Add the tarragon and let cool.

2 MAKE THE DRESSING: Whisk in the mustard, salt, pepper, black and red pepper, and olive oil until completely combined and the mixture has slightly thickened. Stir in the blueberries. Transfer to a jar, cover, and refrigerate until ready to serve.

3 MAKE THE SALAD: Preheat the oven broiler. In a large bowl, toss the mesclun with half of the dressing and divide among 6 chilled plates. Roll the goat cheese rounds in hazelnuts and place on a baking pan. Heat the cheese under the broiler until warmed—1 to 2 minutes. Place one cheese round on top of each salad, drizzle with more vinaigrette, if desired, and serve immediately.

Nutrition information per serving—protein: 7.4 g; fat: 30 g; carbohydrate: 11 g; fiber: 1.9 g; sodium: 210 mg; cholesterol: 13 mg; calories: 336.

BARELY PICKLED BEET AND ORANGE SALAD

MAKES 4 SIDE-DISH SERVINGS

The combination of vinegar, orange juice, and sugar acts as a quick pickling brine for beets.

- 4 beets (about 2 pounds), peeled, each cut into 8 wedges
- 3/4 cup fresh orange juice
- 1/3 cup plus 2 teaspoons raspberry vinegar
- 1 tablespoon packed dark brown sugar
- 1 large clove garlic plus 1/2 teaspoon finely chopped
- 5 sprigs fresh thyme plus 1 teaspoon finely chopped
- 1 teaspoon Dijon mustard
- 1 teaspoon salt
- 1/2 teaspoon ground black pepper
- 1/2 cup olive oil
- 4 ounces mesclun (mixed salad greens)
- 2 oranges, peeled and sectioned
- 1/2 cup crumbled ricotta salata
- 2 tablespoons chopped pecans

1 MAKE THE BEETS: In a pressure cooker, place the beets, orange juice, 1/3 cup vinegar, brown sugar, garlic clove, and thyme sprigs and lock the lid in place following the manufacturer's instructions. Over high heat, bring to high pressure. Reduce the heat just enough to maintain high pressure and cook for 4 minutes. Turn off the heat and, again following manufacturer's instructions, quick-release the pressure. Once all the pressure is released, unlock the lid. Pour the beets and their liquid through a strainer into a large bowl. Discard the thyme sprigs and garlic clove and reserve the beets. Pour the beet liquid back into the pressure-cooker pot and, over high heat, reduce the liquid to 1/4 cup. Remove from heat and let cool. In a medium bowl, whisk together the cooking liquid, mustard, salt, pepper, remaining vinegar, chopped garlic, and chopped thyme. Add the olive oil in a thin stream, whisking constantly.

2 ASSEMBLE THE SALAD: On a serving platter, mound the greens and top with the beets. Drizzle the salad with the beet vinaigrette and top with orange sections. Garnish with the cheese and pecans. Serve immediately.

Nutrition information per serving—protein: 9.4 g; fat: 32.7 g; carbohydrate: 39.6 g; fiber: 8.2 g; sodium: 816 mg; cholesterol: 9.5 mg; calories: 473.

WILTED SPINACH AND RED ONION SALAD

Put this colorful salad together just before serving—for best results.

- 2 tablespoons olive oil
- 1/2 medium red onion, thinly sliced
- 3 cloves garlic, finely chopped
- 2 1-pound bags baby spinach
- 2 tablespoons water
- 3/4 teaspoon salt
- 2 tablespoons sherry vinegar
- 1/2 teaspoon ground black pepper

MAKE THE SALAD: In a large skillet, warm the olive oil over medium heat. Add the onion and garlic; cook 1 minute. Stir in the spinach, water, and salt. Cook 1 minute or just until the spinach leaves start to wilt. Remove from heat and transfer to a large serving bowl. Sprinkle the salad with the vinegar and black pepper. Serve.

Nutrition information per serving—protein: 5 g; fat: 5 g; carbohydrate: 7 g; fiber: 5 g; sodium: 386 mg; cholesterol: 0; calories: 80.

GREENS AND NECTARINES WITH HONEY HAZELNUT DRESSING

This slightly sweet and nut-flavored dressing provides the perfect foil for bitter greens and slices of ripe nectarines.

GREENS:
- 1 bunch arugula
- 1 small head butter lettuce
- 1 small head radicchio
- 4 Belgian endive leaves, sliced lengthwise

DRESSING:
- 3/4 cup vegetable oil
- 1/3 cup sherry vinegar
- 1/4 cup chopped hazelnuts, toasted
- 1/4 cup honey
- 1 clove garlic
- 1/2 teaspoon salt
- 1/4 teaspoon ground black pepper

FRUIT:
- 3 ripe medium nectarines, quartered, pitted, and thinly sliced

1 PREPARE THE GREENS: Trim and wash all the salad greens. Spin dry and place in a large serving bowl. Cover and refrigerate until ready to use.

2 MAKE THE DRESSING: In a blender or food processor fitted with the metal blade, combine the vegetable oil, vinegar, hazelnuts, honey, garlic, salt, and pepper to make an emulsion.

3 TO SERVE: Drizzle the dressing over the greens and toss to mix. Arrange the nectarines on top.

Nutrition information per serving using 2 tablespoons of dressing—protein: 4.5 g; fat: 16 g; carbohydrate: 25 g; fiber: 3 g; sodium: 126 mg; cholesterol: 0; calories: 247.

WARM CABBAGE SLAW WITH MAPLE-BACON DRESSING

MAKES 6 SERVINGS

4 slices bacon, cut crosswise in half

1/2 cup cider vinegar

1/3 cup maple syrup
  (grade B, if available)

1/2 teaspoon ground celery seed

1/4 teaspoon ground black pepper

2 leeks (white part only), trimmed,
  sliced, and rinsed

3 cups shredded green cabbage

1 1/2 cups shredded red cabbage

2 medium carrots, grated
  (about 1/2 cup)

1 MAKE THE DRESSING: In a large skillet, cook the bacon over medium heat until crisp. Transfer to paper towels and discard all but 3 tablespoons fat from the skillet. Add the vinegar, maple syrup, celery seed, and black pepper. Bring to a boil and cook 1 minute. Pour all but 1 tablespoon warm dressing into a small bowl.

2 MAKE THE SLAW: Adjust heat to medium low and add the leeks to the skillet. Cook until slightly softened—about 2 minutes. Add the green and red cabbage and the carrots. Stir in the reserved dressing and cook just until the vegetables soften—3 to 4 minutes. Transfer to serving platter, top with the bacon, and serve immediately.

Nutrition information per serving—protein: 2 g; fat: 9 g; carbohydrate: 18 g; fiber: 2 g; sodium: 155 mg; cholesterol: 46 mg; calories: 158.

BLUE-RIBBON POTATO SALAD

MAKES 8 CUPS

We used russet potatoes in this salad, but you can use a mix of small new red and baby Yukon Gold potatoes for a colorful alternative.

3 pounds baking potatoes, peeled
  and cut into 1-inch pieces

1 1/2 teaspoons salt

1/2 cup extra-virgin olive oil

1/4 cup tarragon or cider vinegar

1 tablespoon fresh chopped tarragon
  leaves

1/2 teaspoon ground black pepper

1 cup chopped celery

1 medium sweet onion, finely chopped
  (about 1 cup)

1/2 cup chopped green onions

2 tablespoons sweet pickle relish

4 hard-cooked large eggs, peeled, and
  grated

1/2 cup mayonnaise

1 COOK THE POTATOES: In a large saucepan, combine the potatoes, 1 teaspoon salt, and enough water to cover. Bring to a boil over high heat and cook the potatoes until easily pierced with a fork—10 to 15 minutes. Drain the potatoes and place them in a large bowl.

2 ASSEMBLE THE SALAD: In a small bowl, whisk together the olive oil, vinegar, tarragon, remaining 1/2 teaspoon salt, and pepper. Pour the olive-oil mixture over the warm potatoes. Stir in the celery, sweet and green onions, and pickle relish. Fold in the eggs and mayonnaise. Cover and refrigerate for at least 2 hours or overnight.

Nutrition information per 1/2-cup serving—protein: 4 g; fat: 14 g; carbohydrate: 24 g; fiber: 2 g; sodium: 241 mg; cholesterol: 57 mg; calories: 238.

FENNEL SLAW WITH RADISHES AND RED ONION ‹ ‹

Try this updated slaw with our Spicy Southern-Fried Chicken.

2 cups thinly sliced fennel bulb

1/2 cup thinly sliced red onion

8 small radishes, quartered (about 1/2 cup)

1/2 cup Rancho Deluxe Dressing (recipe follows)

MAKE THE SLAW: In a large bowl, combine the fennel, onion, and radishes. Pour dressing over the vegetables and toss until well coated. Cover and refrigerate for at least 30 minutes to overnight. Serve chilled.

Nutrition information per serving with dressing—protein: 1.8 g; fat: 22 g; carbohydrate: 6 g; fiber: 2 g; sodium: 337 mg; cholesterol: 1.7 mg; calories: 226.

RANCHO DELUXE DRESSING

This creamy dressing also makes a flavorful partner for steamed new red potatoes.

3/4 cup mayonnaise

1/2 cup buttermilk

2 tablespoons finely chopped fresh flat-leaf parsley

2 tablespoons finely chopped celery leaves

1 tablespoon minced red onion

1 tablespoon fresh lemon juice

2 teaspoons Dijon mustard

1/4 teaspoon dried dillweed

1/4 teaspoon salt

1/4 teaspoon cracked black pepper

MAKE THE DRESSING: In a medium bowl, whisk together mayonnaise and buttermilk. Stir in parsley, celery, onion, lemon juice, mustard, dill, salt, and pepper. Cover and chill 1 hour to overnight. Store, tightly covered and refrigerated, for up to 5 days.

Nutrition information per 1-tablespoon serving– protein: .3 g; fat: 5.5g; carbohydrate: .63 g; fiber: 0; sodium: 78 g; cholesterol: 4.3 mg; calories: 52.7.

GREEN BEANS WITH HONEY MUSTARD VINAIGRETTE

MAKES 4 SERVINGS

Serve this salad hot, cold, or at room temperature.

8 cups water

1 teaspoon salt

1 pound green beans, trimmed and cut crosswise in half

1/4 cup fresh lemon juice

2 tablespoons vegetable oil

1 tablespoon honey

2 tablespoons Dijon mustard

Salt and ground black pepper

Thin strips of pimiento, red bell pepper, or red onion for garnish

1 COOK THE BEANS: In a medium-size saucepan, combine the water and salt and bring to rolling boil. Add the green beans to the saucepan and blanch for about 5 minutes, or until soft. Drain.

2 DRESS THE SALAD: In small bowl whisk together the lemon juice, oil, honey, and mustard. Pour the dressing over the green beans. Sprinkle with salt and pepper to taste. Garnish with pimiento, bell pepper, or onion strips.

Nutrition information per serving—protein: 2.4 g; fat: 5.8 g; carbohydrate: 13.5 g; fiber: .1 g; sodium: 377 mg; cholesterol: 0 mg; calories: 105.

WARM PEAR AND GREEN BEAN SALAD > >

MAKES 8 SERVINGS

Sweet pears, savory green beans, and toasted hazelnuts combine for an intriguing contrast of taste and texture. Serve warm or at room temperature.

1/4 cup extra-virgin olive oil

1 teaspoon salt

1/2 teaspoon ground black pepper

2 pounds green beans, trimmed

4 ripe pears, cored and cut into eight wedges

1 teaspoon sugar

1/2 cup toasted hazelnuts, chopped

DRESSING:

2 tablespoons sherry vinegar

1 teaspoon Dijon mustard

1 small clove garlic, minced

1/4 cup extra-virgin olive oil

1/4 teaspoon salt

1/4 teaspoon ground black pepper

1 ROAST GREEN BEANS AND PEARS: Preheat oven to 400°F. Lightly coat 2 roasting pans with vegetable oil and set aside. In a large bowl, whisk 2 tablespoons oil, 1/2 teaspoon salt, and 1/4 teaspoon pepper. Toss the green beans well with this mixture and place in a roasting pan. In the same large bowl, whisk the remaining oil, salt, and pepper and toss with the pears. Sprinkle the pears with sugar and place in the second roasting pan. Place both pans in the oven. After 30 minutes remove the green beans. Roast the pears 15 more minutes and remove from the oven.

2 PREPARE DRESSING: In a small bowl, whisk together the vinegar, mustard, and garlic. Add the olive oil in a thin stream, whisking constantly. Stir in the salt and pepper. In a salad bowl, toss together the beans, pears, hazelnuts, and dressing. Serve immediately.

Nutrition information per serving—protein: 3.4 g; fat: 18.5 g; carbohydrate: 22.8 g; fiber: 6.4; sodium: 356 mg; cholesterol: 0 mg; calories: 252.

BREADS AND MUFFINS

FIVE-GRAIN BREAD > >

MAKES ABOUT 9 SERVINGS
(ONE 1 1/2-POUND LOAF)

Toast this bread and serve it with your favorite soup. To make a sunflower loaf, substitute $1/2$ cup hulled sunflower seeds for the rice and add 1 more tablespoon of honey. Sprinkle top with sunflower seeds before baking.

- $2^1/2$ cups bread flour
- 1 cup whole-wheat flour
- $1/4$ cup coarse cornmeal
- $1/4$ cup plus 1 tablespoon old-fashioned rolled oats
- $1/4$ cup wheat germ
- $1/4$ cup cooked rice (white or brown)
- $1/4$ cup packed brown sugar
- $2^1/2$ teaspoons instant active dry yeast
- 2 teaspoons salt
- 2 tablespoons honey
- $1/2$ cup buttermilk, warmed to 100°F
- $3/4$ to 1 cup spring water, warmed to 100°F
- 1 tablespoon vegetable oil
- 1 large egg

1 MAKE THE DOUGH: In a large bowl or food processor fitted with the metal blade, combine the flours, cornmeal, $1/4$ cup oats, wheat germ, rice, sugar, yeast, and salt. In a small bowl, combine the honey and buttermilk and stir into the dry mixture. Using a wooden spoon to mix by hand, add the water $1/4$ cup at a time until a stiff dough comes together, or process until dough comes together and rides around the bowl with the blade. On a work surface lightly dusted with whole-wheat flour, knead dough by hand until glossy and elastic—about 10 minutes—or process in food processor for 45 more seconds.

2 PROOF THE DOUGH: Coat a large bowl with the vegetable oil. Shape dough into a ball and place in the bowl, turning dough to coat all sides. Cover bowl with a clean, damp kitchen towel and let rise in a warm, draft-free place until doubled in size—1 to $1^1/2$ hours.

3 FORM THE LOAF: Punch down the dough and shape into a tight ball. Return dough to the floured surface, cover, and let rest for 10 minutes. Sprinkle a baking sheet with cornmeal. Shape the dough into a 10-inch oval, tapering the ends, and place on the baking sheet. Cover with damp kitchen towel and let rise in a warm, draft-free place until doubled in size—about 1 hour.

4 BAKE THE BREAD: Preheat the oven to 350°F. In a small bowl, lightly beat egg with 1 tablespoon of water. Brush loaf with egg wash and sprinkle with remaining tablespoon rolled oats. Using a sharp knife or razor blade, cut 3 diagonal slashes in the top of the dough. Bake in the lower third of the oven until the loaf is golden brown and sounds hollow when lightly tapped—50 to 60 minutes. Cool on a rack. Serve at room temperature or toasted. Store in an airtight container.

Nutrition information per serving—protein: 6.2 g; fat: 2.3 g; carbohydrate: 46.3 g; fiber: 3.3 g; sodium: 453 mg; cholesterol: 1.45 mg; calories: 228.

BOSTON BROWN BREAD

MAKES 2 LOAVES (6 SLICES EACH)

To make this quick bread, you will need two empty standard-size (11½- to 13-ounce) coffee cans. As the bread steams, the batter shrinks slightly, allowing the loaf to slide out easily when done.

- 1 cup all-purpose flour
- 1 teaspoon baking powder
- 1 teaspoon baking soda
- 1 teaspoon salt
- 1½ cups whole-wheat flour
- ½ cup cornmeal
- 2 cups buttermilk
- ¾ cup dark molasses
- 1 cup raisins
- Butter (optional)

1 PREPARE DRY INGREDIENTS: Wash and dry two empty metal coffee cans. Grease insides of cans well. In a large bowl, sift together the all-purpose flour, baking powder, baking soda, and salt. Stir in the whole-wheat flour and the cornmeal.

2 MAKE THE DOUGH: In a large bowl, with an electric mixer on medium speed, beat together the buttermilk and molasses. Reduce speed to low and gradually add the flour mixture, beating well after each addition. Stir in the raisins. Spoon batter evenly into prepared cans. Cover each can loosely with a piece of buttered waxed paper, then top with a larger piece of aluminum foil. Tightly secure aluminum foil with kitchen twine or a rubber band.

3 BAKE THE BREAD: Set a wire rack in a large stockpot and place cans on rack. Add enough boiling water to reach halfway up the cans. Set the pot over high heat and return the water to a boil. Reduce heat to low; cover and simmer 1½ hours, adding more boiling water if needed to maintain the water level.

4 SERVE THE BREAD: To serve, remove the foil and waxed paper from the cans. Turn the loaves out onto a cutting board; slice, and serve with butter, if desired. To store, let the bread cool completely and refrigerate bread in cans, covered with foil and waxed paper, for up to 1 week.

Nutrition information per slice—protein: 5 g; fat: 1 g; carbohydrate: 46 g; fiber: 4 g; sodium: 338 mg; cholesterol: 2 mg; calories: 207.

POTATO CLOVER DINNER ROLLS

‹ ‹

MAKES 20 ROLLS

These light and fluffy rolls, made with buttermilk, yeast, flour, and mashed potatoes, date back to Colonial times when potato breads were common in American kitchens.

- 1 large baking potato (about 10 ounces), peeled and quartered
- 1 cup cold buttermilk
- ¼ cup (½ stick) unsalted butter
- 1 tablespoon sugar
- 2 teaspoons salt
- 1 packet active dry yeast
- 5½ cups bread flour

1 MAKE THE DOUGH: Lightly coat a large bowl with vegetable oil and set aside. In a medium saucepan, place the potatoes and 1½ cups water over medium-high heat. Bring the water to a boil and cook the potatoes until they are easily pierced with a fork—about 15 minutes. In a large bowl, mash the potatoes and ¾ cups of the cooking water. Stir in the buttermilk, butter, sugar, and salt; let cool to room temperature. Add the yeast and stir to dissolve. Stir in the flour until a stiff dough forms. Transfer the dough to a lightly floured work surface and knead until smooth and supple—about 10 minutes. Form the dough into a ball, place it in the prepared bowl, cover with a clean damp towel, and let rise until doubled in volume—about 1 hour.

2 SHAPE THE DOUGH: Preheat oven to 375°F. Lightly coat the cups of two 12-cup muffin pans with cooking spray and set aside. Punch the risen dough down, remove from bowl, and knead lightly. Divide the dough into 60 equal-sized pieces and form each into a small ball. Place 3 balls in each muffin cup, cover with a damp towel, and let rise until doubled in size—about 60 minutes. Bake until the tops of the rolls are golden brown—about 30 minutes. Serve warm or at room temperature.

Nutrition information per roll—protein: 4.7 g; fat: 2.8 g; carbohydrate: 24.7 g; fiber: .9 g; sodium: 227 mg; cholesterol: 6.6 mg; calories: 142.

PRUNE HAZELNUT BREAD > >

MAKES ABOUT 12 SERVINGS
(ONE 10-INCH LOAF)

A satisfying accompaniment to goat cheese or other full-bodied cheeses, this bread is also excellent toasted and spread with cream cheese or butter for breakfast or midafternoon tea.

3/4 cup chopped prunes

1/4 cup Armagnac or other brandy

1 1/2 cups bread flour

1/3 cup rye flour

1 cup whole-wheat flour

2 teaspoons salt

1 packet instant active dry yeast

1 1/4 cups spring water, warmed to 100°F

1 cup chopped hazelnuts

1 tablespoon vegetable oil

1 MAKE THE DOUGH: In a small saucepan, heat the prunes and brandy over medium-low heat for 5 minutes or microwave on high for 30 seconds. Set aside to cool. In a large bowl or food processor fitted with the metal blade, combine the flours, salt, and yeast. Add the water and mix into a rough dough. By hand, on a lightly floured work surface, knead the dough until smooth and elastic—about 10 minutes—or in food processor, mix 45 more seconds. Turn the dough out onto a lightly floured surface and form into a flat rough rectangle. Add the nuts and prunes and fold dough over. Knead gently to distribute the nuts and fruit—2 to 4 minutes. The dough will separate and look crumbly before it comes together, forming a smooth mass. Shape the dough into a ball.

2 PROOF THE DOUGH: Coat a large bowl with vegetable oil and add dough, turning to coat all sides. Cover with a clean, damp kitchen towel and let rise in a warm, draft-free place until doubled in size—1 1/2 to 2 hours. Punch down and let rest 10 minutes.

3 FORM THE LOAF: Flour a 10-inch loaf pan. Shape the dough to fit into the pan and cover with the damp towel. Let rise until doubled in size—about 45 minutes.

4 BAKE THE BREAD: Preheat the oven to 400°F. Rub the entire bread surface with flour and place the loaf in the lower third of the oven. Mist the oven with 3 or 4 sprays of water and bake until the loaf is browned and sounds hollow when tapped—45 to 60 minutes. Cool on a wire rack. Serve at room temperature or toasted. Store in an airtight container.

Nutrition information per serving—protein: 5 g; fat: 9.6 g; carbohydrate: 21.3 g; fiber: 2.3 g; sodium: 428 mg; cholesterol: 0; calories: 186.

THE YEAST OF THE MATTER

There are three different types of yeast available, and they can be used interchangeably. One of the most widely used yeasts is instant active dry yeast, which can be incorporated directly into dry ingredients. Regular active dry yeast, needs to be dissolved in warm water before being added to flour. Both of these types of yeast can be stored in the refrigerator for up to 1 year (be sure to check the sell-by date on the packet). Cake (compressed) Yeast is a moist "brick" that needs to be dissolved in water. It is far more perishable than other yeasts and can be stored in the refrigerator for up to 2 weeks.

RAISIN PUMPERNICKEL BREAD

MAKES ABOUT 9 SERVINGS
(ONE ROUND LOAF)

Here is the loaf for Sunday brunch. The bread is a deep brown, infused with the subtle flavors of cocoa, coffee, molasses, and rye. Toast it and spread with cream cheese and you won't want another thing. Exchange the raisins for 1 table-spoon caraway seeds and you'll have a terrific bread for a Reuben or a corned-beef sandwich.

1 cup whole-wheat flour

1½ cups medium rye flour

1 cup bread flour

1 packet instant active dry yeast

1 tablespoon salt

2 tablespoons Dutch-processed cocoa

1 tablespoon instant espresso powder

½ cup milk, warmed to 100°F

¼ cup spring water, warmed to 100°F

2 tablespoons dark molasses

1 tablespoon vegetable oil

½ cup raisins

½ cup boiling spring water

1 large egg white

1 MAKE THE DOUGH: In a large bowl or food processor fitted with the metal blade, combine the flours, yeast, salt, and cocoa. In a small bowl, stir the espresso powder into the milk and add spring water and molasses. Use a wooden spoon to stir the liquid into the flour mixture or process until the dough comes together. On a lightly floured surface, knead the dough by hand until supple and soft—about 5 minutes—or process in food processor for 45 more seconds.

2 PROOF THE DOUGH: Coat a large bowl with the vegetable oil. Cover with a clean, damp kitchen towel and let rise in a warm, draft-free place until the dough has doubled in size—about 1 hour.

3 HYDRATE AND ADD THE RAISINS: In a medium heatproof bowl, cover the raisins with boiling water and set aside while the dough rises. When the dough has doubled in size, punch down and place on a lightly floured surface. Drain the raisins, place them in the middle of the dough, and knead to incorporate. Form the dough into a ball, cover with the towel, and let rest 15 minutes.

4 SHAPE THE LOAF: Form the dough into a tight 8-inch round loaf. Cover a baker's peel or baking sheet with parchment paper and sprinkle with cornmeal. Place the formed loaf on parchment, cover, and let rise until increased by a third.

5 BAKE THE BREAD: Place a baking stone in the lower third of the oven and preheat the oven to 375°F for 30 minutes (to thoroughly heat the stone). In a small bowl, whisk 1 tablespoon water with the egg white. Using a sharp knife or razor blade, cut 3 diagonal slashes in the top of the dough. Brush the top of the loaf with the egg-white glaze and slide the dough onto the baking stone. Mist the oven with 3 or 4 sprays of water and bake for about 45 minutes. Cool on a rack. Serve at room temperature or toasted. Store in an airtight container.

Nutrition information per serving—protein: 6 g; fat: 1.15 g; carbohydrate: 36.2 g; fiber: 4.56 g; sodium: 654 mg; cholesterol: 1.6 mg; calories: 173.

WHEAT FLOUR 101

Different types of flours are suited to specific baking needs. Here is a guide to the basic types:

> All-purpose flour is the most widely used flour. It is made from a blend of high-gluten hard wheat and low-gluten soft wheat.

> Bread flour is a high-gluten blend of hard-wheat flour with a small amount of malted barley (to improve yeast activity) and vitamin C or potassium bromate (to increase the gluten's elasticity) added. Bread flour is ideal for making yeast breads, since bread needs a strong elastic dough.

> Whole-wheat flour contains the germ, which means it has a higher fiber, nutritional, and fat content than other wheat flours.

> Cake or pastry flour is fine-textured soft-wheat flour with a high-starch content, which, makes for tender cakes and pastries.

> Self-rising flour is an all-purpose flour that contains baking powder and salt added.

SCHIACCIATA CON UVA

MAKES ABOUT 9 SERVINGS
(ONE 9 1/2-INCH FLAT BREAD)

Italians celebrate the grape harvest with this special bread. *Schiacciata* translates to "squashed" or "flattened," *con uva* to "with grapes."

STARTER:

1/3 cup bread flour

1 teaspoon instant active dry yeast

2/3 cup spring water, warmed to 100°F

DOUGH:

2 1/4 cups bread flour

3 tablespoons granulated brown sugar

1 teaspoon instant active dry yeast

1 1/2 teaspoons salt

3/4 cup spring water, warmed to 100°F

2 tablespoons extra-virgin olive oil

1 teaspoon anise seeds

TOPPING:

2 1/2 cups black or red seedless grapes

1/2 cup sweet fortified wine (such as Marsala or Vin Santo)

1 teaspoon vegetable oil

1 tablespoon granulated light brown sugar

1 tablespoon butter

1 MAKE THE STARTER: In a medium bowl, combine the flour and yeast and stir in the water. Cover with a clean, damp kitchen towel and set aside—12 to 24 hours. A loose, bubbly batter will form.

2 MARINATE THE GRAPES: In a small bowl, combine the grapes and wine and let stand—2 hours to overnight. Strain and reserve the wine for another use.

3 MAKE THE DOUGH: In a large bowl or food processor fitted with the metal blade, combine the flour, sugar, yeast, and salt. Add the water, olive oil, and starter and mix to a soft, sticky dough. By hand, on a lightly floured surface, knead the dough until smooth, elastic, and silky—about 10 minutes—or in food processor, mix about 45 more seconds. Shape dough into a ball.

4 PROOF THE DOUGH: Coat a large bowl with vegetable oil and add the dough, turning to coat all sides. Cover with a clean, damp kitchen towel and let rise in a warm, draft-free place until doubled in size—about 1 1/2 hours.

5 FORM THE LOAF: Punch the dough down, add the anise seeds, and knead to incorporate. Form the dough into a tight ball and let it rest 10 minutes. On a lightly floured surface, use a rolling pin to shape the dough into a 14-inch oval. Coat a baking sheet with the vegetable oil and place dough on the sheet. Place the grapes on top of the dough and gently press them into the dough. Cover with the damp towel and let rise until doubled in size—about 30 minutes.

6 BAKE THE BREAD: Preheat the oven to 400°F. Sprinkle the loaf with granulated brown sugar and bake in the middle of the oven until the crust is golden and the grapes are lightly browned—about 45 minutes. Remove from the oven and immediately rub the surface with butter. Cool on a wire rack. Serve at room temperature. Store in an airtight container.

Nutrition information per serving—protein: 3.8 g; fat: 4.5 g; carbohydrate: 39 g; fiber: 1.4 g; sodium: 323 mg; cholesterol: 0; calories: 215.

ROSEMARY RAISIN FOCACCIA WITH PINE NUTS

MAKES ABOUT 8 SERVINGS
(ONE 8- BY 12-INCH FLAT LOAF)

Focaccia—hearth bread—originated in Italy and is quite versatile. For a snack or to accompany soup or salad, try dipping this flat bread in olive oil or cut it into squares, split them, and make sandwiches. Either way, it's irresistible.

4½ cups bread flour

1 packet instant active dry yeast

½ teaspoon sugar

2 teaspoons salt

1¼ cups spring water, warmed to 100°F

½ cup plus 1 tablespoon extra-virgin olive oil

2 tablespoons chopped fresh rosemary leaves, plus 1 sprig

¼ cup golden raisins

⅓ cup toasted pine nuts

2 teaspoons coarse sea salt

1 MAKE THE DOUGH: In a food processor fitted with the metal blade, pulse to combine the flour, yeast, sugar, and salt. Add the water and 4 tablespoons olive oil and process until dough forms a ball—45 seconds. (If your food processor bowl is small, pull out half the dough and process each half for 45 seconds, then knead together by hand.)

2 PROOF THE DOUGH: On a lightly floured surface, knead the dough until supple and soft and form into a ball. Coat a large bowl with 1 tablespoon olive oil, place dough in bowl, and turn to coat all sides. Cover with a clean, damp towel and let rise in a warm, draft-free place until doubled in size—about 1 hour.

3 MAKE THE LOAF: In a small saucepan, combine rosemary and 2 tablespoons olive oil and heat over medium-high heat until olive oil bubbles—about 1 minute. Add raisins and remove from heat. Let cool to room temperature. Coat an 8- by 12-inch glass baking dish with 1 tablespoon olive oil and set aside. Once dough has risen, punch it down, place on a lightly floured surface, and knead in oil, raisin mixture, and pine nuts. Form the dough into a tight ball, cover with the same damp towel, and let dough rest for 15 minutes. On a lightly floured surface, use a rolling pin to form dough into an 8- by 12-inch rectangle about ½-inch thick. Place dough in prepared baking dish, cover with the damp towel, and let the dough rise in a warm, draft-free place—1 to 1½ hours. Dough will be puffy.

4 BAKE THE FOCACCIA: Preheat the oven to 425°F. Use your fingertips to dimple the dough and place small bunches of rosemary leaves in the indentations. Drizzle the remaining tablespoon of oil over the top of the dough and sprinkle with sea salt. Place loaf in the middle shelf of the oven and mist the inside of the oven with 3 or 4 sprays of water. Bake until golden—about 25 minutes. Cool on a wire rack. Serve warm. Store in an airtight container.

Nutrition information per serving—protein: .8 g; fat: 16.5 g; carbohydrate: 5.6 g; fiber: .9 g; sodium: 1069 mg; cholesterol: 0; calories: 166.

OLIVE FOUGASSE

MAKES ABOUT 10 SERVINGS
(TWO 8- BY 10-INCH FLAT BREADS)

Use the best olives and olive oil you can find for this French-style flat bread. It is rolled into a rectangle to form traditional patterns such as sunbursts and tree branches. Make *Fougasse aux Herbes* (Herbed Fougasse) by replacing the olives and salt with 1 tablespoon *herbes de Provence*.

2½ cups bread flour

1 tablespoon instant active
    dry yeast

2 teaspoons sugar

1 teaspoon salt

½ cup milk, warmed to 100°F

½ cup spring water, warmed to 100°F

¼ cup plus 3 tablespoons good quality
    extra-virgin olive oil

⅓ cup pitted, chopped Niçoise or
    kalamata olives

1 teaspoon large-flaked salt
    (such as Maldon) for sprinkling
    (optional)

1 MAKE THE DOUGH: In a food processor fitted with the metal blade, pulse to combine flour, yeast, sugar, and salt. Add the milk, water, and ¼ cup olive oil and process until the dough comes together to form a ball. Process for 45 more seconds and turn the dough out onto a lightly floured work surface. Knead the dough until smooth and elastic and form into a ball.

2 PROOF THE DOUGH: Coat a large bowl with 1 tablespoon olive oil and turn to coat all sides. Cover the bowl with a clean, damp kitchen towel and let rise in a warm, draft-free place until doubled in size—about 1 hour. Punch the dough down and turn it out onto a lightly floured work surface. Press the dough into a rectangle and sprinkle with olives. Fold each corner into the center to form an envelope and knead the olives into the dough. Re-form into a ball, cover with the damp towel, and let rest for 15 minutes.

3 FORM THE LOAVES: Place a baking stone in the middle of the oven and preheat to 375°F for 30 minutes (to thoroughly heat the stone). Divide the dough into two equal pieces. On a lightly floured surface, use a rolling pin to shape each half into an 8- by 10-inch rectangle. Place each rectangle on a parchment-lined baking sheet. Cut 6 to 8 slashes through the dough to form a pattern (e.g., a tree, starburst, or sunflower). Open the slits by pulling them apart with your fingers, coat the top of each loaf with 1 tablespoon olive oil, and let rise—20 to 40 minutes. The dough will be puffy and spring back slowly when lightly pressed with a finger.

4 BAKE THE LOAVES: If using, sprinkle salt over each loaf and slide the loaves (and the parchment underneath) onto the baking stone. Bake until golden brown—15 to 20 minutes. Cool on a rack. Serve at room temperature. Store in an airtight container.

Nutrition information per serving without salt—protein: 3.9 g; fat: 6.3 g; carbohydrate: 25 g; fiber: 1.1 g; sodium: 440 mg; cholesterol: 1.6 mg; calories: 175.

SAFFRON BREAD

MAKES 18 SERVINGS
(TWO 9- BY 5-INCH LOAVES)

The saffron bread often served at Eastertide in Portugal and the Azores inspired our lightly sweetened golden loaves. Try toasting slices, and serve them with jam or cheese.

- ¼ teaspoon saffron threads, crumbled
- 1 cup warm water
- 2 packets active dry yeast
- ½ cup plus 2 tablespoons sugar
- 4¾ cups all-purpose flour
- ¼ cup (½ stick) unsalted butter, softened
- 3 large egg yolks
- 1 large egg

1 MAKE THE DOUGH: In a small bowl, steep the saffron in the warm water for 10 minutes. In a large bowl, combine the yeast, 2 tablespoons sugar, 1 cup flour, and ²/₃ cup of the saffron water. Cover with a clean, damp kitchen towel and let rest for 30 minutes. Coat a large bowl with the butter and set aside. Stir the yeast-and-flour mixture (the sponge) down with a wooden spoon and stir in ½ cup sugar, the remaining saffron water, egg yolks, whole egg, and remaining flour. Continue to stir until a very sticky dough forms—about 3 minutes. Transfer the dough to a lightly floured surface, form it into a ball, and transfer it to the prepared bowl, turning to coat all sides with butter. Cover with a clean, damp kitchen towel and set aside to rise in a warm, draft-free place until the dough doubles in volume—about 1 hour.

2 BAKE THE BREAD: Preheat the oven to 425°F. Punch the dough down and divide it in half. Form both halves into loaves and place in two 9- by 5- by 3-inch loaf pans. Cover with the damp towel and let rise until doubled in volume—about 20 minutes. Bake in the lower third of the oven until the loaves are golden and sound hollow when tapped—20 to 25 minutes. Transfer to a wire rack to cool.

Nutrition information per serving—protein: 4.5 g; fat: 4 g; carbohydrate: 32.5 g; fiber: 1.3 g; sodium: 6.2 mg; cholesterol: 54.2 mg; calories: 186.

ITALIAN HOLIDAY LOAF

MAKES ABOUT 8 SERVINGS
(ONE 8-INCH LARGE ROUND LOAF)

Traditionally made to celebrate Easter, this versatile Italian bread known as *crescia*, is delicious year-round. Flavored with sharp cheese, it is good for breakfast with scrambled eggs, for lunch with soup and salad, or dipped into gravy with a dinner entrée.

- 2 tablespoons olive oil
- ½ cup milk, warmed to 100°F
- 1 packet active dry yeast
- 1 teaspoon sugar
- 2¼ cups all-purpose flour
- ²/₃ cup plus 1 tablespoon grated Parmesan or Romano cheese
- ½ teaspoon salt
- ¼ teaspoon ground black pepper
- 2 large eggs

1 MAKE THE DOUGH: Coat a large bowl with 1 tablespoon of the olive oil and set aside. In a small bowl, stir together the warmed milk, yeast, and sugar and let stand until bubbly. In a large bowl or a food processor fitted with the metal blade combine the flour, ²/₃ cup cheese, salt, and pepper. Add the eggs, yeast mixture, and remaining oil. Process until the dough forms into a ball and rides the blade. Or, by hand, stir with a wooden spoon until a slightly sticky but firm dough forms. Transfer to a lightly floured surface and knead for 15 minutes. Shape the dough into a ball and place in the oiled bowl, turning to coat all sides. Cover the bowl with a clean, damp kitchen towel and let rise in a warm, draft-free place until it doubles in volume—about 1 hour.

2 SHAPE THE LOAF: Lightly oil an 8-inch round pan and set aside. Punch down the dough and transfer it to a lightly floured surface. Divide the dough in half, then divide one dough half into three equal-sized pieces and, using your palms, roll each piece into an 18-inch-long strand. Braid the strands, attach the ends to form a circle, and place in the prepared pan. Form the remaining dough into a ball and place it in the center of the braided circle. At this point the two pieces might not touch each other or the sides of the pan. Cover the pan with a damp towel and let rise in a warm, draft-free place until it doubles in volume and the braid and ball touch each other—50 to 60 minutes. Preheat the oven to 350°F.

3 BAKE THE BREAD: Sprinkle the top of the risen loaf with the remaining cheese. Bake the bread in the lower third of the oven until the crust is golden and the loaf sounds hollow when tapped—about 30 minutes. Transfer to a wire rack to cool.

Nutrition information per serving—protein: 9.5 g; fat: 8 g; carbohydrate: 29 g; fiber: 1.4 g; sodium: 312 mg; cholesterol: 61.9 mg; calories: 228.

PIZZA BIANCA

MAKES TWO 12-INCH SQUARE FLATBREADS

Daniel and Sharon Leader, owners of Bread Alone, in Boiceville, N.Y., created this crisp snack bread based on a similar popular sandwich bread found in Rome and throughout Southern Italy.

- 3½ cups unbleached all-purpose flour
- 1½ cups cool water (about 60°F)
- ¼ ounce cake yeast (about 1½ firmly packed teaspoons) or
- 1 tablespoon good-quality active dry yeast, such as SAF
- 2¼ teaspoons kosher salt
- 1 tablespoon extra-virgin olive oil
- ½ tablespoon minced fresh rosemary leaves
- ½ teaspoon coarse sea salt

1 MAKE THE DOUGH: In a large bowl, using a wooden spoon, combine the flour and water, stirring for about 60 seconds. Cover the bowl with a clean, damp towel and let rest for 30 minutes. Using a mixer with a dough hook attachment or your hands, knead in the yeast. Add no additional flour except to dust hands while kneading. Knead the dough for 10 minutes, add the kosher salt, and knead 3 to 5 more minutes, until the dough is elastic and has a slight sheen. Dough will be very sticky. Place the dough in a lightly oiled bowl, cover with plastic wrap, and let rise in a warm, draft-free place until double in volume—about 3 hours.

2 SHAPE AND BAKE THE LOAVES: Place a large baking stone in the lower third of the oven and preheat oven to 475°F. Divide the dough in half, shape each piece into a disk, and place each on a large, lightly floured baking sheet or peel. Let the dough rest for 45 minutes. Cover each half of dough with a lightly oiled piece of waxed paper or plastic wrap and, using a rolling

pin, flatten the dough into two 12- by 12-inch squares. Let the dough rest 15 minutes more. Brush the dough lightly with olive oil and sprinkle with rosemary and sea salt and bake until bread is golden brown—20 to 25 minutes.

Nutrition information per 4-inch square piece—protein: 2.5 g; fat: 1 g; carbohydrate: 18.6 g; fiber: .8 g; sodium: 141 mg; cholesterol: 0; calories: 96.

SAVORY CORNMEAL COOKIES

MAKES ABOUT FIFTY 1-INCH COOKIES

A cross between a cracker and a biscuit, these airy little bites can be served alongside chili or as an hors d'oeuvre.

- 1 cup yellow or white cornmeal
- ½ cup all-purpose flour
- ¾ teaspoon salt
- 1 teaspoon sugar
- 1 teaspoon baking powder
- ⅛ teaspoon ground red pepper
- ¼ teaspoon cracked black pepper
- 1 cup grated Asiago or sharp Cheddar cheese
- 2 tablespoons butter, melted
- 1 large egg
- ⅔ cup water

1 PREPARE THE BAKING SHEETS: Line two baking sheets with parchment paper. Preheat the oven to 400°F.

2 MAKE THE COOKIE DOUGH: In a medium bowl, combine the cornmeal, flour, salt, sugar, baking powder, and ground red and black peppers. Stir in the cheese. In a small bowl, whisk together the melted butter, egg, and water. Use a wooden spoon to stir the egg mixture into the flour mixture until a smooth ball of dough forms. Drop rounded teaspoons of dough onto prepared baking sheets.

3 BAKE THE COOKIES: Bake in the middle of the oven until golden—12 to 14 minutes. Remove from baking sheet and cool on a wire rack. Store in an airtight container for up to 2 days.

Nutrition information per serving—protein: 1.1 g; fat: 1.3 g; carbohydrate: 3 g; fiber: .2 g; sodium: 49.6 mg; cholesterol: 7.5 mg; calories: 27.5.

CHOCOLATE BREAD > >

Serve this impressive chocolate bread warm along with a glass of milk, and children may never ask for cookies again!

2^1/$_2$ cups bread flour

^{1}/$_3$ cup sugar

^{1}/$_2$ cup plus 2 tablespoons Dutch-processed cocoa

1 packet instant active dry yeast

1 teaspoon salt

1^1/$_3$ cups spring water, warmed to 100°F

1 large egg yolk, at room temperature

1 tablespoon unsalted butter, softened

1 tablespoon vegetable oil

^{3}/$_4$ cup coarsely chopped high-quality semisweet chocolate

1 MAKE THE DOUGH: In a large bowl or food processor fitted with the metal blade, combine the flour, sugar, ^{1}/$_2$ cup cocoa, yeast, and salt. In a medium bowl, whisk together the water and egg yolk. Add the egg mixture to the dry ingredients and stir or process to form a soft dough. By hand, on a lightly floured surface, knead butter into the dough and continue to knead until dough is smooth and supple—about 10 minutes—or in food processor, mix for 45 more seconds.

2 PROOF THE DOUGH: Coat a large bowl with vegetable oil and add dough ball, turning to coat all sides. Cover with a clean, damp kitchen towel and let rise in a warm, draft-free place until doubled in size—about 1 hour.

3 FORM THE LOAF: Punch dough down. Turn out on a lightly floured surface, knead by hand a few moments, and divide dough into three equal pieces. Form each piece of dough into a tight 8-inch ball. Cover with the damp towel and let rest for 15 minutes. Roll each of the three balls into a 12-inch-long rope. On a baking sheet lined with parchment paper, place the three ropes and form into a braid. Cover with the damp towel and let rise until doubled in size.

4 BAKE THE BREAD: Preheat the oven to 350°F. Dust the braided loaf with the remaining 2 tablespoons cocoa. Bake in the center of the oven to a deep mahogany color—about 40 minutes. Remove from oven, sprinkle chopped chocolate over the hot loaf, and place on a rack to cool. Serve warm or at room temperature. Store in an airtight container.

Nutrition information per serving—protein: 5 g; fat: 7.3 g; carbohydrate: 39 g; fiber: 2.7 g; sodium: 227 mg; cholesterol: 24 mg; calories: 233.

SKILLET CORNBREAD

1 tablespoon butter

1 tablespoon vegetable oil

1 cup all-purpose flour

1 cup yellow or white cornmeal

1 teaspoon baking powder

1 teaspoon baking soda

1 teaspoon salt

^{1}/$_2$ teaspoon cream of tartar

1 8-ounce can cream-style corn

^{1}/$_2$ cup milk

1 large egg

^{1}/$_2$ cup drained canned whole corn kernels

1 PREPARE THE SKILLET: Preheat the oven to 425°F. Place the butter and vegetable oil in a 9-inch cast-iron skillet (alternatively, use any 9-inch round baking dish). Place skillet in the oven.

2 MAKE THE DOUGH: In a large bowl, combine the flour, cornmeal, baking powder, baking soda, salt, and cream of tartar. In a medium bowl, combine the cream-style corn, milk, and egg. Stir the milk mixture into the flour mixture just until combined. Fold in the corn kernels.

3 MAKE THE CORNBREAD: Remove skillet from the oven and carefully spoon the batter into it. Bake the cornbread until center feels firm when gently pressed—20 to 25 minutes. Serve warm.

Nutrition information per serving—protein: 5 g; fat: 5 g; carbohydrate: 34 g; fiber: 3 g; sodium: 521 mg; cholesterol: 32 mg; calories: 198.

HERB POPOVERS <<

We developed this recipe using *herbs de Provence,* but any dried herb or blend of herbs can be used.

> **6 large eggs**
>
> **2 cups milk**
>
> **6 tablespoons butter, melted**
>
> **2 cups all-purpose flour**
>
> **1 teaspoon herbes de Provence**
>
> **1 teaspoon salt**

1 PREPARE THE BAKING CUPS: Heat oven to 375°F. Generously grease eight 7-ounce ovenproof custard cups; place the cups on a baking pan and set aside. Alternatively, use a nonstick popover pan.

2 MAKE THE DOUGH: In a large bowl, with an electric mixer on medium speed, beat the eggs until frothy. Beat in the milk and butter. Reduce speed to low; beat in the flour, herbs, and salt.

3 BAKE THE POPOVERS: Divide batter among the prepared custard cups. Bake 1 hour. Using a sharp knife, pierce the side of each popover, allowing steam to escape. Continue baking until browned—about 10 minutes longer. Turn out and serve immediately.

Nutrition information per popover—protein: 10 g; fat: 15 g; carbohydrate: 27 g; fiber: .8 g; sodium: 420 mg; cholesterol: 188 mg; calories: 283.

EASTER MORNING BISCUITS

These crisp, honey-sweetened biscuits—our version of a Greek Easter favorite, *koulouraki*—are just perfect for dunking in morning coffee at Easter or any time of year. They're made from a simple non-rising dough that's similar to cookie dough and are quick and easy to prepare.

> **3 cups all-purpose flour**
>
> **1 teaspoon baking powder**
>
> **1/2 teaspoon salt**
>
> **1/2 cup butter (1 stick), softened**
>
> **1/3 cup plus 1 tablespoon honey**
>
> **1/3 cup packed light brown sugar**
>
> **2 large eggs**
>
> **2 tablespoons milk**
>
> **1/2 teaspoon pure vanilla extract**
>
> **3 tablespoons orange juice**

1 MAKE THE DOUGH: Sift the flour, baking powder, and salt together into a medium bowl. In a large bowl, with an electric mixer on medium speed, beat the butter, 1/3 cup honey, and sugar until they are light and fluffy. With the mixer running, add the eggs one at a time until thoroughly incorporated. Add the milk, vanilla, and 2 tablespoons orange juice and beat on medium speed until combined. Gradually add the flour mixture and beat for 1 more minute until all flour is incorporated and a soft dough forms. Cover the bowl with plastic wrap and refrigerate the dough for 30 minutes.

2 BAKE THE BISCUITS: Preheat the oven to 350°F. In a small bowl, combine the remaining honey and orange juice to make a glaze; stir until smooth, and set aside. Divide the dough into 16 equal-sized pieces and form each into either an S-shaped serpentine or a twist. For serpentines, roll each dough piece into a "rope" approximately 8 inches long, bend the rope into an S, and coil each end. To form twists, fold the 8-inch rope in half and twist the ends of each side over each other 3 times. Place the biscuits on a baking sheet and bake for 12 minutes. Remove the biscuits from the oven, brush with the orange glaze, and continue to bake until golden—about 15 more minutes. Cool on a wire rack. Serve with coffee or tea.

Nutrition information per biscuit—protein: 3.4 g; fat: 6.7 g; carbohydrate: 28 g; fiber: .8 g; sodium: 102 mg; cholesterol: 42.4 mg; calories: 185.

PUMPKIN BISCUITS

Our fluffy biscuits prove that pumpkin isn't just for pie. Try them buttered for breakfast or split and stuffed with ham or turkey for lunch.

4 cups all-purpose flour

2^1/$_2$ tablespoons baking powder

2 teaspoons salt

2 teaspoons ground ginger

^{1}/$_2$ teaspoon ground red pepper

1 cup (2 sticks) cold unsalted butter

1^1/$_2$ cups unsweetened pumpkin puree

1 tablespoon honey

^{1}/$_2$ cup buttermilk

1 MAKE THE DOUGH: Preheat the oven to 400°F. In a large bowl, combine the flour, baking powder, salt, ginger, and ground red pepper. Cut the chilled butter into small pieces; Using a pastry cutter, two knives, or your hands, cut the butter into the flour mixture until the mixture resembles coarse meal. Set aside. In a small bowl, combine the pumpkin puree and honey. Add the pumpkin mixture to the flour mixture and stir until just combined. Add the buttermilk and stir just until mixture clings together and is combined.

2 ROLL OUT THE BISCUITS: Lightly coat a baking sheet with vegetable oil and set aside. Turn the biscuit dough out onto a lightly floured surface and knead about 10 times. Roll the dough out to ^{3}/$_4$-inch thickness and cut biscuits out with a 3^1/$_2$-inch round cutter; gather the scraps, gently press together, and repeat until all of the dough is used. Place the biscuits 1 inch apart on the prepared baking sheet and bake until golden—25 to 30 minutes. Transfer to a wire rack to cool.

Nutrition information per biscuit—protein: 6.4 g; fat: 19 g; carbohydrate: 43.6 g; fiber: 3.3 g; sodium: 729 mg; cholesterol: 50.1 mg; calories: 370.

SESAME AND POPPY SEED CRACKERS

Homemade crackers are easy to make, and the resulting crisps can host almost any cheese, from a semisoft or soft-ripened one such as Brie to a semihard one like goat's-milk Cheddar.

3 cups all-purpose flour

2 teaspoons baking powder

2 teaspoons salt

^{1}/$_2$ cup (1 stick) unsalted butter, cut into small pieces and chilled

1 cup plain yogurt

^{3}/$_4$ cup sesame seeds, toasted

^{1}/$_3$ cup poppy seeds

2 large eggs

1 tablespoon sugar

1 PREPARE THE DOUGH: Preheat the oven to 350°F. In a food processor fitted with the metal blade, pulse together the flour, baking powder, and salt. Add the butter and pulse until the mixture resembles coarse meal. Transfer the flour mixture to a large bowl and add the yogurt, ^{1}/$_2$ cup sesame seeds, and poppy seeds. Stir just until the ingredients are incorporated. Divide the dough into quarters, wrap in plastic wrap, and chill for 10 minutes.

2 BAKE THE CRACKERS: Lightly coat a baking sheet with vegetable oil and set aside. In a small bowl, lightly beat the eggs and sugar together until the sugar dissolves; set aside. On a lightly floured surface, roll the dough out to a 10- by 16-inch rectangle about ^{1}/$_4$-inch thick. Brush the dough with the egg wash and sprinkle evenly with the remaining sesame seeds. Cut into 2- by 5-inch rectangles and bake on the prepared baking sheet until browned—about 25 minutes. Transfer crackers to a wire rack to cool completely and store in an airtight container until ready to serve (for up to 1 week).

Nutrition information per cracker—protein: 2.8 g; fat: 5.9 g; carbohydrate: 10.9 g; fiber: .9 g; sodium: 173 mg; cholesterol: 22 mg; calories: 106.

WHOLE GRAIN AND PEPPER CRACKERS

MAKES THIRTY-SIX 3-INCH
TRIANGULAR CRACKERS OR FORTY
2-INCH SQUARE CRACKERS

Surprisingly simple to make, our whole grain crackers reward the cook with their mellow, nutty flavor and subtle peppery bite. Stored in an airtight container, they will last for up to a week—but we bet they'll quickly be devoured, with cheese or on their own.

$^1/_4$ cup old-fashioned rolled oats

$^1/_4$ cup bran

1 cup all-purpose flour

$1^1/_4$ teaspoons baking powder

$^1/_2$ teaspoon sugar

$^1/_2$ teaspoon kosher salt

$^1/_4$ teaspoon baking soda

$^1/_4$ cup ($^1/_2$ stick) unsalted butter, cut into small pieces and chilled

$^1/_3$ cup buttermilk

1 teaspoon ground black pepper

1 large egg, lightly beaten

1 MAKE THE DOUGH: In a food processor fitted with a metal blade, pulse the oats and bran until coarsely ground. Add the flour, baking powder, sugar, $^1/_4$ teaspoon salt, and baking soda and pulse to combine. Add the butter and process until the flour mixture resembles coarse meal. Add the buttermilk and pepper and continue to process until the dough forms a ball and rides the blade. Divide in half, wrap in plastic wrap, and refrigerate for 30 minutes.

2 BAKE THE CRACKERS: Preheat the oven to 350°F. Line a baking sheet with parchment paper and set aside. Roll the dough out on a lightly floured surface to a 9- by 9-inch square about $^1/_4$-inch thick. Using a sharp knife, cut the dough into 3-inch triangles or 2-inch squares. Transfer the crackers to the prepared baking sheet, brush them with some of the beaten egg, and sprinkle with some of the remaining salt. Repeat with the remaining dough and bake crackers until golden brown—about 15 minutes. Transfer the crackers to a wire rack to cool completely, and store in an airtight container until ready to serve.

Nutrition information per 3-inch cracker—protein: .7 g; fat: 1.5 g; carbohydrate: 3.6 g; fiber: .4 g; sodium: 58.8 mg; cholesterol: 6.5 mg; calories: 29.4.

BANANA-OATMEAL PANCAKES WITH MAPLE-RUM SYRUP

MAKES 3 SERVINGS (9 PANCAKES)

To serve a larger group, this recipe can easily be doubled or tripled.

$1^1/_3$ cups buttermilk

$^1/_2$ cup quick-cooking rolled oats

1 cup all-purpose flour

1 teaspoon baking powder

$^1/_2$ teaspoon salt

1 tablespoon vegetable oil

1 large egg

$^1/_2$ teaspoon pure vanilla extract

$1^1/_2$ cups coarsely chopped ripe bananas (about 2 large)

$^3/_4$ cup maple syrup (grade A, if available)

1 teaspoon dark rum (or $^1/_2$ teaspoon rum extract)

$^1/_4$ teaspoon ground cinnamon

3 tablespoons chopped pecans, toasted

1 MAKE THE BATTER: Preheat the oven to 200°F. In a small bowl, combine the buttermilk and oats. Set aside 10 minutes. In a large bowl, combine the flour, baking powder, and salt.

2 In a medium bowl, whisk together the vegetable oil, egg, and vanilla. Add the egg mixture and oat mixture to the flour mixture, combining well. Fold in the chopped bananas. If mixture seems too thick, add 1 to 2 tablespoons water.

3 MAKE THE PANCAKES: Heat a nonstick griddle or skillet over medium-high heat. Lightly coat with vegetable oil. For each pancake, spoon $^1/_3$ cup batter onto hot griddle. Cook until the tops bubble and the edges are crisp—3 to 5 minutes. Turn the pancakes over and cook 1 minute more. Repeat with the remaining batter and keep the pancakes warm in the oven.

4 MAKE THE SYRUP: In a small saucepan, combine the maple syrup, rum, and cinnamon over low heat until warm. Top the pancakes with the warm syrup and toasted pecans; serve.

Nutrition information per serving—protein: 15 g; fat: 15 g; carbohydrate: 126 g; fiber: 6 g; sodium: 615 mg; cholesterol: 75 mg; calories: 672.

MULTIGRAIN BLUEBERRY PANCAKES

MAKES ABOUT 4 CUPS BATTER
(SIXTEEN 4-INCH PANCAKES)

Four grains offer a wholesome twist on the classic blueberry pancake.

1 cup all-purpose flour

3/4 cup whole-wheat flour

1/3 cup yellow cornmeal

1/3 cup old-fashioned rolled oats

2 tablespoons sugar

2 teaspoons baking powder

1 teaspoon salt

1/2 teaspoon baking soda

1/2 teaspoon ground nutmeg

1 3/4 cups buttermilk

1/4 cup (1/2 stick) unsalted butter, melted

1/3 cup honey

3 large eggs

1 cup fresh blueberries

1 MAKE THE BATTER: In a large bowl, combine the flours, cornmeal, oats, sugar, baking powder, salt, baking soda, and nutmeg. Using a whisk, add buttermilk, butter, honey, and eggs to dry mixture until a smooth batter forms. Gently fold in the blueberries.

2 MAKE THE PANCAKES: Preheat the oven to 250°F. Lightly coat a nonstick skillet or griddle with vegetable oil and heat until hot over medium-high heat. Pour 1/4 cupfuls of batter to form pancakes and cook until the tops bubble and the edges begin to crisp. Turn each pancake over and continue to cook until both sides are golden brown. Transfer the pancakes to a baking pan and place in oven to keep warm until ready to serve. Repeat until all batter is used. Serve hot.

Nutrition information per pancake—protein: 4.2 g; fat: 4.5 g; carbohydrate: 23.3 g; fiber: 1.5 g; sodium: 276 mg; cholesterol: 48.6; calories: 146.

BLACK RASPBERRY BUTTERMILK SCONES > >

MAKES 16 SCONES

These tender scones contain a sweet surprise—a pool of black raspberry jam baked between the pastry layers.

1 1/2 cups all-purpose flour

1 1/2 cups cake flour

1 tablespoon baking powder

1 teaspoon salt

1 cup (2 sticks) unsalted butter, cut into 1-inch pieces

1 cup buttermilk

1 tablespoon grated lemon zest

1/2 cup black raspberry jam

1 1/2 teaspoons sugar

1 MAKE THE DOUGH: Preheat the oven to 400°F. In a food processor fitted with the metal blade, place the flours, baking powder, and salt and pulse until combined. Add the butter and pulse until the mixture resembles coarse meal. Add the buttermilk and zest and pulse until the dough is just combined.

2 SHAPE THE SCONES: Line a baking sheet with parchment paper and set aside. Place an 18-inch sheet of parchment paper on a work surface and sprinkle it lightly with flour. Transfer the dough to the paper and, with floured hands, gently press the dough into a 12- by 12-inch square; the dough should be about 3/4 inch thick. Cut out two 6-inch circles, reshape the remaining dough into a 3/4-inch-thick square, and cut out 1 more 6-inch circle. Gather the remaining scraps and form into 1 final 6-inch circle. Place 1/4 cup of jam on two of the circles. Top each with the remaining dough rounds and pinch the sides shut. Using a knife, score the top of each scone with a large cross marking 4 quadrants. Sprinkle the tops with sugar. Transfer scones to the prepared pan and bake until golden—35 to 40 minutes. Transfer to a wire rack to cool. Split or cut on the scores. Serve warm or at room temperature.

Nutrition information per scone—protein: 2.6 g; fat: 11.8 g; carbohydrate: 20.4 g; fiber: .6 g; sodium: 225 mg; cholesterol: 31.6 mg; calories: 197.

CINNAMON-PECAN STICKY BUNS

< <

MAKES 10 BUNS

3¼ cups bread flour

1 packet instant active dry yeast

3 tablespoons sugar

1 teaspoon salt

½ cup milk

½ cup (1 stick) plus 2 tablespoons
    unsalted butter, cut into small pieces

3 large eggs

1 tablespoon grated lemon zest

1 tablespoon fresh lemon juice

1¼ cups packed dark brown sugar

½ cup light corn syrup

3 tablespoons unsalted butter,
    melted

1½ cups pecan halves (6 ounces),
    plus ¼ cup finely chopped

¼ cup sour cream

1 tablespoon ground cinnamon

1 large egg yolk

1 MAKE THE DOUGH: In a food processor fitted with the metal blade, place ³/₄ cup flour, yeast, 2 tablespoons sugar, and salt and pulse to mix. In a small saucepan, heat the milk and ¹/₂ cup butter until warm—about 115°F. Add the milk mixture to dry ingredients and process for 30 seconds. With the motor running, add the eggs, one at a time. Add lemon zest, juice, and remaining 2¹/₂ cups flour and process for 30 more seconds. Remove the dough and place on a lightly floured surface, knead for 5 minutes by hand, and form into a ball.

2 PROOF THE DOUGH: Coat a large bowl with 1 tablespoon butter and add the ball of dough, turning to coat all sides. Cover with a clean, damp kitchen towel and let dough rise in a warm, draft-free place until doubled in size—about 1 hour. Place the dough on a lightly floured work surface and punch it down. Cover with the damp towel and let rest for 15 minutes.

3 MAKE THE GLAZE AND FILLING: Coat a 10-inch round baking pan with remaining 1 tablespoon butter and set aside. In a medium bowl, stir together 1 cup brown sugar, corn syrup, melted butter, and pecan halves. Spread the mixture on the bottom of the prepared baking pan and set aside. Stir together the sour cream, chopped pecans, remaining ¹/₄ cup brown sugar, remaining tablespoon sugar, cinnamon, and egg yolk in a small bowl until combined. Set aside.

4 FORM THE BUNS: Preheat the oven to 400°F. Roll the dough into a 20- by 12-inch rectangle. Keeping one of the longer sides toward you, spread the sour cream mixture evenly over the dough and roll the dough into a log. Lightly pinch the seam to seal it and slice the log into 10 two-inch-thick pinwheel-like pieces. Place pieces, cut-side down, about 1 inch apart on the prepared pan. Cover with a clean, damp towel and let rise in a warm, dry place until doubled in size and buns are touching—about 1 hour.

5 BAKE THE BUNS: Place the buns on the center rack in the oven and bake until golden brown—35 to 40 minutes. Remove buns from the oven. Let sit for 2 minutes and invert onto a serving plate. Cool buns 5 minutes and serve warm.

Nutrition information per bun—protein: 9.8 g; fat: 32.7 g; carbohydrate: 68 g; fiber: 2.5 g; sodium: 272 mg; cholesterol: 130 mg; calories: 585.

CARROT-GINGER BRAN MUFFINS
> >

MAKES 8 MUFFINS

Carrot adds sweetness to these bran muffins, and the ginger adds spice. They're especially wonderful served warm from the oven.

- 3/4 cup all-purpose flour
- 1/2 cup wheat bran
- 1/2 cup packed dark brown sugar
- 1 teaspoon baking powder
- 1/2 teaspoon baking soda
- 1/2 teaspoon salt
- 1/2 teaspoon ground ginger
- 1/4 teaspoon ground cinnamon
- 6 tablespoons vegetable oil
- 1/4 cup applesauce
- 1 large egg
- 2 carrots, shredded (about 1/2 cup tightly packed)
- 1 tablespoon minced crystallized ginger
- 2 teaspoons grated peeled fresh ginger

MAKE THE MUFFINS: Preheat the oven to 375°F. Place 8 paper liners in the cups of a muffin pan and set aside. In a medium bowl, combine the flour, bran, sugar, baking powder, baking soda, salt, ginger, and cinnamon and set aside. In a large bowl, whisk together the vegetable oil, applesauce, and egg. Add the carrots, crystallized ginger, and fresh ginger and stir to combine. Add the dry ingredients to the egg mixture and stir until just combined. Divide the batter equally among the prepared muffin cups. Bake until the tops spring back when lightly touched—20 to 25 minutes. Transfer muffins to a wire rack to cool completely.

Nutrition information per muffin—protein: 2.7 g; fat: 11.2 g; carbohydrate: 22.4 g; fiber: 2.3 g; sodium: 274 mg; cholesterol: 26.6 mg; calories: 193.

RHUBARB-ALMOND MUFFINS

MAKES 16 MUFFINS

Sweet prunes balance rhubarb's tartness in this easy-to-prepare recipe.

- 2/3 pound rhubarb, tops removed and ends trimmed
- 2 1/2 cups all-purpose flour
- 3/4 cup chopped almonds
- 1 teaspoon baking powder
- 1 teaspoon baking soda
- 1/2 teaspoon ground nutmeg
- 1/2 teaspoon salt
- 1/4 teaspoon ground cinnamon
- 1 cup packed light brown sugar
- 1 1/4 cups buttermilk
- 1/2 cup vegetable oil
- 1 large egg
- 1 tablespoon pure vanilla extract
- 1/2 cup chopped pitted prunes

1 PREPARE THE RHUBARB: Preheat the oven to 375°F. Lightly coat sixteen 2 1/2-inch muffin-pan cups with vegetable oil. Wash the rhubarb stalks; coarsely chop and set aside.

2 MAKE THE BATTER: In a large bowl, combine the flour, almonds, baking powder, baking soda, nutmeg, salt, and cinnamon.

3 In a medium bowl, with an electric mixer on medium speed, beat the brown sugar, buttermilk, oil, egg, and vanilla until combined. Stir into the flour mixture just until moistened; the batter will be lumpy. Fold the rhubarb and prunes into batter. Spoon the batter into muffin cups.

4 BAKE THE MUFFINS: Bake the muffins until a cake tester inserted in center of a muffin comes out clean—18 to 20 minutes. Let cool in pans 5 minutes. Transfer the muffins to a wire rack and let cool completely. Store in an airtight container for up to 3 days.

Nutrition information per muffin—protein: 5 g; fat: 11 g; carbohydrate: 36 g; fiber: 2 g; sodium: 171 mg; cholesterol: 14 mg; calories: 252.

SAUCES, PRESERVES, AND CONDIMENTS

APPLE BUTTER

MAKES 3 1/2 CUPS

Simmering the apples and spices fills the kitchen with the aroma of autumn. We used Fuji apples, but you could substitute Macoun or Rome apples with equally delicious results.

5 pounds cooking apples, (such as Fuji), about 10 cored and quartered

1 cup apple cider

2 tablespoons orange juice

1 cup packed dark brown sugar

1/2 cup sugar

MAKE THE APPLE BUTTER: In a large Dutch oven, combine the apples, cider, and orange juice and bring to a boil over high heat. Reduce the heat and simmer, covered, stirring occasionally, until apples are soft—30 to 40 minutes. Remove the pan from the heat. In small batches, puree the apples and any cooking liquid through a food mill. Return the puree to the Dutch oven, add the sugars, and bring to a boil, stirring constantly. Cook, continuing to stir until the puree thickens slightly—about 10 minutes. Reduce heat to low, partially cover, and simmer for 1 hour. Transfer the butter to a clean jar and cool completely. Store refrigerated for up to 1 month.

Nutrition information per 1-tablespoon serving—protein: .1 g; fat: .1 g; carbohydrate: 12.6 g; fiber: .8 g; sodium: 1.2 mg; cholesterol: 0; calories: 49.

PERFECT STRAWBERRY PRESERVES

MAKES 8 HALF-PINT JARS

This heirloom recipe yields the tastiest results when you choose small, uniform berries of which at least a quarter are underripe. The product is a wonderful cross between syrup and jam.

2 pints small best-quality strawberries

1 1/2 tablespoons cider vinegar (5 percent acidity)

4 cups sugar

1 MAKE THE PRESERVES: Combine strawberries and vinegar in a large saucepan. Bring the mixture to a boil over high heat, shaking the pan occasionally, for 3 minutes. add the sugar and bring to a full boil. Continue to boil for 6 minutes, occasionally working the pan in a circular motion. Remove from heat, cover, and allow to stand overnight.

2 PROCESS THE JAM: Sterilize eight 1/2 pint jars and keep hot. Bring the strawberry mixture to a boil over high heat and ladle into the hot jars, leaving 1/4 inch headspace. Securely cap each jar and process using the boiling-water canning method (see below) for 10 minutes. Store in a cool dark pantry for up to 1 year.

Nutrition information per 2-tablespoon serving—protein: .1 g; fat: 0; carbohydrate: 13.2 g; fiber: .1 g; sodium: .2 mg; cholesterol: 0; calories: 51.

CANNING SAFETY

Any preserve that is processed in a boiling-water canner for less than 10 minutes requires sterilized jars. To do this, submerge the jars in boiling water for 10 minutes and keep them in hot water until you are ready to fill them. Lids do not need to be sterilized, but they must be hot: heat them in simmering water for 10 minutes. To reduce bacterial growth in filled jars, insert a long wooden skewer into the jars to help remove the air bubbles. Be sure to wipe the rims dry before sealing the jars. Process the jars in the boiling-water canner for the amount of time specified in the recipe. Once the jars have cooled, test them for an airtight seal by pressing the center of each lid. If it is flat, the jar is properly sealed. Any jar that has not sealed properly must be stored in the refrigerator and its contents consumed within 2 to 3 days.

BLACKBERRY-CASSIS JAM

MAKES 2 CUPS

This decadent cassis-spiked jam is used to fill Lemon Blackberry Cake (see recipe on page 185). It is also wonderful drizzled over pancakes or as a topping for ice cream.

- **5 cups fresh or frozen blackberries**
- **1 cup plus 2 tablespoons cassis**
- **1/2 cup sugar**
- **1 tablespoon grated lemon zest**
- **2 tablespoons fresh lemon juice**
- **2 tablespoons cornstarch**

MAKE THE JAM: In a medium nonreactive saucepan, combine blackberries, 1 cup cassis, sugar and lemon zest and juice, and cook over medium-low heat until berries begin to soften—about 10 minutes. Use a slotted spoon to remove only the berries. Place them in a medium bowl, lightly mash them, and strain the resulting liquid back into the saucepan. Set the strained berries aside. Dissolve the cornstarch in the remaining 2 tablespoons of cassis and stir the mixture into the hot berry juice. Bring the liquid to a boil, reduce heat to medium-low, and cook, stirring often to avoid burning, until the liquid thickens and is reduced to half its original volume—about 2 cups. Stir the reserved blackberries into the liquid. Remove from heat and let cool completely.

Nutrition information per 2-tablespoon serving—protein: .3 g; fat: .2 g; carbohydrate: 20.2 g; fiber: 2 g; sodium: 1.2 mg; cholesterol: 0; calories: 108.

TOMATO JAM

MAKES 2 CUPS

Use up any end-of-season tomatoes in this spicy jam—try it on grilled steak at your next cookout.

- **3 pounds beefsteak tomatoes (about 5 large)**
- **3 tablespoons olive oil**
- **1 small onion, diced (about 1/2 cup)**
- **1 medium clove garlic, minced**
- **1 teaspoon ground red pepper**
- **1 teaspoon ground black pepper**
- **1 teaspoon coriander seeds**
- **1 teaspoon mustard seeds**
- **1/2 teaspoon cumin seeds**
- **1 cup cider vinegar**
- **3/4 cup sugar**
- **1/4 cup dry sherry**

1 BLANCH THE TOMATOES: Using a paring knife, cut a small x on the bottom of each tomato. Bring a large pot of water to a boil, drop the tomatoes into the water, and let them cook about 30 seconds. Using a slotted spoon, remove the tomatoes and immediately plunge them into a bowl of ice water. Remove the cooled tomatoes and, using the paring knife, gently peel off their skins. Chop the skinned tomatoes and set aside.

2 MAKE THE JAM: In a large saucepan, heat oil over medium heat and sauté the onions for 3 minutes. Add the garlic and cook until the onions soften—about 2 more minutes. Add the remaining ingredients, including the chopped tomatoes. Increase the heat to medium high and cook until the tomato mixture comes to a boil. Reduce heat to medium and simmer until most of the liquid has evaporated. Cool completely. Store refrigerated in an airtight container for up to 1 month.

Nutrition information per 1-tablespoon serving—protein: .5 g; fat: 1.5 g; carbohydrate: 7.5 g; fiber: .7 g; sodium: 4.3 mg; cholesterol: 0 mg; calories: 43.

BASIC MAYONNAISE

MAKES 1/2 CUP

A culinary classic, homemade mayonnaise can easily be varied by using a flavored oil such as walnut or basil, or by adding a couple table-spoons of fresh-chopped herbs or capers.

1 large egg yolk, at room temperature
  *see note
1¹/₂ tablespoons fresh lemon juice
¹/₂ teaspoon Dijon mustard
¹/₄ teaspoon salt
¹/₂ cup plus 1 tablespoon vegetable oil

MAKE THE MAYONNAISE: In a large bowl, whisk together the egg yolk, lemon juice, mustard, and salt. While whisking, add the oil in a very thin continuous stream until all oil is incorporated. Serve immediately or refrigerate in an airtight container for 2 to 3 days.

Nutrition information per 1-tablespoon serving—protein: .4 g; fat: 16 g; carbohydrate: .3 g; fiber: 0; sodium: 75.4 mg; cholesterol: 26.6 mg; calories: 144.

Note: Young children, pregnant women, the elderly, and anyone with compromised health should avoid eating foods made with uncooked eggs.

GREEN GODDESS MAYONNAISE

MAKES 3/4 CUP

Inspired by San Francisco's classic green god-dess dressing, this herbed mayonnaise can be spread on sandwiches or used as a base for dips and dressings.

¹/₂ cup mayonnaise
1 anchovy fillet, drained
¹/₄ cup chopped fresh chives
¹/₄ cup chopped fresh parsley
1 teaspoon fresh lemon juice
1 teaspoon white wine vinegar

MAKE THE MAYONNAISE: In a food processor fitted with the metal blade, place all ingredients and process until herbs are finely chopped and ingredients are combined and smooth. Store covered in the refrigerator for up to 2 days.

Nutrition information per 1-tablespoon serving—protein: .3 g; fat: 7.4 g; carbohydrate: .8 g; fiber: .1 g; sodium: 75 mg; cholesterol: 5.9 mg; calories: 69.4.

CLASSIC VINAIGRETTE

MAKES 1 CUP

An essential in every cook's repertoire, this basic vinaigrette can dress everything from mesclun mix to fresh steamed beans or sliced ripe tomatoes

¹/₃ cup red wine vinegar
1 tablespoon minced shallot
¹/₂ teaspoon chopped fresh thyme leaves
¹/₄ teaspoon salt
¹/₄ teaspoon ground black pepper
³/₄ cup light olive oil

MAKE THE VINAIGRETTE: In a medium bowl, whisk together the vinegar, shallots, thyme, salt, and pepper together. While whisking, add the oil in a slow continuous stream until fully incorporated. Serve immediately.

Nutrition information per 1-tablespoon serving—protein: 0; fat: 13.5 g; carbohydrate: 1 g; fiber: 0; sodium: 44.5 mg; cholesterol: 0; calories: 122.

WARM PINE NUT VINAIGRETTE

MAKES 1/4 CUP

Add another dimension to roasted meats or poultry by drizzling them with this richly flavored balsamic vinaigrette. We particularly like it with Cornish Hens Baked in Salt Dough (see recipe on page 45), or, of course, on salads.

3 tablespoons unsalted butter
3 tablespoons pine nuts
¹/₄ teaspoon salt
¹/₄ teaspoon ground black pepper
2 teaspoons aged balsamic vinegar
2 teaspoons chopped fresh parsley
¹/₂ teaspoon chopped fresh sage leaves

MAKE THE VINAIGRETTE: In a small saucepan, melt the butter over medium heat, add the pine nuts and cook until the butter just begins to turn brown. Remove from heat and let cool slightly. Stir in the remaining ingredients and serve immediately.

Nutrition information per 1-tablespoon serving—protein: 1.8 g; fat: 12.2 g; carbohydrate: 1.7 g; fiber: .38 g; sodium: 136 mg; cholesterol: 23.3 mg; calories: 116.

LEMON-FETA DRESSING

MAKES 3/4 CUP

4 ounces feta cheese, broken into chunks

3 tablespoons plain yogurt

2 tablespoons fresh lemon juice

1 tablespoon honey

1 tablespoon olive oil

1 clove garlic, peeled

MAKE THE DRESSING: In a blender or food processor fitted with the metal blade, combine all ingredients and puree until the mixture reaches a smooth and pourable consistency—2 to 3 minutes. Store covered and refrigerated for up to 2 days.

Nutrition information per 1-tablespoon serving—protein: 1.9 g; fat: 3.3 g; carbohydrate: 2.3 g; fiber: 0; sodium: 107 mg; cholesterol: 8.9 mg; calories: 46.

CREAMY RANCH DRESSING

MAKES 3/4 CUP

Proof that homemade is better than store-bought, this dressing is so good you'll never want to buy bottled again. Serve it as a dipping sauce for fresh vegetables or toss with steamed veggies, steamed potatoes, or green salad.

1/3 cup mayonnaise

1/4 cup buttermilk

1/4 cup sour cream

2 tablespoons chopped green onion

2 tablespoons finely chopped fresh parsley

1 tablespoon cider vinegar

1 teaspoon Dijon mustard

1 small clove garlic, minced

1/4 teaspoon ground black pepper

1/4 teaspoon salt

MAKE THE DRESSING: In a medium bowl, place all ingredients and whisk to combine. Use immediately or store in the refrigerator for up to 2 days.

Nutrition information per 1-tablespoon serving—protein: .5 g; fat: 5.9 g; carbohydrate: 1 g; fiber: .1 g; sodium: 97.9 mg; cholesterol: 5.9 mg; calories: 57.6.

PUMPKIN SEED PESTO

MAKES 1 1/2 CUPS

This versatile pesto works well as a sauce for pasta, a seasoning for steamed rice, or spread on bread for turkey sandwiches.

1/2 cup salted, roasted hulled pumpkin-seeds (pepitas)

2 tablespoons grated Parmesan cheese

2 cloves garlic, peeled

1 cup loosely packed fresh basil leaves

1/2 cup chopped fresh parsley

2 teaspoons grated lemon zest

2 tablespoons fresh lemon juice

1/2 cup extra-virgin olive oil

MAKE THE PESTO: In a food processor fitted with the metal blade, combine the pumpkin seeds, Parmesan, and garlic. Process until the seeds are finely ground—about 30 seconds. Add the basil, parsley, lemon zest and juice and pulse in the olive oil until the herbs are chopped and olive oil is just incorporated. Serve immediately, refrigerate for up to 2 days, or freeze for up to 2 months until ready to use.

Nutrition information per 1/4-cup serving—protein: 2.3 g; fat: 19.8 g; carbohydrate: 4.6 g; fiber: 2.4 g; sodium: 72.8 mg; cholesterol: 1.6 mg; calories: 199.

BLUEBERRY-BAY VINEGAR

MAKES 2 1/4 CUPS

Making this flavored vinegar is a great way to use up a bounty of seasonal berries. It also provides the base for Blueberry Vinaigrette (see recipe on page 128).

4 cups fresh blueberries

2 bay leaves

2 cups white wine vinegar

MAKE THE VINEGAR: In a large glass jar, place blueberries and bay leaves and pour in the vinegar. Store covered in refrigerator for 2 to 10 days. When vinegar is flavored to your liking, strain through several layers of cheesecloth or a coffee filter. Discard blueberries and bay leaves. Store in refrigerator for up to 2 months.

Nutrition information per 1-tablespoon serving—protein: .1 g; fat: .1 g; carbohydrate: 3.6 g; fiber: .5 g; sodium: 1.1 mg; cholesterol: 0; calories: 15.

SPICED CRANBERRY SAUCE WITH ORANGE

Add a little pizzazz to your holiday dinners. Star anise and ginger give our updated cranberry sauce a subtle celebratory spice.

- 4 whole allspice berries
- 2 whole star anise
- 3/4 cup sugar
- 1/4 cup orange juice
- 1 12-ounce bag fresh cranberries, rinsed
- Zest of 1/2 orange removed with a vegetable peeler and cut into 1/2-inch-long pieces

MAKE THE SAUCE: Gather the allspice and star anise in a 4-inch square of cheesecloth and tie into a bundle. In a small saucepan, combine the sugar, orange juice, 1/4 cup water, and the spice bundle set over medium heat. Cook, stirring occasionally, until the sugar melts and the liquid begins to bubble. Remove from heat and let the spices steep for 10 minutes. Return the pan to the stovetop, add the cranberries and the zest, and cook over medium-high heat until the berries just begin to pop—about 7 minutes. Remove pan from the heat, remove the sachet, transfer the mixture to a serving bowl, and chill. Can be refrigerated for up to 3 days.

Nutrition information per serving—protein: .2 g; fat: .1 g; carbohydrate: 25.2 g; fiber: 1.5 g; sodium: .7 mg; cholesterol: 0; calories: 97.5.

HONEY-SHALLOT KETCHUP

A far cry from store-bought, this ketchup is thick and chunky with an assertive yet sweet bite. It enlivens everything from big, juicy steaks to simple hamburgers.

- 1 tablespoon extra-virgin olive oil
- 2 shallots, minced
- 1 clove garlic, minced
- 1/3 cup cider vinegar
- 2 tablespoons honey
- 3 pounds tomatoes, peeled, seeded, and chopped
- 1 teaspoon kosher salt
- 1 sprig fresh thyme
- 1/2 teaspoon whole allspice berries
- 1/8 teaspoon ground cloves
- 1/8 teaspoon ground coriander

MAKE THE KETCHUP: In a large skillet, heat the olive oil over low heat. Add the shallots and garlic and cook until soft—about 10 minutes. Add the vinegar and honey, increase heat to medium, and cook for 2 minutes. Add remaining ingredients and bring the mixture to a boil. Reduce heat to low and simmer until the mixture has reduced and thickened—about 40 minutes. Remove and discard the thyme and allspice and let the ketchup cool. Store refrigerated in a covered container for up to 1 month.

Nutrition information per 1-tablespoon serving—protein: .3 g; fat: .4 g; carbohydrate: 2.5 g; fiber: .3 g; sodium: 47.1 mg; cholesterol: 0; calories: 12.8.

TOMATO RELISH

MAKES 1 CUP

In addition to complementing Minted Lamb Patties (see recipe on page 62), this relish makes a zesty topping for bruschetta.

- 1 cup large cherry tomatoes (about 6 ounces), quartered
- 1/3 cup chopped pitted kalamata olives
- 1 tablespoon finely chopped fresh parsley
- 1 tablespoon fresh lemon juice
- 1 tablespoon olive oil

MAKE THE RELISH: In a medium bowl, combine all ingredients. Best if used the same day.

Nutrition information per 1/4-cup serving—protein: .7 g; fat: 8.4 g; carbohydrate: 4.1 g; fiber: .6 g; sodium: 305 mg; cholesterol: 0; calories: 92.

SWEET-CORN RELISH

MAKES SIX 1-PINT JARS

Now that supersweet hybrid corns are for sale at every roadside stand, you can make a relish that is both pungent and sweet, ideal to top a hamburger. Silver Queen is our favorite, but you can find others.

- 10 large ears corn, husked and silked
- 3 large onions, coarsely chopped (about 6 cups)
- 1 large green bell pepper, coarsely chopped (about 1 cup)
- 1 red or orange bell pepper, coarsely chopped (about 1 cup)
- 1 poblano pepper, seeded and coarsely chopped (about 1/2 cup)
- 2 cups cider vinegar (5 percent acidity)
- 1 cup sugar
- 2 teaspoons kosher salt
- 1 1/2 teaspoons dry mustard
- 1/2 teaspoon celery seeds
- 1/4 teaspoon ground turmeric

1 MAKE THE RELISH: Cut the corn off the cobs and scrape the corn milk from the cobs. Place the corn, its milk, and all the remaining ingredients in a large stockpot and bring to a boil over high heat. Reduce heat to medium low and simmer for 10 minutes.

2 PROCESS THE RELISH: Sterilize six 1-pint jars and keep hot. Pour the hot corn relish into the hot jars, leaving 1/4 inch headspace. Remove any air bubbles, securely cap each jar, and process using the boiling-water canning method (see page 164) for 15 minutes. Cool jars, check for proper seals, and store in a cool, dark place for up to 1 year.

Nutrition information per 1/2-cup serving—protein: 2.4 g; fat: .8 g; carbohydrate: 23.6 g; fiber: 2.3 g; sodium: 187 mg; cholesterol: 0; calories: 98.

SPICY RHUBARB CHUTNEY

MAKES 2 CUPS

This chutney can be used to glaze pork tenderloin; it also makes an excellent condiment for baked ham or lamb chops.

- 1¼ pounds rhubarb, tops removed and ends trimmed
- ½ cup packed light brown sugar
- ¼ cup cider vinegar
- ¼ cup chopped onion
- ½ teaspoon ground coriander
- ½ teaspoon ground ginger
- ¼ teaspoon dry mustard
- ¼ teaspoon salt
- ⅓ cup chopped dried apricots
- ⅓ cup dried cherries
- 2 tablespoons chopped fresh cilantro leaves

1 Wash the rhubarb stalks; coarsely chop and set aside.

2 In a 4-quart saucepan, combine the brown sugar, vinegar, onion, coriander, ginger, mustard, and salt. Bring to a boil. Cook over high heat, uncovered, 3 minutes, stirring constantly. Stir in the rhubarb, apricots, and cherries; reduce heat to medium-low and let simmer until the rhubarb is just tender but not broken up—10 to 15 minutes. Remove from heat, stir in the cilantro, and let cool 10 minutes. Refrigerate until ready to use.

Nutrition information per ¼-cup serving—protein: 1 g; fat: .2 g; carbohydrate: 26 g; fiber: 3 g; sodium: 77 mg; cholesterol: 0; calories: 104.

HOT PEPPER SAUCE

MAKES 1/2 CUP

Just the tiniest drop of this potent sauce will add a lot of heat and peppery spice to a dish. Use it with a bit of caution as it is about 50% hotter than hot pepper sauces found at the grocery.

- 1 tablespoon olive oil
- 2 cloves garlic, chopped
- 1 small tomato, peeled, seeded, and chopped (about ¼ cup)
- ½ cup distilled white vinegar
- ½ pound red Scotch bonnet peppers, seeded and minced *see note
- 1 teaspoon salt

MAKE THE SAUCE: In a medium saucepan, heat the oil over medium-low heat. Add the garlic and cook until soft—about 1 minute. Add the tomato and cook until soft—about 1 minute. Add the vinegar, chilies, and salt and simmer for 2 minutes. Transfer the mixture to a covered bowl and refrigerate for 2 days. Strain the mixture through a sieve; discard solids. Store in an airtight container. The hot sauce will keep in the refrigerator for 3 months.

Nutrition information per 1/4-teaspoon serving—protein: .1 g; fat: .1 g; carbohydrate: 1.3 g; fiber: 0; sodium: 23.4 mg; cholesterol: 0; calories: 6.4.

Note: When cooking with hot peppers such as scotch bonnets, wear gloves and avoid touching any part of the body (especially the eyes) without first thoroughly washing your hands.

ROASTED EGGPLANT SALSA > >

This zesty Mediterranean combination of eggplant, olives, and capers is great with grilled or roasted meats, on rounds of toast, or layered in sandwiches and wraps.

- 1 large eggplant, cut crosswise into $1/2$-inch-thick slices
- 1 medium onion, cut into $1/4$-inch-thick rounds
- 3 cloves garlic, coarsely chopped
- $1/4$ cup olive oil
- 1 teaspoon salt
- $1/2$ teaspoon ground black pepper
- $1/4$ teaspoon crushed red pepper
- $1/4$ cup roasted red pepper, cut into $1/4$-inch pieces
- $1/4$ cup kalamata olives, pitted and chopped
- $1/4$ cup capers, drained
- 1 tablespoon balsamic vinegar
- 1 tablespoon fresh lemon juice

1 ROAST THE VEGETABLES: Preheat the oven to 400°F. In a large bowl, place the eggplant, onions, garlic, oil, salt, pepper, and crushed red pepper and toss to combine. Transfer vegetables to a baking sheet and roast for 20 minutes. Turn vegetables over and continue to roast until soft and lightly browned—about 20 minutes.

2 ASSEMBLE THE SALSA: Let the vegetables cool and chop into $1/2$-inch pieces. In a large bowl, place the vegetables and add the remaining ingredients. Toss to combine and refrigerate. Salsa will keep in the refrigerator, covered, for up to 3 days.

Nutrition information per 1-tablespoon serving—protein: .2 g; fat: 1.5 g; carbohydrate: 1.3 g; fiber: .4 g; sodium: 92.7 mg; cholesterol: 0; calories: 18.5.

PICKLED GARLIC, SHALLOTS, AND PEARL ONIONS

Our update of the classic pickled onions, this recipe combines three different kinds of allium. Using vermouth in the pickling liquid gives a wonderfully crisp herbal accent to the pickles.

- 2 cups white wine vinegar (5 percent acidity)
- 2 cups vermouth
- 3 tablespoons sugar
- 2 teaspoons kosher salt
- 4 small sprigs each fresh thyme, rosemary, and dill
- 2 teaspoons whole black peppercorns
- $1^{1}/3$ cups small shallots, peeled
- $1^{1}/3$ cups pearl onions
- 1 cup peeled garlic cloves
- 4 small bay leaves
- 4 small dried chile peppers (optional)

1 PREPARE THE VEGETABLES: In a large nonreactive saucepan, combine the vinegar, vermouth, sugar, salt, herbs, and peppercorns and bring to a boil over high heat. Boil mixture for 5 minutes, reduce heat to medium, and keep hot. Sterilize four $1/2$-pint jars and layer the remaining ingredients into the jars while they are still hot.

2 PROCESS THE VEGETABLES: Pour the hot vinegar mixture over the filled jars, leaving $1/4$-inch headspace. Remove any air bubbles, securely cap each jar, and process using the boiling-water canning method (see page 164) for 10 minutes. Cool jars, check for proper seals, and store in a cool, dark place for up to 1 year. Thoroughly cooled, unprocessed pickled vegetables will keep in the refrigerator for up to 2 months.

Nutrition information per $1/2$-cup serving—protein: 1.7 g; fat: .1 g; carbohydrate: 15.8 g; fiber: .7 g; sodium: 330 mg; cholesterol: 0; calories: 106.

CAKES AND COOKIES

PEAR UPSIDE-DOWN CAKE > >

MAKES 10 SERVINGS (ONE 8-INCH CAKE)

We adapted this recipe from a cake served at Remi Restaurant in New York. We couldn't resist it for its country flavors and simplicity. A Teflon-coated cake pan will work just as well as a spring-form pan.

1 3/4 cups sugar

6 tablespoons (3/4 stick) unsalted butter

2 peeled Bartlett pears, one sliced crosswise into 1/4-inch-thick pieces and the other cut into 1/2-inch-thick wedges

1/4 cup plus 2 tablespoons all-purpose flour

1/4 cup plus 1 tablespoon cornmeal

1/2 teaspoon baking powder

1/4 teaspoon salt

2 large eggs

4 large egg yolks

1 MAKE THE CARAMEL: Preheat the oven to 325°F. In a small saucepan, place 1 cup of sugar over medium-high heat and cook until the sugar liquifies and becomes amber in color. Stir in 2 tablespoons butter and pour the caramel into an 8-inch spring-form cake pan, taking care to coat the pan bottom evenly. Arrange the pear pieces in a single layer on top of the caramel and set aside.

2 MAKE THE CAKE BATTER: Sift together the flour, cornmeal, baking powder, and salt and set aside. In a large bowl, with an electric mixer on medium-high speed, beat the remaining sugar and butter until light and fluffy. Add the eggs and egg yolks one at a time, mixing until thoroughly combined with each addition. Reduce mixer speed to low, add the dry ingredients, and mix until combined. Gently spread the batter evenly over the pears and bake until cake is golden brown and a tester inserted into the center comes out clean—about 45 minutes. Cool slightly and release the cake from the pan. Invert the cake onto a serving plate and remove the spring-form pan base. Serve warm or at room temperature.

Nutrition information per serving—protein: 3.4 g; fat: 10.3 g; carbohydrate: 46.8 g; fiber: 1.2 g; sodium: 90.5 mg; cholesterol: 146 mg; calories: 286.

TOASTED COCONUT COFFEE CAKE

MAKES 12 SERVINGS
(ONE 9-INCH CAKE)

2 1/4 cups all-purpose flour

1 1/2 cups sweetened flaked coconut

3/4 cup packed light brown sugar

1 1/2 tablespoons ground cinnamon

6 tablespoons (3/4 stick) unsalted butter, melted

3/4 (1 1/2 sticks) unsalted butter, softened

1 teaspoon baking powder

1/2 teaspoon salt

5 large egg yolks

1/3 cup sugar

1 1/2 teaspoons pure vanilla extract

1/2 cup sour cream

1 MAKE THE COFFEE-CAKE TOPPING: In a small bowl, combine 1/2 cup flour, coconut, 1/2 cup brown sugar, and cinnamon. Toss in melted butter and set aside.

2 MAKE THE BATTER: Preheat the oven to 325°F. Lightly coat a 9-inch round springform pan with softened butter and set aside. Combine the remaining flour, baking powder, and salt in a bowl and set aside. Using an electric mixer set on high speed beat the egg yolks, remaining brown sugar, granulated sugar, and vanilla until the mixture is thick and pale yellow—about 2 minutes. Mix in the remaining butter and the sour cream. Reduce the mixer speed to low, add the flour mixture, and mix.

3 BAKE THE CAKE: Pour batter evenly into the prepared pan, sprinkle with topping, and bake on the middle rack of the oven until a toothpick inserted into the center of the cake comes out clean—55 to 60 minutes. Cool in pan on a wire rack for 1 hour. Release the cake from the pan. Serve warm.

Nutrition information per serving—protein: 4.4 g; fat: 24.6 g; carbohydrate: 37.9 g; fiber: 1.6 g; sodium: 159 mg; cholesterol: 140 mg; calories: 386.

BERRY-DOTTED ANGEL FOOD CAKE

< <

MAKES 12 SERVINGS
(ONE 10-INCH ROUND CAKE)

To achieve a light, airy angel food cake every time, follow these basic steps: Avoid overbeating the egg whites—they become dry and grainy, making it hard to fold in the flour; never oil the cake pan—the batter needs to "grab" the pan as it rises in order to reach maximum height; finally, cool the cake inverted, either over a tall narrow-necked bottle or resting on four tall inverted glasses, until it is completely cool.

- 1 cup plus 1 tablespoon cake flour
- 1 tablespoon cornstarch
- 1$\frac{1}{4}$ cups sugar
- $\frac{3}{4}$ teaspoon salt
- 12 large egg whites (about 1$\frac{1}{3}$ cups), at room temperature
- 1 teaspoon cream of tartar
- 1$\frac{1}{2}$ teaspoons pure vanilla extract
- 1$\frac{1}{2}$ cups assorted small firm raspberries (black, red, and golden)

1 MAKE THE BATTER: Preheat oven to 350°F. Over a surface covered with a large sheet of waxed or parchment paper, sift 1 cup cake flour, cornstarch, $\frac{1}{2}$ cup sugar, and salt. Resift into a large bowl and set aside. In a large bowl, with an electric mixer on low speed, whip the egg whites and cream of tartar until foamy—about 3 minutes. Add the remaining $\frac{3}{4}$ cup sugar and vanilla, increase mixer speed to medium high, and beat just until egg whites form stiff peaks. Do not over-beat. Set aside.

2 ASSEMBLE THE CAKE: Sift a third of the reserved flour mixture over the beaten egg whites and gently fold together. Sift another third of the flour and fold it in. Add the berries in an even layer and sift the remaining flour over the berries. Fold gently until combined. Gently and evenly place the batter into a 10-inch tube pan and bake on the middle rack of oven until cake is golden brown and springs back when lightly touched—40 to 50 minutes. Let cool completely, inverted—about 90 minutes. Gently run a knife along the outside edge of the pan and along the inside tube. Turn out onto a plate and serve.

Nutrition information per serving—protein: 4.4 g; fat: .2 g; carbohydrate: 31 g; fiber: 1 g; sodium: 189 mg; cholesterol: 0; calories: 142.

BAKING INGREDIENTS
Some Substitutions

In a pinch you can use the following substitutions:

> Buttermilk—For every cup of buttermilk, substitute 1 cup plain yogurt. Or make sour milk by measuring 1 tablespoon vinegar or lemon juice into a liquid measuring cup and adding enough milk to equal 1 cup. Let it stand for 5 minutes before using.

> Cake Flour—For 1 cup cake flour, measure 1 cup all-purpose flour, remove 2 tablespoons of the flour, and replace it with 2 tablespoons cornstarch. Whisk the flour and cornstarch together to combine them thoroughly.

> Baking Powder—For 1 teaspoon baking powder, substitute $\frac{1}{4}$ teaspoon baking soda plus $\frac{5}{8}$ teaspoon cream of tartar, or use $\frac{1}{4}$ teaspoon baking soda plus $\frac{1}{2}$ cup buttermilk or sour milk. Substitute for $\frac{1}{2}$ cup of the liquid called for in the recipe.

> Unsalted Butter—Use salted butter and reduce the amount of salt in the recipe by about $\frac{3}{8}$ teaspoon per stick of butter used.

MORAVIAN SUGAR CAKE

MAKES 12 SERVINGS
(ONE 10-INCH ROUND CAKE)

Said to have originated in Moravia which is now a region of the Czech Republic, this most unusual cake combines a sweet yeasted-potato dough and a rich brown sugar-cinnamon topping. Our version includes a buttery apple filling that makes it even more scrumptious.

1 medium baking potato, peeled and cut
  into 1-inch pieces

1¹/8 teaspoons dry active yeast
  (¹/2 packet)

2 tablespoons water warmed to 110°F

6 tablespoons (³/4 stick) unsalted butter,
  cut into pieces

¹/2 cup milk

¹/3 cup sugar

1 large egg

³/4 teaspoon salt

3 cups all-purpose flour, sifted

TOPPING:

¹/3 cup packed light brown sugar

¹/3 cup sugar

¹/4 teaspoon ground cinnamon

3 tablespoons heavy cream

¹/4 cup (¹/2 stick) unsalted butter

FILLING:

8 small McIntosh apples, peeled, cored,
  and cut into wedges

2 tablespoons unsalted butter

2 tablespoons sugar

1 MAKE THE DOUGH: Coat a large bowl with oil and set aside. Place the potato in a small saucepan, cover with water and bring to a boil over high heat. Cook until fork tender—about 20 minutes. In a small bowl, combine the yeast and water and let dissolve. Mash the cooked potato and place ¹/2 cup potato, the butter, yeast mixture, and milk in the bowl of a standing mixer fitted with the paddle attachment, stir until combined. Add the sugar and egg and mix to combine. Add the salt and flour and mix on low speed until well blended—about 3 minutes. Transfer the dough to a lightly floured surface and knead until smooth—about 3 minutes. Add additional flour as necessary to prevent the dough from sticking. Transfer the dough to the prepared bowl, turning to coat all sides. Cover the bowl with a clean, damp kitchen towel and set aside to rise in a warm, draft-free place until it has doubled in size—60-90 minutes. Refrigerate dough for at least 1 hour or as long as 24.

2 SHAPE THE DOUGH: Butter a 10-inch round pan and set aside. Punch down the dough, transfer it to a lightly floured surface and divide in half. Shape the dough into 2-ounce rounds and place in the prepared pan in a circular pattern, leaving ¹/4 inch between each round. Place excess dough in a smaller pan or refrigerate for another use. Cover with a clean, damp towel and let rise in a warm place until dough has doubled—about 45 minutes. Preheat oven to 350°F.

3 MAKE THE TOPPING: Combine the brown sugar, sugar, cinnamon, cream, and butter in a small saucepan and bring to a boil over high heat. Simmer until well combined—about 1 minute. Set aside and allow to cool.

4 BAKE AND ASSEMBLE THE CAKE: Brush the cake top and in between the creases generously with the topping. Place the cake pan on the center rack and bake until golden and sounds hollow when tapped—about 35 minutes. Invert pan onto a large plate and set plate on a wire rack to cool. Sauté apples in 2 tablespoons butter and 2 tablespoons sugar until golden. Set aside. Slice the cake in half. Transfer the bottom layer to a serving plate, place the apples on the bottom half of the cake, and replace the top. Cover the top of the cake with the remaining topping and serve.

Nutrition information per serving—protein: 4.7 g; fat: 14.2 g; carbohydrate: 54.4 g; fiber: 2.6 g; sodium: 149 mg; cholesterol: 55.3 mg; calories: 358.

THE IMPORTANCE OF MEASURING

Following these simple guidelines will guarantee your baking success. Measure liquids in glass or clear plastic liquid measuring cups. Dry ingredients, like flour and sugar, should always be measured in cups from dry measuring cups. When measuring dry ingredients, use the dip and sweep method, leveling off the contents with a knife without tapping or shaking the cup. Do not sift flour unless called for in a recipe. If a recipe calls for sifted flour, sift the flour before measuring. If it calls for an amount of flour sifted, measure the flour, then sift it.

BANANA-CARAMEL CAKE

MAKES 12 SERVINGS
(ONE 9-INCH 2-LAYER CAKE)

Banana cake + caramel icing = heaven on a plate.

2¹/₂ cups cake flour

2¹/₂ teaspoons baking powder

¹/₂ teaspoon baking soda

¹/₂ teaspoon salt

¹/₂ cup (1 stick) unsalted butter, softened

1¹/₄ cups sugar

2 large eggs

1¹/₂ teaspoons pure vanilla extract

¹/₂ cup buttermilk

1 cup mashed very ripe bananas
(about 2 bananas)

Caramel Icing (recipe follows)

1 MAKE THE BATTER: Preheat the oven to 350°F. Using a small brush, lightly coat two 9-inch cake pans with softened butter or vegetable oil. Dust with flour, tap out any excess, and set aside. Over a surface covered with a large sheet of waxed or parchment paper, sift the flour, baking powder, baking soda, and salt. Into a medium bowl, resift the flour mixture and set aside. In a large bowl, with an electric mixer on medium-high speed, beat the butter until light—about 1 minute. Add the sugar and continue to beat for 2 more minutes. Add the eggs, one at a time, beating thoroughly after each addition, and mix in the vanilla. Reduce mixer speed to low and add the flour mixture by thirds, alternating with the buttermilk and bananas and ending with the dry ingredients. Mix just enough to blend the batter after each addition.

2 BAKE THE CAKE: Divide the batter equally between the pans and bake on the middle rack of oven until a tester inserted into each cake layer comes out clean—25 to 30 minutes. Cool in the cake pans on a wire rack for 15 minutes. Using a knife, loosen the cake layers from the pan sides and invert the layers onto the wire rack to cool completely.

3 ICE THE CAKE: Use a serrated knife to trim the mounded side of the cake layers, if necessary. Line the edges of a cake plate with 3-inch-wide strips of waxed or parchment paper and place a cake layer, trimmed side down, on top. Place 1 cup Caramel Icing on top of the layer and spread evenly. Place the second layer, trimmed side down, on the first and cover the top and sides with the remaining icing.

Nutrition information per serving—protein: 3.5 g; fat: 23.8 g; carbohydrate: 77.8 g; fiber: .7 g; sodium: 291 mg; cholesterol: 74.8 mg; calories: 528

CARAMEL ICING

MAKES 2 1/2 CUPS

Be sure to have a candy thermometer on hand—it will help you to get this icing right every time.

3 cups packed light brown sugar

1¹/₂ cups heavy cream

¹/₂ teaspoon fresh lemon juice

5 tablespoons cold butter, cut into
pieces

MAKE THE ICING: In a medium saucepan, with a candy thermometer attached, stir sugar, heavy cream, and lemon juice together. Cook the mixture, without stirring, over medium-high heat to soft-ball stage (238°F). Remove from heat and let the caramel mixture cool to 140°F. Place the butter on top of the cooled caramel mixture. Remove the thermometer and, using a handheld mixer set on medium-high speed, beat the caramel until it thickens enough to hold its shape, lightens in color, and changes from translucent to opaque—about 5 minutes. Apply icing immediately.

PUMPKIN SPICE CAKE > >

MAKES 16 SERVINGS
(ONE 8-INCH 3-LAYER CAKE)

Three layers high, this dark, moist cake is impressive to look at and delicious to eat—especially when slathered with Pumpkin Cream Cheese Frosting.

- 3/4 cup (1½ sticks) unsalted butter, softened
- 1 cup packed dark brown sugar
- 1 cup granulated sugar
- 3 large eggs
- 1 cup unsweetened pumpkin puree
- ½ cup buttermilk
- 1 teaspoon pure vanilla extract
- 2 cups all-purpose flour
- 2 teaspoons baking powder
- 1½ teaspoons ground cinnamon
- 1 teaspoon baking soda
- ½ teaspoon fresh grated nutmeg
- Pumpkin-Cream Cheese Frosting (recipe follows)

1 PREPARE THE CAKE PANS: Preheat the oven to 350°F. Lightly coat three 8-inch cake pans with softened butter. Cut three 8-inch circles out of parchment paper and fit one into the bottom of each cake pan. Lightly coat the paper circles with butter and set pans aside.

2 MAKE THE BATTER: In a large bowl, with an electric mixer on medium speed, cream the butter until smooth. Add the sugars and mix until smooth. Add the eggs, one at a time, beating well after each addition, until the mixture is smooth and light. Set aside. In a medium bowl, combine the pumpkin puree, buttermilk, and vanilla and set aside. In a large bowl, combine the flour, baking powder, cinnamon, baking soda, and nutmeg and set aside. In thirds, alternately add the flour mixture and buttermilk mixture to the butter mixture, blending well after each addition until smooth.

3 BAKE THE CAKE: Pour batter into the prepared pans and bake until a toothpick inserted into the middle of each cake comes out clean—35 to 40 minutes. Cool the cakes in the pans on wire racks for 30 minutes. Remove cakes from pans and return to the wire racks until completely cool.

4 ASSEMBLE THE CAKE: Place one layer on a cake plate and top with one-third recipe of Pumpkin Cream-Cheese Frosting. Repeat with the second and third layers. Serve or store refrigerated for up to 4 days.

Nutrition information per serving—protein: 4.6 g; fat: 17.7 g; carbohydrate: 60.8 g; fiber: 1.5 g; sodium: 195 mg; cholesterol: 86.8 mg; calories: 414.

PUMPKIN-CREAM CHEESE FROSTING

MAKES 3 1/2 CUPS

This is a dreamy frosting for Pumpkin Spice Cake or just about any flavor cake—chocolate, yellow, pound cake—or cupcakes.

- 1 8-ounce package cream cheese, softened
- ¼ cup unsweetened pumpkin puree
- ¼ cup (½ stick) unsalted butter, softened
- 1 teaspoon grated orange zest
- 1 tablespoon fresh orange juice
- ½ teaspoon pure vanilla extract
- 4 cups confectioners' sugar, sifted

MAKE THE FROSTING: In a large bowl, with an electric mixer on medium speed, beat the cream cheese, pumpkin puree, butter, orange zest and juice and vanilla until smooth. Add the sugar and continue to beat until light and creamy—about 5 more minutes.

Nutrition information per 1/4-cup serving—protein: 1.3 g; fat: 9 g; carbohydrate: 29.4 g; fiber: .2 g; sodium: 48.9 mg; cholesterol: 26.7 mg; calories: 199.

LEMON-BLACKBERRY CAKE < <

MAKES 12 SERVINGS
(ONE 9-INCH 2-LAYER CAKE)

3 cups cake flour

1$^1/_2$ teaspoons baking powder

1 teaspoon salt

$^1/_2$ teaspoon baking soda

1 cup (2 sticks) butter, softened

2$^1/_2$ cups sugar

5 large eggs

1 teaspoon pure vanilla extract

$^1/_4$ cup plus 2 tablespoons fresh
    lemon juice

$^3/_4$ cup buttermilk

Blackberry-Cassis Jam
    (see recipe on page 165)

Lemon Buttercream Frosting
    (recipe follows)

1 MAKE THE BATTER: Preheat the oven to 350°F. Using a small brush, lightly coat two 9-inch cake pans with softened butter or vegetable oil. Dust with flour and tap out any excess. Set aside. In a medium bowl, sift together the flour, baking powder, salt, and baking soda and set aside. In a large bowl, with a mixer on medium speed, cream the butter and sugar until light and fluffy. Add the eggs one at a time, blending each thoroughly before adding the next. Scrape down the side of the bowl and beat in vanilla extract. Reduce mixer speed to low and add the flour mixture by thirds, alternating with the lemon juice and buttermilk and ending with the dry ingredients.

2 BAKE THE CAKE: Divide the batter equally between the pans and spread evenly. Bake on the middle rack of the oven until the tops spring back when lightly touched and a tester inserted in the center of each cake layer comes out clean—20 to 30 minutes. Cool in the cake pans on a wire rack for 15 minutes. Using a knife, loosen the cake layers from the sides of the pans and invert the layers onto the wire rack to cool completely.

3 FROST THE CAKE: Use a serrated knife to trim the cake layers to make them level, if necessary. Line the edges of a cake plate with 3-inch-wide strips of waxed or parchment paper and place a cake layer on top. Use a pastry bag or a plastic zip-top bag with a corner cut off to pipe a $^1/_2$-inch-thick ring of Lemon Buttercream Frosting around the edge of the cake layer. Spread 1$^1/_2$ cups Blackberry-Cassis Jam inside the buttercream ring and top with the second layer. Place 1 cup Lemon Buttercream Frosting on top of the cake and cover the entire cake with a thin coating of frosting. Chill cake for at least 1 hour. Remove cake from refrigerator and cover with the remaining frosting. Remove paper strips and serve at room temperature. Store refrigerated for up to 4 days.

Nutrition information per serving—protein: 7.3 g; fat: 49.7 g; carbohydrate: 102 g; fiber: 3.2 g; sodium: 354 mg; cholesterol: 256 mg; calories: 891.

LEMON BUTTERCREAM FROSTING

MAKES 3 CUPS

$^1/_2$ cup egg whites (about 3 large eggs)

1 cup sugar

2 cups (4 sticks) unsalted butter,
    cut into small pieces

1 tablespoon grated lemon zest

1 tablespoon fresh lemon juice

MAKE THE FROSTING: In a large stainless-steel bowl placed over a pot filled with 1 inch of simmering water, place the egg whites and sugar. Use a whisk to beat the mixture until it is very hot to the touch (about 160°F). Remove from heat and, using a mixer set on high speed, immediately begin whipping the mixture until it is cool, thick, and glossy and has tripled in volume—about 5 minutes. Reduce mixer speed to medium and add the butter—about a quarter cup at a time—allowing 5 to 10 seconds in between each addition. Add the lemon zest and lemon juice and continue to beat until smooth and fluffy.

MAPLE WALNUT CAKE

MAKES 12 SERVINGS
(ONE 8-INCH 2-LAYER CAKE)

2½ cups all-purpose flour

2 teaspoons baking powder

2 teaspoons baking soda

½ teaspoon salt

½ teaspoon ground cinnamon

½ cup (1 stick) unsalted butter, softened

½ cup sugar

2 large eggs

1½ cups maple syrup

2 teaspoons pure vanilla extract

½ cup water

1 cup finely chopped walnuts

6 walnut halves

Maple-Sugar Frosting (recipe follows)

1 MAKE THE BATTER: Preheat the oven to 350°F. Using a small brush, lightly coat two 9-inch cake pans with softened butter or vegetable oil. Dust with flour and tap out any excess. Set aside. In a medium bowl, sift together the flour, baking powder, baking soda, salt, and cinnamon. Set aside. In a large bowl, with a mixer on high speed, beat the butter and sugar for one minute. Add the eggs, one at a time, and beat for 1 minute after each addition. Add 1 cup maple syrup and vanilla. Reduce mixer speed to low and add the flour mixture by thirds, alternating with the water and ending with the dry ingredients. Gently stir in the chopped walnuts.

2 BAKE THE CAKE: Divide the batter equally between the two prepared pans and spread evenly. Bake on the middle rack of the oven until a tester inserted into the center of each cake layer comes out clean—about 30 minutes. Cool in the cake pans on a wire rack for 10 minutes. Using a knife, loosen the cake layers from the sides of the pans and invert the layers onto the wire rack to cool completely.

3 MAKE THE CAKE GARNISHES: Lightly coat a sheet pan with vegetable oil and arrange the walnut halves about three to four inches apart. In a small saucepan, heat the remaining ½ cup maple syrup over medium-high heat. Cook the syrup until it reaches hard-crack stage (300°F), or when a drop placed in a glass of cold water becomes hard and brittle. Remove from heat and carefully spoon boiled syrup over the walnuts, allowing it to run in streams around the sheet pan. Set aside to let cool completely.

4 FROST THE CAKE: Use a serrated knife to level the mounded sides of the cake layers, if necessary. Line the edges of a cake plate with 3-inch-wide strips of waxed or parchment paper and place a cake layer, trimmed side down, on top. Place 1 cup Maple-Sugar Frosting on top of the layer and spread evenly. Place the second layer, trimmed side down, on the first and cover the top and sides of the cake with the remaining icing. Decorate the top of the cake with candied walnuts and the hardened maple sugar. Remove paper strips and serve. Store at room temperature for up to 4 days.

Nutrition information per serving—protein: 4.5 g; fat: 18.4 g; carbohydrate: 93.3 g; fiber: 1 g; sodium: 845 mg; cholesterol: 77.6 mg; calories: 549.

MAPLE-SUGAR FROSTING

MAKES 3 CUPS

2¼ cups confectioners' sugar

½ cup packed dark brown sugar

½ cup (1 stick) unsalted butter

⅛ teaspoon salt

½ cup maple syrup

1 teaspoon pure vanilla extract

2–4 tablespoons milk

MAKE THE FROSTING: In a medium bowl, with a mixer on medium speed, beat sugars, butter, and salt until combined. Continue beating and add the maple syrup in a slow stream. Add the vanilla. Increase speed to medium high and continue to beat until light and fluffy. If necessary, add up to 4 tablespoons of milk to achieve a smooth spreading consistency.

FRESH BERRY SHORTCAKE WITH SPICED SYRUP

Fragrant spices add a new dimension to this traditional summer dessert.

SPICED BERRIES:

1 1/2 cups water

1 cup granulated sugar

1/3 cup fresh lemon juice

2 1-inch-thick slices fresh ginger

1 3-inch cinnamon stick

1 whole star anise, crushed

1 vanilla bean, split

1 tablespoon Cognac or brandy (optional)

1 pint fresh blueberries

1 pint fresh strawberries, hulled and halved

1/2 pint fresh raspberries

SHORTCAKES:

2 cups self-rising all-purpose flour

3 tablespoons granulated sugar

1/2 cup (1 stick) unsalted butter

3/4 cup milk

1/2 cup plus 1 tablespoon heavy cream

1 teaspoon confectioners' sugar

1 MAKE THE SPICED BERRIES: In a 2-quart saucepan, combine the water, granulated sugar, lemon juice, ginger, cinnamon, star anise, and vanilla bean. Bring to a boil over high heat. Reduce heat to medium and simmer for 25 minutes. Remove from heat and strain the mixture through a fine sieve, discarding spices. Stir in the Cognac, if using, and set spice mixture aside to cool completely. Add the blueberries, strawberries, and raspberries to the spice mixture. Set aside.

2 MAKE THE SHORTCAKES: Preheat the oven to 400°F. Lightly coat a baking sheet with vegetable oil. In a medium bowl, combine the flour and granulated sugar. With a pastry blender or 2 knives, cut in the butter until the mixture resembles coarse crumbs. Stir in the milk until a very soft dough forms, being careful not to overwork the dough. Divide the dough into six equal pieces and drop onto the prepared baking sheet. Lightly pat each piece into a round and brush them with 1 tablespoon heavy cream. Bake until shortcakes are golden brown—about 20 minutes. Transfer to a wire rack to cool completely.

3 ASSEMBLE THE CAKE: In a medium bowl, with an electric mixer on high speed, beat the remaining 1/2 cup heavy cream and confectioners' sugar until stiff peaks form. Cut each shortcake horizontally in half. Place each bottom half on a dessert plate. Spoon about 3/4 cup berry mixture over each bottom half. Spoon a heaping tablespoon of whipped cream on top of the berry mixture. Place the matching shortcake half on top. Drizzle each plate with spiced syrup.

Nutrition information per serving—protein: 7 g; fat: 26 g; carbohydrate: 88 g; fiber: 5 g; sodium: 480 mg; cholesterol: 76 mg; calories: 593.

CHOCOLATE ESPRESSO TORTE

MAKES 12 SERVINGS
(ONE 9- BY 9-INCH CAKE)

This elegant cake, flavored with coffee and chocolate, is topped with a glistening ganache glaze.

21 ounces semisweet chocolate, chopped

1$\frac{1}{2}$ cups (3 sticks) unsalted butter

2 tablespoons instant espresso powder
    or instant coffee crystals

5 large eggs, separated

$\frac{3}{4}$ cup sugar

1 tablespoon pure vanilla extract

$\frac{1}{2}$ cup all-purpose flour

$\frac{1}{4}$ teaspoon salt

$\frac{1}{2}$ teaspoon cream of tartar

1 tablespoon light corn syrup

2 tablespoons heavy cream

1 MAKE THE CAKE BATTER: Preheat the oven to 350°F. Butter a 9- by 9-inch square cake pan and line the bottom of the pan with parchment paper. Butter the parchment paper and set aside. In a double boiler, over low heat, melt 9 ounces of the chocolate and $\frac{3}{4}$ cup butter, and the espresso powder together. Remove from heat and set aside. In a large bowl, with an electric mixer on medium speed, beat the egg yolks until foamy—15 to 30 seconds. Add $\frac{1}{2}$ cup sugar and continue to beat until thick and pale—about 3 minutes. Reduce the mixer speed to low and add the chocolate mixture, vanilla, flour, and salt. In a medium bowl, using a mixer on medium speed, beat the egg whites and cream of tartar to soft peaks. Add the remaining 1/4 cup sugar in a thin, steady stream and beat until stiff peaks form. Fold the beaten whites into the chocolate mixture by thirds.

2 BAKE THE CAKE: Pour the batter into the prepared pan and bake until a cake tester inserted in the center of the cake comes out clean—about 35 minutes. Let the cake cool for 30 minutes. Invert the cake onto a wire rack set over a baking sheet.

3 MAKE THE GANACHE GLAZE: In a double boiler, melt the remaining 12 ounces chocolate over low heat. When melted, remove from heat and stir in the remaining $\frac{3}{4}$ cup butter, softened, until combined. Stir in the corn syrup and heavy cream. Let the mixture cool until the glaze is thick enough to coat yet still pours easily—2 to 3 minutes. Pour the glaze onto the center of the cake and use a spatula to smooth it evenly over the top and sides. Allow the glaze to set for 10 minutes. Carefully transfer the cake to a serving platter.

Nutrition information per serving—protein: 3 g; fat: 40.4 g; carbohydrate: 46.4 g; fiber: .1 g; sodium: 32.8 mg; cholesterol: 154 mg; calories: 548.

PISTACHIO SEMOLINA HONEY CAKE

MAKES 10 SERVINGS
(ONE 10-INCH ROUND CAKE)

The combination of semolina, a coarse-ground durum wheat, and the infusion of honey gives this cake its rich texture.

CAKE:

4 large eggs

2/3 cup sugar

$\frac{1}{2}$ cup vegetable oil

$\frac{3}{4}$ cup all-purpose flour

$\frac{3}{4}$ cup semolina

1$\frac{1}{2}$ teaspoons baking powder

$\frac{1}{2}$ teaspoon salt

1 cup finely ground pistachios

1 teaspoon grated lemon zest

SYRUP:

1 cup plus 2 tablespoons honey

1 cup water

1 tablespoon fresh lemon juice

1 1-inch piece honeycomb (optional)

2 tablespoons chopped pistachios
    (optional)

1 MAKE THE CAKE: Heat the oven to 350°F. Lightly coat a 10-inch springform pan with vegetable oil. In a large bowl, with mixer on high speed, beat the eggs and sugar until thick and pale—about 5 minutes. Reduce mixer speed to low and drizzle in the oil, beating until blended. In a medium bowl, mix the flour, semolina, baking powder, and salt. Whisk into the egg mixture until combined. Stir the ground pistachios and lemon zest into the batter. Spread the batter into the prepared pan.

2 BAKE THE CAKE: Place the cake on the middle rack of the oven and bake until golden and a cake tester or toothpick inserted into the center comes out clean—30 to 35 minutes.

3 MAKE THE SYRUP: Stir 1 cup honey, water, and lemon juice into a 1-quart saucepan and bring to a boil over high heat. Boil until reduced by half—about 10 minutes. Let cool to room temperature.

4 SOAK THE CAKE: Using a toothpick or skewer, poke deep holes into the hot cake in the pan. Drizzle half of the syrup evenly over the top of the cake, allowing it to be absorbed, then pour the remaining syrup over the cake. Let cake cool completely.

5 TO SERVE: Carefully transfer cake to a cake plate. Drizzle remaining 2 tablespoons honey over the top of the cake. Garnish with a piece of honeycomb and pistachio nuts, if desired.

Nutrition information per serving—protein: 7 g; fat: 21 g; carbohydrate: 65 g; fiber: 2.5 g; sodium: 303 mg; cholesterol: 85 mg; calories: 460.

STACKED APPLESAUCE CAKE

MAKES 16 SERVINGS
(ONE 9-INCH 3-LAYER CAKE)

The three layers of our easy-to-make variation of the traditional Kentucky Apple Stack Cake float on pillows of spiced whipped cream.

- 3 cups all-purpose flour
- 1 tablespoon baking soda
- 1½ teaspoons baking powder
- ¾ teaspoon ground cinnamon
- ¾ teaspoon ground nutmeg
- ¼ teaspoon ground cloves
- ¾ cup (1½ cups) unsalted butter, softened
- 1½ cups granulated sugar
- 2 large eggs
- 3 teaspoons pure vanilla extract
- 3 cups unsweetened applesauce
- Cinnamon Whipped Cream (recipe follows)
- 2 tablespoons confectioners' sugar (optional)

1 MAKE THE BATTER: Preheat the oven to 350°F. Using a small brush, lightly coat three 9-inch cake pans with softened butter or vegetable oil. Dust with flour and tap out any excess. Set aside. In a medium bowl, combine the flour, baking soda, baking powder, cinnamon, nutmeg, and cloves. Set aside. In a large bowl, with an electric mixer on medium-high speed, beat the butter for one minute. Add the sugar and continue to beat until blended. Add the eggs and vanilla and beat for 2 more minutes. Reduce speed to low and add the flour mixture by thirds, alternating it with the applesauce and ending with the dry ingredients.

2 BAKE THE CAKE: Divide the batter equally among the pans and spread evenly. Bake on the middle rack of the oven until a tester inserted in the center of each cake layer comes out clean—35 to 40 minutes. Let cool in the cake pans on a wire rack to room temperature. Using a knife, loosen the cake layers from the sides of the pans and invert the layers onto a wire rack.

3 FINISH THE CAKE: Place one cake layer on a cake plate or stand. Spread half of the Cinnamon Whipped Cream on the layer. Place a second layer over the first and repeat. Top with the final layer and sprinkle with confectioners sugar, if desired, and serve. Store refrigerated for up to 4 days.

Nutrition information per serving—protein: 3.7 g; fat: 20 g; carbohydrate: 48.7 g; fiber: 1.5 g; sodium: 303 mg; cholesterol: 64 mg; calories: 384.

CINNAMON WHIPPED CREAM

MAKES 4 CUPS

- 2 cups very cold heavy cream
- ¾ cup confectioners' sugar
- 1 teaspoon ground cinnamon
- ½ teaspoon pure vanilla extract

MAKE THE WHIPPED CREAM: In a large bowl, using a mixer set on medium-high speed, beat the cream, sugar, cinnamon, and vanilla until stiff peaks form. Do not overbeat.

HOT CHOCOLATE CAKE

MAKES 12 SERVINGS
(ONE SINGLE-LAYER 9-INCH ROUND CAKE)

A hint of cayenne pepper gives this chocolate cake a unique and warming flavor.

- ¼ cup unsweetened cocoa, plus 1 tablespoon for dusting
- 1 cup all-purpose flour
- ½ teaspoon salt
- ½ teaspoon baking powder
- ¼ teaspoon ground cinnamon
- ¼ teaspoon ground red pepper
- 8 ounces bittersweet chocolate
- ½ cup (1 stick) plus 2 tablespoons unsalted butter
- 4 large eggs
- ½ cup granulated sugar
- ⅓ cup packed dark brown sugar
- 1 teaspoon pure vanilla extract

1 MAKE THE BATTER: Preheat the oven to 350°F. Butter one 9-inch round cake pan and line the bottom with parchment paper. Butter the parchment paper and dust the pan with 1 tablespoon cocoa. Set aside. In a medium bowl, sift together the flour, ¼ cup cocoa, salt, baking powder, cinnamon, and ground red pepper and set aside. In a double boiler set over simmering water, melt 6 ounces chocolate and the butter. Set aside. In a large bowl, with an electric mixer on medium-high speed, beat the eggs and sugars until the mixture thickens and increases in volume—about 5 minutes. Reduce mixer speed to low, add the chocolate mixture and the vanilla, and beat until combined. Gradually add the flour mixture and beat until incorporated. Pour batter into prepared pan. Bake on the middle shelf of the oven until cake springs back when lightly touched in the center—30 to 40 minutes. Cool the cake in the pan on a wire rack for 20 minutes. Invert the cake onto the wire rack, remove the parchment paper, and let cool completely. Transfer the cake to a serving dish.

2 MAKE THE GLAZE: Melt the remaining bittersweet chocolate and drizzle over the top of the cake.

Nutrition information per serving—protein: 5.1 g; fat: 19.1 g; carbohydrate: 30.3 g; fiber: 1.6 g; sodium: 130 mg; cholesterol: 96.9 mg; calories: 290.

EASY CHOCOLATE PARTY CAKE

> >

MAKES 16 SERVINGS
(ONE 8-INCH 2-LAYER CAKE)

Some people call this a "dump" cake—all the ingredients are dumped into one bowl, mixed into a smooth batter, and baked into moist, fudgy layers.

- 2 cups all-purpose flour
- 1½ cups milk
- ⅔ cup granulated sugar
- ⅔ cup packed dark brown sugar
- ½ cup unsweetened cocoa
- ¾ cup (1½ sticks) butter
- 3 large eggs
- 2 teaspoons pure vanilla extract
- 1 teaspoon baking powder
- 1 teaspoon baking soda
- ½ teaspoon salt
- Fudgy Cream Cheese Frosting (recipe on page 192)

1 MAKE THE BATTER: Preheat the oven to 350°F. Using a small brush, lightly coat two 8-inch cake pans with softened butter. Dust with flour and tap out any excess. Set aside. In a large bowl, with an electric mixer on low speed, combine the flour and the remaining 10 ingredients. Increase the mixer speed to medium and continue to beat for 3 more minutes.

2 BAKE THE CAKE: Divide the batter equally between the pans and spread evenly. Bake on the middle rack of the oven until the tops spring back when lightly touched. Cool in the cake pans on a wire rack for 10 minutes. Using a knife, loosen the cake layers from the pan sides. Invert the cake layers onto the wire rack to cool completely.

3 FROST THE CAKE: Use a serrated knife to level the tops of the cake layers, if necessary. Line the edges of a cake plate with 3-inch-wide strips of waxed or parchment paper and place a cake layer, trimmed side down, on top. Place ½ cup Fudgy Cream-Cheese Frosting on top of the layer and spread evenly. Place the second layer on the first and cover the top and sides with the remaining frosting. Remove paper strips and serve. Store refrigerated for up to 4 days.

Nutrition information per serving—protein: 8.1 g; fat: 25.7 g; carbohydrate: 64.8 g; fiber: 3.5 g; sodium: 350 mg; cholesterol: 120 mg; calories: 503.

FUDGY CREAM CHEESE FROSTING

MAKES 1 3/4 CUPS

This rich frosting is wickedly good, and it needs no cooking!

1 8-ounce package cream cheese, softened

1/4 cup (1/2 stick) butter, softened

3 tablespoons milk

3 cups sifted confectioners' sugar

2/3 cup unsweetened cocoa

1/8 teaspoon salt

1 1/2 teaspoons pure vanilla extract

MAKE THE FROSTING: In a medium bowl, with an electric mixer on medium speed, beat the cream cheese, butter, and milk together until smooth. Add the sugar, cocoa, and salt and continue to beat until blended. Reduce mixer speed to low, add the vanilla, and beat until smooth. Cover and chill for at least 30 minutes before using.

RHUBARB-PECAN OATMEAL BARS

MAKES 16 BARS

Simple to make, these luscious bar cookies pack plenty of healthful ingredients—just right for a lunchbox treat or an afternoon pick-me-up.

1 1/2 cups all-purpose flour

1 1/2 cups old-fashioned rolled oats

1 cup packed light brown sugar

1/2 teaspoon ground cinnamon

1/2 teaspoon salt

3/4 cup (1 1/2 sticks) butter, softened

2 cups thickened Chunky Rhubarb Sauce (recipe on page 193)

1/2 cup chopped pecans

1 PREPARE THE BAKING PAN: Heat the oven to 375°F. Lightly coat a 13- by 9-inch baking pan with vegetable oil.

2 MAKE THE DOUGH: In a medium bowl, combine the flour, oats, brown sugar, cinnamon, and salt. Add the butter and stir with a fork until the mixture resembles coarse crumbs.

3 Press two-thirds of the crumb mixture into the bottom of the pan. Spread the thickened Chunky Rhubarb Sauce evenly over the crumb layer. Top with the remaining crumb mixture and pecans.

4 BAKE THE BAR COOKIES: Bake until the top is golden and the rhubarb sauce bubbles—25 to 30 minutes. Let cool on wire rack to room temperature. Cut into 16 pieces and store in an airtight container for up to 3 days.

Nutrition information per bar—protein: 3 g; fat: 12 g; carbohydrate: 35 g; fiber: 2 g; sodium: 164 mg; cholesterol: 23 mg; calories: 251.

TIPS FOR FROSTING A CAKE

> Place the cake on a rigid surface for frosting, a serving plate or cardboard round is ideal. If you frost the cake on the plate on which it will be served, place strips of wax paper around the bottom of the cake, sliding them slightly underneath, these will protect the plate and can be pulled out once the cake is frosted.

> Stiff frosting will not go on easily; so if it has been chilled, bring the icing to room temperature before starting.

> Use a generous amount of icing to build up a good layer. Trying to spread a skimpy amount of icing means pressing against the sides and getting crumbs into the icing.

> Begin by coating the sides of the cake; spreading any excess icing from the sides onto the top of the cake and add more to coat.

> To make swoops in the icing, use the back of a teaspoon or tablespoon, depending on the size of swoop required. The rounded tip of an inch-wide offset spatula will make large, dramatic swoops.

> If you have a piping bag, use it to ice the cake, piping the top in ever-decreasing circles then spreading it smooth. Or use an offset spatula; position the spatula almost flat, halfway across the top of the cake to spread the icing smoothly; dip the blade of the spatula in hot water, shake it off and draw it across the cake top, smoothing the surface.

CHUNKY RHUBARB SAUCE

MAKES ABOUT 3 1/2 CUPS

This sauce is delicious served over ice cream or pound cake. To use it in our Rhubarb-Pecan Oatmeal Bars, you'll need to thicken it: Mix 2 tablespoons cornstarch with 3 tablespoons water and stir into the rhubarb mixture. Cook, stirring, until sauce is clear and thickened.

- 2 pounds rhubarb, tops removed, ends trimmed, and cut into 1-inch pieces
- 3/4 cup sugar
- 1 teaspoon grated orange zest
- 1/3 cup fresh orange juice
- 1/4 teaspoon ground nutmeg
- 1/4 teaspoon salt

MAKE THE SAUCE: In a 4-quart saucepan, combine the rhubarb, sugar, orange zest and juice, nutmeg, and salt. Bring to a boil. Reduce heat to low, cover, and simmer until thickened—about 15 minutes. Cool to room temperature. Refrigerate until ready to use.

Nutrition information per 1/4 cup—protein: .6 g; fat: 0; carbohydrate: 14 g; fiber: 2 g; sodium: 41 mg; cholesterol: 0; calories: 58.

CHOCOLATE-COCONUT MACAROONS

MAKES 20 MACAROONS

These popular cookies are spectacular on their own, but to dress them up for a party we dipped the cloudlike confections in bittersweet chocolate.

- 2 large egg whites
- 1/2 cup sugar
- 1/2 teaspoon pure vanilla extract
- 2 tablespoons all-purpose flour
- 2 1/2 cups sweetened, flaked coconut
- 3 1/2 ounces bittersweet chocolate
- 1 teaspoon vegetable oil

1 PREPARE THE BATTER: Preheat the oven to 350°F. In a large bowl, with an electric mixer on medium speed, beat the egg whites until soft peaks form. With the mixer still running, gradually add the sugar in a steady stream and mix until well blended. Add the vanilla extract and continue to beat until mixture becomes soft and glossy peaks form. Add the flour and beat until stiff peaks form. Gently fold in the coconut. Allow the macaroon mixture to rest for 10 minutes.

2 BAKE THE MACAROONS: Line a baking pan with parchment paper. Place heaping tablespoons of the macaroon batter on the pan, two inches apart. Use thumb and index finger to pinch each small mound of batter into a pyramid shape. Bake until golden brown—about 13 minutes. Remove from oven and let the macaroons rest in the baking pan for 2 minutes. Transfer macaroons, with the parchment, to a wire rack to cool. When completely cool, carefully peel macaroons off the parchment.

3 DIP THE MACAROONS: In a heatproof dish set over simmering water, or in the top of a double boiler, place the chocolate. Melt, stirring occasionally to prevent burning. Remove from heat and stir in the oil. Dip the tip of each macaroon into the melted chocolate. Place dipped macaroons on a wire rack and let cool until set. Store in an airtight container for up to 1 week.

Nutrition information per macaroon—protein: 1.2 g; fat: 6.1 g; carbohydrate: 13.5 g; fiber: .7 g; sodium: 36.2 mg; cholesterol: 0; calories: 106.

ICED APPLE COOKIES > >

2 cups all-purpose flour

1 teaspoon baking soda

1 teaspoon ground cinnamon

$^1/_2$ teaspoon salt

$^1/_4$ teaspoon ground cloves

$^1/_4$ teaspoon ground nutmeg

$1^1/_3$ cups packed light brown sugar

$^3/_4$ cup ($1^1/_2$ sticks) plus 2 tablespoons
   unsalted butter, softened

1 large egg

1 cup pecans, chopped

1 cup raisins

1 Red Delicious apple, chopped (1 cup)

$^1/_2$ cup plus 2 tablespoons apple cider

3 cups confectioners' sugar

1 MAKE THE BATTER: Preheat the oven to 350°F. Combine the flour, baking soda, cinnamon, salt, cloves, and nutmeg in a medium bowl. In a large bowl, with an electric mixer on medium speed, cream the sugar and $^3/_4$ cup butter until light and fluffy. Add the egg and beat until incorporated. Gradually add the flour mixture and beat until combined. Stir in the pecans, raisins, apples, and $^1/_4$ cup apple cider.

2 BAKE THE COOKIES: Drop by heaping table-spoon, 2 inches apart, onto parchment-lined baking sheets. Flatten each mound slightly and bake—18 to 22 minutes. Cool on a wire rack.

3 In a small bowl, stir together the sugar, remaining cider, and remaining butter until smooth. Drizzle about 1 tablespoon icing over each cookie. Store in an air-tight container for up to 4 days.

Nutrition information per cookie—protein: 3.3 g; fat: 16.7 g; carbohydrate: 46.9 g; fiber: 1.6 g; sodium: 173 mg; cholesterol: 43.2 mg; calories: 340.

BISCOTTI COOKIE SAMPLER

With our easy basic recipe you can make Fruit Triangles, Chocolate Macadamia Chubbies, and Orange Ginger Crisps.

BASIC RECIPE:

6 tablespoons ($^3/_4$ stick) unsalted butter

$^3/_4$ cup sugar

2 large eggs

$1^3/_4$ cups all-purpose flour

1 teaspoon baking powder

$^1/_4$ teaspoon salt

FRUIT TRIANGLES:

$^1/_3$ cup dried cranberries

$^1/_3$ cup golden raisins

Grated zest of 1 lemon

2 tablespoons turbinado sugar

CHOCOLATE-MACADAMIA CHUBBIES:

$^3/_4$ cup macadamia nuts, chopped

2 tablespoons Dutch-processed cocoa

1 ounce semisweet chocolate, melted

ORANGE GINGER-CRISPS:

$^1/_3$ cup chopped crystallized ginger

Grated zest of 1 lemon

Grated zest of $^1/_2$ orange

1 MAKE THE DOUGH: Preheat the oven to 325°F. Line a baking sheet with parchment paper and set aside. In a large bowl, with an electric mixer on medium speed, beat the butter and sugar together until light and fluffy. Add the eggs and beat to incorporate. Reduce mixer speed to low and gradually add the flour, baking powder, and salt plus additional ingredients as per each biscotti variation.

2 SHAPE AND BAKE THE BISCOTTI: For Fruit Triangles, press the dough into a 9- by 9-inch square on the prepared baking sheet and sprinkle with turbinado sugar. For Chocolate-Macadamia Chubbies or Orange-Ginger Crisps, shape the dough into two 1-inch logs and place on the prepared baking sheet. Bake all until firm—25 to 30 minutes. Cool completely on a wire rack. Slice Fruit Triangles into 18 triangles; Chocolate Macadamia Chubbies into thirty $^3/_4$-inch-thick slices; and Orange Ginger Crisps into fifty $^1/_4$-inch-thick slices. Toast in the oven until crisp—3 to 5 minutes per side.

Nutrition information per $^3/_4$-inch plain cookie—protein: 1.2 g; fat: 2.7 g; carbohydrate: 10.6 g; fiber: .2 g; sodium: 35.1 mg; cholesterol: 20.4 mg; calories: 71.2.

LEMON ICEBOX COOKIES < <

Freeze the dough of these slice-and-bake cookies for up to one month. Just thaw and slice for fresh-baked cookies anytime.

3/4 cup (1 1/2 sticks) unsalted butter, softened

1/2 cup packed light brown sugar

1/2 cup granulated sugar

1 large egg

2 tablespoons honey

1 tablespoon grated lemon zest

1 teaspoon pure lemon extract

2 cups all-purpose flour

1 teaspoon baking powder

1 teaspoon baking soda

1/4 cup confectioners' sugar

1 MAKE THE DOUGH: In a large bowl, with an electric mixer on medium speed, beat the butter and sugars until light and fluffy. Add the egg, honey, zest, and extract and beat until combined. Reduce mixer speed to low and add the flour, baking powder, and baking soda. Mix until well blended and a sticky dough forms. Remove dough from the bowl and divide in half. On a sheet of parchment or waxed paper, form each dough half into a log about $1\frac{1}{2}$ inches in diameter. Tightly wrap in the paper and refrigerate until dough is firm—2 to 3 hours.

2 BAKE THE COOKIES: Preheat oven to 325°F. Line a baking sheet with parchment paper. Unwrap one log of the dough and slice off $\frac{5}{8}$-inch-thick rounds. Place cookie-dough rounds 2 inches apart on the baking sheet. Rewrap remaining dough and keep chilled until ready to bake. Bake until the cookies are golden—11 to 13 minutes. With a spatula, carefully transfer cookies to wire racks to cool completely. Sprinkle the top of each cookie with a thin, even layer of confectioners' sugar. Store in an airtight container for up to 4 days or freeze, without confectioners' sugar, for up to 4 weeks.

Nutrition information per cookie—protein: 1.7 g; fat: 7.3 g; carbohydrate: 17 g; fiber: .4 g; sodium: 95 mg; cholesterol: 29 mg; calories: 139.

SIMPLE SHORTBREAD COOKIES

The embodiment of versatility, this basic cookie dough lends itself to nearly endless variations and possibilities. The list of ingredients for shortbread (butter, flour, and sugar) has remained much the same since its precursor, short cakes, appeared in the British Isles in the 16th century. We've added vanilla and salt to heighten flavor.

1 3/4 cups (3 1/2 sticks) unsalted butter, cut into 1-inch pieces

1 cup sugar

2 teaspoons pure vanilla extract (optional)

4 1/2 cups all-purpose flour

1/2 teaspoon salt (optional)

1 MAKE THE DOUGH: Preheat the oven to 350°F. In a large bowl, with an electric mixer on medium speed, beat the butter and sugar until light and fluffy. If desired, add vanilla and beat until combined. Reduce mixer speed to low; gradually beat in the flour, and salt, if using, until a dough forms.

2 SHAPE THE COOKIES: Between 2 sheets of floured parchment paper, roll out half of the dough to a $\frac{1}{8}$-inch thickness. Remove the top sheet of paper and cut out as many shapes as possible, leaving $\frac{1}{4}$-inch space in between. Press together the trimmings. Roll out the dough again and cut more shapes. Repeat with the remaining half of dough.

3 BAKE THE COOKIES: Bake until the cookies are golden and feel slightly firm to the touch—7 to 9 minutes. Transfer the cookies to wire racks to cool completely. Store in an airtight container for up to 4 days or freeze for up to 2 weeks.

Nutrition information per cookie—protein: 1 g; fat: 7 g; carbohydrate: 13 g; fiber: .3 g; sodium: 24 mg; cholesterol: 18 mg; calories: 118.

PIES AND TARTS

BLUEBERRY AND PEACH PIE > >

MAKES 10 SERVINGS (ONE 10-INCH PIE)

Make the most of two of summer's favorite fruits—succulent blueberries and juicy, sweet peaches—by baking a homemade pie topped with a flaky lattice crust. It s a wonderful finale to any meal.

PASTRY:

2 1/2 cups all-purpose flour

3/4 cup sugar

1/2 teaspoon salt

3/4 cup (1 1/2 sticks) plus 2 tablespoons cold unsalted butter, cut into small pieces

3–5 tablespoons ice water

1/2 teaspoon pure vanilla extract

FILLING:

3 cups fresh peaches, peeled, pitted, and sliced

2 cups fresh blueberries

3/4 cup plus 1 tablespoon sugar

3 tablespoons cornstarch

1/2 teaspoon ground cinnamon

1/2 teaspoon grated lemon zest

1 large egg, lightly beaten

1 MAKE THE PASTRY: In a large bowl, combine the flour, sugar, and salt. Add butter and use your fingers or a pastry cutter to incorporate it into the flour until mixture resembles coarse meal. Using a fork, mix in the vanilla and 3 tablespoons ice water, one at a time, adding remaining water as necessary, just until the mixture begins to cling together. Gather into a ball and flatten into 2 equal-sized disks. Wrap tightly in plastic wrap and refrigerate for 1 to 2 hours (or up to overnight).

2 BLIND-BAKE THE CRUST: Preheat the oven to 425°F. On a floured surface, roll 1 pastry disk into a circle 1/4 inch thick and at least 12 inches in diameter. Transfer the dough to a 10-inch pie pan. Trim the dough, leaving a 1/2-inch overhang. Fold the overhanging pastry under itself and pinch the dough to crimp it around the rim. Cut out a circle of parchment paper to cover the bottom of the dough and line it with pie weights or dried beans. Bake for 10 minutes, then remove the weights and paper. Cool on a wire rack. Lower oven temperature to 375°F.

3 MAKE THE LATTICE TOPPING: Remove remaining pastry disk from the refrigerator. On a floured surface, roll into a thin circle. Use a pizza wheel or pastry cutter to cut 1-inch-wide strips. Transfer to a parchment-lined baking sheet, cover with plastic wrap, and refrigerate while making the filling.

4 MAKE THE FILLING: In a large bowl, place blueberries and peaches. In a small bowl, combine the sugar, cornstarch, cinnamon, and lemon zest. Add the contents of the small bowl to the blueberries and peaches and gently toss to coat fruit. Pour the filling into the baked piecrust. Place dough strips on top of the filling in a crisscross pattern to form a lattice. Trim the ends, leaving a 1/2-inch overhang, and crimp the edges. Lightly brush the lattice with beaten egg and sprinkle with sugar.

5 BAKE THE PIE: Loosely cover the crimped edge of the crust with a foil collar to prevent overbrowning. Place pie on the middle shelf of the oven and bake until the filling bubbles and the crust is golden brown—about 45 minutes. Cool on a wire rack. Serve at room temperature.

Nutrition information per serving—protein: 6.2 g; fat: 22 g; carbohydrate: 87 g; fiber: 3.3 g; sodium: 172 mg; cholesterol: 77.2 mg; calories: 559.

TIPS FOR PERFECT PASTRY DOUGH

Have butter as cold as possible. Ideally, chop it into small pieces and freeze it for a short while (20-30 minutes) before starting. If you have cold hands, rub the butter into the flour with your fingertips. If your hands are hot, it's best to use a pastry cutter or two knives. After mixing, allow the dough to rest for at least 30 minutes to give the gluten time to relax, this makes the dough less elastic and easier to roll.

CHERRY PIE

The ingredients for the pie crust should be very cold, so put them in the freezer for 20 to 30 minutes before you start. The decorative slits in the top crust let the steam escape and show off the gorgeous red cherries beneath.

- 1 cup all-purpose flour
- 3 tablespoons packed dark brown sugar
- 1/4 teaspoon salt
- 7 tablespoons unsalted butter
- 3 tablespoons ice water
- 1 pound sweet or sour cherries (about 3 cups), pitted
- 3 tablespoons sugar (2/3 cup if using sour cherries)
- 2 tablespoons cornstarch
- 2 teaspoons grated lemon zest
- 1 tablespoon fresh lemon juice

1 MAKE THE PASTRY: In a large bowl, combine the flour, brown sugar, and 1/8 teaspoon salt. Cut in 6 tablespoons of the butter using a pastry blender, two knives, or your hands until the mixture resembles coarse meal. Add water 1 tablespoon at a time; mix until just combined. Pat the dough into a 5-by 6-inch rectangle, cover tightly with plastic wrap, and chill for at least 30 minutes.

2 MAKE THE PIES: Preheat the oven to 350°F. Melt the remaining butter and set aside. Combine the cherries, sugar, cornstarch, lemon zest and juice, melted butter, and remaining 1/8 teaspoon salt and set aside. Divide the dough into 4 equal pieces and roll each piece to a 1/8-inch thickness and fit two of the rolled-out pieces into two 4-inch pie plates. Fill each with half the cherry mixture and drape the remaining two doughs over the pies and crimp the edges to seal. Cut slits into the tops of the pies and bake until golden.

Nutrition information per 1/2 sour-cherry pie—protein: 4.6 g; fat: 20.8 g; carbohydrate: 78.6 g; fiber: 2.5 g; sodium: 143 mg; cholesterol: 54.4 mg; calories: 508.

Nutrition information per 1/2 sweet-cherry pie—protein: 4.8 g; fat: 21.5 g; carbohydrate: 62 g; fiber: 2.9 g; sodium: 140 mg; cholesterol: 54.4 mg; calories: 408.

MIXED BERRY CROSTATA   < <

Crostata is Italian for "tart" and this free-form version is simple to make and very adaptable. You can substitute equal amounts of peaches, plums, or apricots for the berries or use half berries, half stone fruits.

- 1 1/4 cups plus 1 tablespoon all-purpose flour
- 1/4 cup plus 2 tablespoons granulated sugar
- 1/8 teaspoon salt
- 1/2 cup (1 stick) unsalted butter, softened
- 2 large eggs, beaten
- 1 cup fresh raspberries
- 1 cup fresh blackberries
- 1 tablespoon fresh lemon juice
- 1 tablespoon turbinado sugar (optional)

1 MAKE THE PASTRY: Combine 1 1/4 cups flour, 1/4 cup sugar, and salt in a large bowl. Form a well in the center of the dry ingredients and place the butter and 1 egg in the well. Using your hands, mix the ingredients into a soft, pliable dough. Form it into a 4-inch disk and place it on a lightly floured parchment paper. Lightly dust the dough with flour and roll it into a 10-inch circle. Place dough with parchment on a baking sheet, cover the dough with plastic wrap, and chill for 10 minutes. Preheat the oven to 375°F.

2 MAKE THE CROSTATA: In a small bowl, mix remaining flour and sugar and set aside. Remove the dough from the refrigerator and evenly spread the flour-and-sugar mixture on the dough, leaving a 1-inch-wide border around the edge. Place berries on top of the mixture and sprinkle with lemon juice. Fold the 1-inch border over top of the berries to form a 9-inch crostata.

3 BAKE THE CROSTATA: Lightly brush the top of the crostata dough with remaining beaten egg, and sprinkle with turbinado sugar, if desired. Bake on the middle rack of the oven—about 35 minutes. Remove from the oven and slide the crostata with the parchment paper onto a wire rack. Cool for 1 hour. Serve warm or at room temperature.

Nutrition information per serving—protein: 5.4 g; fat: 17.5 g; carbohydrate: 41.3 g; fiber: 2.8 g; sodium: 68.2 mg; cholesterol: 112 mg; calories: 340.

TARRAGON-ROSEMARY STRAWBERRY TART

MAKES 8 SERVINGS

Zip up a classic strawberry tart with the faint perfume of anise by adding tarragon to the crust and tarragon and rosemary to the syrup. Other berries to try: raspberries, blackberries, or a combination of both.

FILLING:

3 cups vanilla-flavored yogurt

PASTRY:

1¼ cups all-purpose flour

¼ cup sugar

1 tablespoon chopped fresh tarragon leaves

¼ teaspoon baking powder

¼ teaspoon salt

½ cup (1 stick) butter, cut into pieces

1 large egg

1 egg yolk

SYRUP:

¾ cup sugar

½ cup water

2 tablespoons chopped fresh tarragon leaves, plus a sprig

1 tablespoon chopped fresh rosemary leaves

1 tablespoon fresh lemon juice

2 pints fresh strawberries, hulled

1 PREPARE THE YOGURT: Place the yogurt in a strainer lined with a large coffee filter. Set over a bowl and let drain, covered, in the refrigerator, 4 hours to overnight.

2 MAKE THE PASTRY: In a medium bowl, combine the flour, sugar, tarragon, baking powder, and salt. With pastry blender or 2 knives, cut the butter into the dry ingredients until mixture resembles coarse crumbs. In a small bowl, beat together the egg and egg yolk. Add to the flour mixture, mixing lightly with a fork until the dough is moist enough to hold together when lightly pressed. Shape into a ball and flatten into a disk, cover with plastic wrap, and refrigerate for at least 1 hour.

3 BAKE THE CRUST: Preheat the oven to 375°F. Between 2 sheets of floured waxed paper, roll the dough out to an 11-inch round. Remove the top sheet of waxed paper and invert the dough into a 9-inch fluted tart pan with removable bottom. Remove the remaining sheet of waxed paper and fold over the edge of the dough to fit into the pan. With a fork, pierce the bottom of the crust. Bake until the edges are lightly browned and the bottom is firm to the touch—12 to 15 minutes. Set on a wire rack to cool.

4 MAKE THE SYRUP: Prepare Syrup: In a 1-quart saucepan, combine the sugar, water, tarragon, and rosemary. Heat to boiling over medium-high heat. Reduce heat to low and cook until thickened—7 to 10 minutes. Remove from heat and stir in the lemon juice. Let cool completely.

5 ASSEMBLE THE TART: Remove the side from the pan. Evenly spread the thickened yogurt over the bottom of the crust. Place the strawberries, cut side down, in a decorative pattern on top of the yogurt. Brush the strawberries with syrup and serve the remaining syrup in a pitcher. Garnish with a sprig of tarragon.

Nutrition information per serving—protein: 8 g; fat: 14 g; carbohydrate: 57 g; fiber: 2 g; sodium: 241 mg; cholesterol: 87 mg; calories: 382.

RHUBARB CUSTARD PIE WITH PECAN CRUST

MAKES 8 SERVINGS

Celebrate the first spring rhubarb with this wonderful new recipe. The nutty crust contrasts nicely with the creamy filling.

CRUST:

½ cup pecan halves

1⅓ cups all-purpose flour

½ cup sugar

½ cup (1 stick) butter, cut into pieces and chilled

2 large egg yolks

1 tablespoon pure vanilla extract

1 large egg white

1 teaspoon water

CUSTARD:

1¼ pounds rhubarb, tops removed, ends trimmed, and coarsely chopped (4 cups)

⅔ cup sugar

1 teaspoon grated lemon zest

¼ teaspoon salt

2 large eggs

1 large egg yolk

1¼ cups heavy cream

1½ tablespoons cornstarch

1 MAKE THE CRUST: Heat the oven to 400°F. In a food processor fitted with the metal blade, process the pecans until finely ground. Add the flour and sugar; process until combined. Add the butter, egg yolks, and vanilla; process until the mixture resembles coarse crumbs. Press into the bottom and sides of a 9-inch round pie plate; crimp along the edge, forming a decorative crust. With the tines of a fork, prick the bottom and sides of crust. In a small bowl, mix together egg white and water. Brush bottom and side of crust with the egg-white mixture. Bake until golden brown—10 to 12 minutes. Transfer to a wire rack and let cool completely.

2 FILL THE PIE: Reduce the oven temperature to 350°F. In a large bowl, combine the rhubarb, sugar, lemon zest, and salt. Spoon into the crust. In a medium bowl, beat together the eggs and egg yolk. Add the cream and cornstarch; mix together. Spoon over the rhubarb mixture.

3 FINISH THE PIE: Cover the edge of the crust with aluminum foil to prevent overbrowning and bake until the custard is firm—25 to 30 minutes. Transfer to a wire rack and let cool completely. Serve.

Nutrition information per serving—protein: 7 g; fat: 33 g; carbohydrate: 51 g; fiber: 3 g; sodium: 207 mg; cholesterol: 212 mg; calories: 525.

APPLE-CHEDDAR CRUMBLE PIE

> >

MAKES 10 SERVINGS

Mix local apple varieties to yield a heavenly perfumed pie.

PASTRY:

1¼ cups all-purpose flour

½ teaspoon salt

⅛ teaspoon ground red pepper

½ cup (1 stick) cold unsalted butter, cut into pieces

¾ cup grated sharp Cheddar cheese

3–4 tablespoons ice water

FILLING:

1 pound tart apples, such as Rhode Island Greening, Cortland, or Granny Smith, peeled, cored, and thinly sliced (3 cups)

3 pounds sweet apples, such as Rome Beauty or Jonathan, peeled, cored, and thinly sliced (3 cups)

1 teaspoon grated lemon zest

¼ cup fresh lemon juice

¾ cup sugar

2 tablespoons all-purpose flour

½ teaspoon ground cinnamon

¼ teaspoon salt

¼ teaspoon freshly grated nutmeg

⅛ teaspoon ground allspice

CRUMBLE TOPPING:

⅓ cup all-purpose flour

3 tablespoons packed brown sugar

3 tablespoons cold unsalted butter, cut into small pieces

½ cup grated sharp Cheddar cheese

1 MAKE THE PASTRY: In a large bowl, combine the flour, salt, and ground red pepper. Add the butter and, using a pastry cutter, two knives, or your hands, cut the butter into the flour until the mixture resembles coarse meal. Add the grated cheese and toss. Add cold water, by the tablespoon, until a rough dough forms. Gather the dough into a ball, flatten into a ³/₄-inch-thick disk, and tightly wrap in plastic. Refrigerate for 30 minutes. On a lightly floured surface, roll out the dough into an 11-inch circle about ¼ inch thick. Transfer dough to a 9-inch pie pan, turn overhanging dough under itself to form an edge along the top of the pan, and crimp the edge. Chill for 30 minutes. Preheat the oven to 425°F. Line the crust with parchment paper and fill with pie weights or dried beans. Bake until the crust is lightly browned—about 15 minutes. Cool on a rack and remove the pie weights.

2 MAKE THE FILLING: Add both types of cut apples to a large bowl and toss with the lemon zest and juice. In a small bowl, mix the sugar, flour, cinnamon, salt, nutmeg, and allspice. Sprinkle the spice mixture over the apples and toss to mix thoroughly. Spoon the apples into the prepared crust.

3 MAKE THE CRUMBLE TOPPING: In a small bowl, with a fork, toss the flour, brown sugar, butter, and grated Cheddar cheese. Sprinkle the top of the pie with the crumble mixture.

4 BAKE THE PIE: Place the pie in the middle of the oven and bake until the topping is golden brown—50 to 60 minutes. Cool on a rack for at least 30 minutes. Serve warm or at room temperature.

Nutrition information per serving—protein: 5.9 g; fat: 17.8 g; carbohydrate: 47.4 g; fiber: 12.5 g; sodium: 251 mg; cholesterol: 49 mg; calories: 366.

DOUBLE LEMON TART

MAKES 8 SERVINGS (ONE 9-INCH TART)

This tart can be made ahead of time and chilled, then caramelized under a broiler just before serving.

CRUST:

2 cups all-purpose flour

1/2 cup granulated sugar

1/2 teaspoon salt

1 tablespoon finely chopped
    rosemary leaves

1 cup (2 sticks) cold unsalted butter,
    cut into small pieces

FILLING:

1 cup lemon sections (about 6 lemons)

1/4 cup lemon juice

1 3/4 cups granulated sugar

3 large eggs

2 large egg whites

1/2 teaspoon salt

1 lemon, sliced into very thin rounds

3 tablespoons superfine sugar

1 MAKE THE CRUST: Preheat the oven to 350°F. In a food processor fitted with the metal blade, combine the flour, sugar, salt, and rosemary. Add butter and pulse until the mixture resembles a coarse meal.

Or, by hand, combine the flour and sugar in a bowl. Using your fingers, a pastry cutter, or two knives, mix the butter into the flour mixture until mixture resembles coarse meal. Place the mixture in an 11-inch tart pan and press it into the bottom and along the side of the pan. Bake the crust until golden brown along the edges—15 to 20 minutes. Remove from the oven and cool on a wire rack—about 15 minutes.

2 MAKE THE FILLING: In a nonreactive saucepan, place lemon sections, juice, and sugar. Cook over medium heat, stirring occasionally, until sugar dissolves. Remove from the heat. In a medium bowl, lightly whisk the eggs, whites, and salt. While continually stirring, slowly pour the lemon mixture into the eggs. Pour the filling into the cooled crust, arrange the lemon slices on top of the custard, and bake on the middle rack of the oven until the custard is set—about 30 minutes. If the edges begin to overbrown, cover the crust with a collar of aluminum foil or pie shields. Cool completely on a wire rack.

3 CARAMELIZE THE TART: Refrigerate the tart to chill it completely. Just before serving, heat an oven broiler and position the rack on the uppermost shelf. Sprinkle the superfine sugar over the chilled tart and place it under the broiler. Watching it closely as the sugar begins to bubble and brown, carefully rotate it to ensure even browning. Remove the tart once the sugar has caramelized to a golden-brown color—2 to 3 minutes. Serve immediately.

Nutrition information per serving—protein: 7.2 g; fat: 25.3 g; carbohydrate: 46 g; fiber: 2.3 g; sodium: 309 mg; cholesterol: 142 mg; calories: 430.

BUTTERMILK CHESS PIE

MAKES 8 SERVINGS

Smooth, sweet, and tangy, this dessert is a Deep South favorite.

PASTRY:

1 cup all-purpose flour

1 teaspoon salt

1/2 cup (1 stick) cold unsalted butter, cut into small pieces

1 large egg yolk, beaten

1/4 cup buttermilk

FILLING:

4 large egg yolks

1 cup sugar

1/2 cup all-purpose flour

3 tablespoons unsalted butter, melted

1/2 teaspoon baking soda

2 cups buttermilk

2 tablespoons grated lemon zest

2 tablespoons fresh lemon juice

1 MAKE THE PASTRY: In a medium bowl, combine the flour and salt. Add the butter and use your fingers or a pastry cutter to incorporate it into the flour until mixture resembles coarse meal. Using a fork, mix in the egg yolk and buttermilk just until the mixture begins to cling together. Gather into a ball and flatten into a disk. Wrap tightly in plastic wrap and refrigerate 1 to 2 hours.

2 BLIND-BAKE THE CRUST: Preheat the oven to 425°F. On a floured surface, roll the pastry out to an 11-inch circle and transfer it to a 9-inch pie plate. Trim up to 1/2 inch of pastry to even the edge and fold the overhanging pastry under itself. Pinch the dough to crimp it around the rim. Cut out a circle of parchment paper to cover the bottom of the dough and line it with pie weights or dried beans. Bake for 10 minutes, remove the weights and paper, and continue to bake until the crust is golden—8 to 10 more minutes. Let cool on a wire rack. Lower oven temperature to 350°F.

3 MAKE THE FILLING: In a medium bowl, with an electric mixer on medium speed, beat the egg yolks and sugar until pale yellow. Add the flour and butter and continue to beat until incorporated. Stir in the baking soda, buttermilk, lemon juice, and zest. Pour the filling into the baked piecrust.

4 BAKE THE PIE: Loosely cover the crimped edge of the crust with a foil collar to prevent overbrowning. Place pie on the middle shelf of the oven and bake until the custard is set and lightly browned and a knife inserted into the center comes out clean—about 40 minutes. Cool on a wire rack. Serve at room temperature or chilled.

Nutrition information per serving— protein: 6.6 g; fat: 21 g; carbohydrate: 46 g; fiber: .78 g; sodium: 425 mg; cholesterol: 182 mg; calories: 401.

CEREAL TARTS WITH YOGURT AND FRESH FRUIT ‹ ‹

MAKES 8 SERVINGS

A quick, fresh and healthful treat. The crispy tart shells are made with crushed cereal, almonds, and maple syrup and bake in just ten minutes. Yogurt makes a creamy high-protein filling.

- 5 cups cornflakes
- 1 cup pecan halves
- 1/4 cup (1/2 stick) unsalted butter, melted
- 6 tablespoons maple syrup
- 1 16-ounce container plain yogurt
- 1 16-ounce container vanilla yogurt
- 2 2/3 cups fresh fruit (such as grapes, blueberries and raspberries)

1 MAKE THE TART SHELLS: Preheat the oven to 350°F. Place eight 4-inch round tart pans with removable bottoms on a baking sheet and set aside. In the bowl of a food processor fitted with a metal blade, place the cornflakes and pecans and process until combined—about 10 short pulses. Transfer the cereal mixture to a large bowl, drizzle with the melted butter, and toss to combine. Stir in the maple syrup. Evenly divide the cereal mixture among the tart pans and press along the bottoms and sides to form shells. Bake for 10 minutes. Transfer to a wire rack to cool.

2 ASSEMBLE THE TARTS: Remove the shells from the molds and transfer each to a serving plate. Top each tart shell with 1/4 cup of the yogurt and 1/3 cup fruit. Serve immediately.

Nutrition information per serving—protein: 7.8 g; fat: 18.6 g; carbohydrate: 39.9 g; fiber: 1.7 g; sodium: 245 mg; cholesterol: 28.3 mg; calories: 350.

CHOCOLATE BOURBON PECAN PIE

MAKES 12 SERVINGS (ONE 11-INCH PIE)

This over-the-top flavor combination is a real crowd pleaser. Serve it with whipped cream.

- 1 3/4 cups plus 2 tablespoons all-purpose flour
- 1/2 cup plus 3 tablespoons sugar
- 3/4 teaspoon salt
- 3/4 cup (1 1/2 sticks) unsalted butter, cut into small pieces and chilled
- 3-6 tablespoons ice water
- 1 cup light corn syrup
- 3 large eggs
- 5 tablespoons unsalted butter, melted
- 1/4 cup bourbon
- 2 teaspoons pure vanilla extract
- 4 ounces bittersweet chocolate, grated
- 2 cups chopped pecans plus 1/2 cup pecan halves

1 MAKE THE PASTRY: In a food processor fitted with the metal blade, place the flour, 2 tablespoons sugar, and 1/4 teaspoon salt and pulse until combined. Add the cold butter and pulse until mixture resembles coarse meal. Drizzle in 3 to 6 tablespoons ice water, 1 tablespoon at a time, and pulse until a dough just begins to form. Gather the dough into a disk, wrap in plastic, and chill until firm—about 45 minutes.

2 BLIND-BAKE THE CRUST: Preheat the oven to 400°F. Roll out the dough to a 13-inch circle, place into an 11-inch pie plate, and crimp the edges. Line with parchment paper and fill with pie weights. Bake for 10 minutes, remove weights, and bake for 5 more minutes.

3 MAKE THE FILLING: Lower the oven setting to 350°F. In a large bowl, combine the corn syrup, remaining sugar, eggs, melted butter, bourbon, vanilla, and remaining salt and set aside. Sprinkle the chocolate and chopped nuts over the bottom of the pie shell and pour the egg-vanilla mixture on top. Place the pecan halves in a decorative pattern on top of the filled pie and bake until golden and set—about 45 minutes. Transfer the pie to a wire rack and let cool for 90 minutes. Pie will keep covered for up to 3 days.

Nutrition information per serving—protein: 6.4 g; fat: 37.9 g; carbohydrate: 55.3 g; fiber: 2.1 g; sodium: 185 mg; cholesterol: 97.3 mg; calories: 571.

PUMPKIN CREAM PIE WITH CANDIED CRANBERRIES   > >

MAKES 8 MINI-PIES

With our easy ginger snap cookie crust there's no fuss or muss. You simply mix the cookie crumbs and butter in a bowl, then pat it into the pie plate.

CRUST:

3 cups gingersnap cookie crumbs

2 tablespoons ground cinnamon

3/4 cup (1 1/2 sticks) unsalted butter, melted

TOPPING:

2 cups sugar

1 cup fresh cranberries

FILLING:

1/2 cup milk

1 teaspoon unflavored gelatin

1 cup pureed pumpkin

3/4 cup sugar

2 tablespoons brandy or Cognac

1/4 teaspoon ground nutmeg

1/4 teaspoon ground cloves

4 large egg yolks

1 cup heavy cream, whipped to stiff peaks

1 MAKE THE TART SHELLS: Preheat the oven to 350°F. In a large bowl, combine the cookie crumbs, 2 teaspoons cinnamon, and melted butter. Cover the bottom and sides of eight 3 1/2-inch tartlet pans with removable bottoms with the crumb mixture. Transfer the tartlet shells to a baking sheet and bake for 10 minutes. Transfer to a wire rack and let cool completely.

2 MAKE THE CRANBERRY TOPPING: In a small saucepan, bring 2 cups sugar and 1/2 cup water to a boil over high heat. Add the cranberries and cook until cranberries just begin to soften. With a slotted spoon, remove the cranberries to a small bowl and set aside. Reserve the cranberry syrup for another use.

3 MAKE THE FILLING: Fill a large bowl with ice and water and set aside. Place the milk in a small bowl, sprinkle the gelatin over it, and set aside. In large saucepan, combine the pumpkin puree, 3/4 cup sugar, brandy, remaining cinnamon, nutmeg, cloves, and egg yolks. Cook the pumpkin mixture over medium heat, whisking constantly until it begins to bubble and a thermometer reads 140°F. Stir in the milk mixture and cook 1 more minute, transfer the mixture to a medium bowl and place over the prepared ice bath. Stirring occasionally, until cool—about 10 minutes. Fold the whipped cream into the chilled pumpkin mixture, spoon about 1/4 cup plus 2 tablespoons filling into each crust, and smooth the tops. Chill for 6 hours or overnight. Top each tartlet with a spoonful of candied cranberries, and serve cold.

Nutrition information per serving—protein: 5.5 g; fat: 24.9 g; carbohydrate: 46 g; fiber: 3 g; sodium: 177 mg; cholesterol: 173 mg; calories: 428.

TOMATO AND CAMEMBERT TART

< <

This superb tart is also delicious made with French muenster cheese. Serve it as an appetizer, or with a green salad for lunch.

PASTRY:

1½ cups all-purpose flour

6 tablespoons (¾ stick) cold unsalted butter, cut into small pieces

½ teaspoon salt

½ teaspoon coarsely ground black pepper

½ cup plus 2–3 tablespoons extra-virgin olive oil

1 tablespoon water

FILLING:

1 tablespoon Dijon mustard

½ cup grated Gruyère

4 plum tomatoes, cut into ½-inch-thick slices and seeded

6 ounces Camembert, cut into ⅛-inch-thick slices

¼ cup chopped fresh parsley

¼ cup chopped fresh basil leaves

1 teaspoon finely chopped fresh rosemary leaves

1 tablespoon fresh thyme leaves

1 small bay leaf, finely crumbled

1 clove garlic, minced

1 MAKE THE PASTRY: Using a pastry blender or 2 knives, combine the flour, butter, salt, and pepper until the mixture resembles coarse meal. Using a fork, mix in 2 tablespoons oil and the water just until the bottom of the mixture begins to cling together. If necessary, add an additional tablespoon oil. Gather into a ball, flatten into a disk, wrap in plastic wrap, and chill for 30 minutes.

2 BAKE THE TART: Preheat the oven to 375°F. Roll out the chilled dough into a 14-inch circle and place it into a tart pan; set aside. Spread the mustard over the bottom of the tart shell. Sprinkle the Gruyère evenly over the mustard and alternately place the tomato and Camembert over the Gruyère. In a small bowl, mix the remaining ½ cup extra-virgin olive oil, all of the herbs, and the garlic together and brush two-thirds of the mixture over the tart. Bake on the middle shelf of the oven for 35 minutes. Remove the tart and brush it with the remaining oil. Serve warm.

Nutrition information per serving—protein: 6.2 g; fat: 22.3 g; carbohydrate: 13.5 g; fiber: .9 g; sodium: 259 mg; cholesterol: 30.7 mg; calories: 276.

PEAR TART WITH BLUE CHEESE STREUSEL

MAKES 8 SERVINGS

Some people can't choose between dessert and cheese, this rich tart allows them to savor both at the same time.

1 recipe pastry dough (recipe follows)

¼ cup plus 2 tablespoons all-purpose flour

6 tablespoons plus 1 teaspoon packed light brown sugar

⅓ cup finely chopped blanched almonds

1¼ cups crumbled blue cheese

1½ pounds pears (about 4 medium), peeled, cored, and cut into ½-inch-thick lengthwise slices

1 tablespoon fresh lemon juice

2 tablespoons unsalted butter, softened

1 MAKE THE STREUSEL: Preheat the oven to 350°F. Roll the pastry dough out into a 13-inch circle, transfer it to a baking sheet, cover with plastic wrap, and refrigerate at least 20 minutes. In a medium bowl, combine the flour, ¼ cup brown sugar, and almonds. Using a pastry blender, 2 knives, or your fingers, cut in ¾ cup blue cheese until the mixture resembles coarse meal. Set aside.

2 MAKE THE FILLING: In a large bowl, combine the pears, lemon juice, remaining blue cheese, butter, and 2 tablespoons brown sugar; toss to coat, and set aside.

3 MAKE THE TART: Sprinkle the prepared dough with two-thirds of the streusel mixture, leaving a 2-inch-wide border around the edge. Top with the pear filling followed by the remaining streusel. Fold the 2-inch border over the top of the streusel and sprinkle the folded crust with the remaining brown sugar. Bake until pears are tender and crust is golden brown—45 to 50 minutes. Cut into wedges and serve warm or at room temperature.

Nutrition information per serving—protein: 8.5 g; fat: 21.8 g; carbohydrate: 40.7 g; fiber: 3.3 g; sodium: 332 mg; cholesterol: 50.9 mg; calories: 384.

PASTRY DOUGH

MAKES 1 PASTRY SHELL(ONE CRUST PIE)

This dough can be frozen for up to 1 month—just be sure to chill it before freezing so the gluten in the flour is allowed to relax.

1¼ cups all-purpose flour

⅛ teaspoon salt

7 tablespoons cold unsalted butter, cut into small pieces

3–4 tablespoons ice water

MAKE THE PASTRY: In a large bowl, combine the flour and salt. Using a pastry cutter, two knives, or your fingers, quickly cut the butter into the flour until the mixture resembles coarse meal. Add the cold water by the tablespoon until a rough dough forms. Gather the dough and shape it into a ¾-inch-thick disk. Wrap the dough tightly in plastic wrap and chill for 30 minutes.

Nutrition information per serving—protein: 2.8 g; fat: 5.9 g; carbohydrate: 10.9 g; fiber: .9 g; sodium: 173 mg; cholesterol: 22 mg; calories: 106.

WILD MUSHROOM TART

MAKES 6 SERVINGS (ONE 9-INCH TART)

This savory tart is sturdy enough to travel. After it cools, wrap tightly and serve at room temperature.

PASTRY:

1½ cups all-purpose flour

½ teaspoon salt

½ cup (1 stick) butter, cut into small pieces

2–3 tablespoons ice water

FILLING:

1 cup apple cider

3 tablespoons olive oil

⅓ cup chopped shallots

8 ounces white mushrooms, sliced

4 ounces wild mushrooms (such as cremini, shiitake, or chanterelle), sliced

¾ cup dried porcini mushrooms

¼ cup Calvados, applejack, or hard cider

½ cup chopped fresh flat-leaf parsley

½ teaspoon salt

¼ teaspoon ground black pepper

4 large eggs

¾ cup heavy cream

1 cup grated smoked mozzarella or smoked Gouda

½ cup grated Parmesan cheese

1 MAKE THE PASTRY: In a food processor fitted with the metal blade, combine the flour, salt, and butter. Pulse until the mixture is mealy—about 6 pulses. With processor running, add water, one tablespoon at a time, until the dough comes together, no longer than 15 seconds. Gather the dough into a rough ball, flatten into a 7-inch disk, and wrap in plastic wrap. Refrigerate for 1 hour minimum or up to 24 hours. Preheat the oven to 375°F.

2 FORM THE CRUST: Roll out the dough between 2 sheets of plastic wrap, creating a circle 2 inches larger than bottom of tart pan. Remove the top sheet of plastic wrap and turn dough over into a 9-inch tart pan with a removable bottom. Carefully remove the bottom sheet of plastic wrap. Tuck the dough into the pan and trim the edges evenly with the top of the pan. Freeze for 10 minutes. Line the bottom of the prepared pan with waxed paper and weight down with pie weights or dried beans. Bake 20 minutes, remove weights, and cool on a wire rack.

3 MAKE THE FILLING: Reheat the oven to 375°F. In a small saucepan or microwaveable container, bring the cider to a boil. Pour the hot cider over the dried porcini mushrooms and let hydrate for 20 minutes. Set aside. Heat the oil in a large skillet and sauté all fresh mushrooms and shallots about 10 minutes. Add the porcini mushrooms, along with their liquid, and the Calvados. Cook on medium-low heat for about 15 minutes or until almost all liquid is absorbed. Stir in the parsley, salt, and pepper.

4 In a large bowl, combine the eggs, heavy cream, and cheeses. Stir in the mushroom mixture. Pour into the prepared crust.

5 BAKE THE TART: Bake until a toothpick inserted in the center comes out clean and the top has browned—30 to 35 minutes. Cool on a wire rack and serve at room temperature. May be prepared the day before and refrigerated. Reheat in a 350°F oven 20–25 minutes to bring to room temperature before serving.

Nutrition information per serving—protein: 25 g; fat: 45 g; carbohydrate: 48 g; fiber: 6.6 g; sodium: 654 mg; cholesterol: 245 mg; calories: 710.

DESSERTS

CRANBERRY GRANOLA SPICED APPLES

MAKES 6 SERVINGS

These baked apples capture fall's aromas and flavors.

6 Rome Beauty apples

1 tablespoon fresh lemon juice

STUFFING:

½ cup dried cranberries

½ cup granola

2 tablespoons packed light brown sugar

½ teaspoon ground cinnamon

¼ teaspoon ground nutmeg

2 tablespoons butter, cut into small pieces

RASPBERRY GLAZE

3 tablespoons fresh lemon juice

¼ cup seedless raspberry jam

1 MAKE THE APPLES: Preheat the oven to 350°F. Lightly coat a baking dish with vegetable oil. Wash, dry, and core the apples, leaving the bottoms intact. Brush apple flesh with lemon juice. Arrange apples in the baking dish.

2 MAKE THE STUFFING: In a small bowl, toss together the cranberries, granola, brown sugar, cinnamon, and nutmeg. Spoon into apples and top with butter pieces.

3 MAKE THE GLAZE: In a glass bowl, heat the lemon juice and jam together in a microwave oven at 100 percent power until the mixture bubbles—about 30 seconds. Brush the apples with the mixture and drizzle extra topping into the filled apples.

4 BAKE AND SERVE: Place baking dish on the middle rack of oven and bake uncovered until apples are soft—about 55 minutes. Serve warm.

Nutrition information per serving—protein: 1.9 g; fat: 7.5 g; carbohydrate: 52 g; fiber: 6 g; sodium: 47 mg; cholesterol: 10 mg; calories: 259.

MIXED-BERRY PAVLOVA

MAKES 12 SERVINGS
(ONE 9-INCH PAVLOVA)

Named for the famous Russian ballerina Anna Pavlova, this fabulous dessert showcases summer berries between layers of crispy meringue and soft whipped cream.

½ lemon

6 large egg whites, at room temperature

⅛ teaspoon salt

2 teaspoons balsamic vinegar

1 tablespoon plus 1 teaspoon pure vanilla extract

1¼ cups sugar

4 cups heavy cream

2 pints mixed berries

1 PREPARE THE BAKING SHEETS: Preheat the oven to 200°F. Line two baking sheets with parchment paper and, using a pencil, trace a 9-inch-diameter circle on each. Turn parchment over—penciled side down—and set the lined baking sheets aside.

2 MAKE THE MERINGUES: Use the lemon to wipe the inside of a large metal bowl and the beaters of an electric mixer. Add the egg whites and salt to the bowl and beat on low speed until foamy. Add vinegar and 1 teaspoon vanilla and beat until combined. Increase mixer speed to medium and add the sugar in a slow stream. Increase speed to medium high and continue beating until egg whites form satiny, stiff peaks. Do not overbeat. Place half of the meringue in the center of each of the traced circles and, using a spatula, spread it evenly to fill the circles. Bake until meringues are completely dry—about 3 hours. Leaving the meringues on the parchment paper, transfer to a wire rack to cool completely—about 45 minutes.

3 MAKE THE WHIPPED CREAM: In a large bowl, combine the cream and the remaining tablespoon vanilla. With an electric mixer, beat on medium-high speed until soft peaks form—about 3 minutes. Keep chilled until ready to use.

4 ASSEMBLE THE PAVLOVA: Place one meringue disk on a cake plate or cake stand and top with half of the whipped cream and half of the berries. Place the remaining meringue disk over the first layer and top with the remaining cream followed by the berries.

Nutrition information per serving—protein: 3.8 g; fat: 29.5 g; carbohydrate: 27.9 g; fiber: 1.4 g; sodium: 79 mg; cholesterol: 109 mg; calories: 385.

HOLIDAY FRUIT SALAD WITH POMEGRANATE SYRUP

This syrup is well worth the effort it takes to prepare. You'll find yourself using it for everything from flavoring spritzers to glazing pork roasts. Add it to vinaigrettes or, as we've done here, to sweeten winter fruits.

POMEGRANATE SYRUP:

2 large pomegranates

2/3 cup sugar

1 tablespoon fresh lemon juice

FRUIT SALAD:

2 pints strawberries, hulled and halved

3 cups fresh or drained canned pineapple chunks

2 bananas, peeled and sliced

3 oranges, peeled, seeded, and sliced

1 pink grapefruit, peeled and sectioned

Pomegranate seeds (optional)

1 MAKE THE SYRUP: Quarter the pomegranates, peel off the rind, and pull the fruit apart into pieces. Carefully pull out the red seeds. Wrap a handful of seeds in cheesecloth and press hard to release all juice into a bowl. Discard spent seeds. Repeat the process until all the juice has been extracted from the remaining seeds. Alternately, process seeds in a blender. Pour this liquid into a clear container and refrigerate for up to 8 hours. Sediment will settle to the bottom. Ladle the clear liquid into a saucepan, and add the sugar and lemon juice. Heat until the sugar dissolves, then cook until the syrup reduces and thickens a little—about 5 minutes. Pour into a container, cover, and refrigerate.

2 MAKE FRUIT SALAD: In a clear glass bowl, place the strawberries, pineapple, bananas, oranges, and grapefruit sections. Toss with two or three tablespoons pomegranate syrup. Cover and refrigerate until serving time. Garnish with pomegranate seeds, if desired.

Nutrition information per serving—protein: 1.8 g; fat: 1 g; carbohydrate: 34.2 g; fiber: 4.6 g; sodium: 2.2 mg; cholesterol: 0; calories: 138.

CHAMPAGNE, FRUIT, AND MARSALA CREAM PARFAITS

Marsala, a fortified wine from Sicily, subtly flavors the creamy layers between the marinated summer fruit in this elegant dessert.

2 medium peaches, cut into 3/4-inch-thick slices (1 1/2 cups)

3 medium apricots, cut into 3/4-inch-thick slices (1 1/2 cups)

2 medium plums, cut into 3/4-inch-thick slices (1 1/2 cups)

2 medium nectarines, cut into 3/4-inch-thick slices (2 cups)

1 1/2 cups fresh cherries, pitted

1/2 cup fresh raspberries

1/4 cup honey

1/2 cup Champagne

1 cup heavy cream

1/4 cup sweet Marsala wine

1 tablespoon confectioners' sugar

1 MARINATE THE FRUIT: In a large bowl, place the peaches, apricots, plums, nectarines, cherries, and raspberries. In a small bowl, combine the honey and Champagne. Pour the Champagne mixture over the fruit and gently toss to coat fruit evenly.

2 PREPARE THE PARFAITS: In a medium bowl, with an electric mixer on medium-high speed, beat the heavy cream, Marsala, and sugar together until soft peaks form. Place 1/2 cup fruit salad in each of 8 parfait glasses, top with 2 tablespoons whipped cream, and add another 1/2 cup of fruit. Top each with the remaining 2 tablespoons cream. Serve immediately.

Nutrition information per serving—protein: 1.2 g; fat: .6 g; carbohydrate: 24.5 g; fiber: 2.3 g; sodium: 1.5 mg; cholesterol: 0; calories: 108.

FIG, RASPBERRY, AND HONEY TRIFLE

MAKES 10 SERVINGS

The trifle, a layered custard, cake, and fruit dessert, originated in England. It is served in a footed glass bowl, encouraging a creative arrangement of the layers. Make this luscious dessert the day before you plan to serve it to allow all of the flavors to meld.

CUSTARD:

5 cups milk

1 cup sugar

1/2 cup cornstarch

1/2 teaspoon salt

4 large egg yolks

2 teaspoons pure vanilla extract

FRUIT FILLING:

3/4 cup honey

2 tablespoons orange juice

12 fresh figs, halved

4 cups fresh raspberries

CAKE:

1 16-ounce loaf pound cake

1/2 cup seedless raspberry jam

1/4 cup cream sherry

HONEYWHIPPED CREAM:

1 1/2 cups heavy cream

3 tablespoons honey

1 MAKE THE CUSTARD: One day in advance, in a 4-quart saucepan, combine the milk, sugar, cornstarch, and salt. Bring to a boil over medium heat, stirring constantly, until thickened and bubbly; remove from heat. In a small bowl, beat the egg yolks until frothy, then stir in a small amount of the hot milk mixture. Stir the egg-yolk mixture back into the remaining milk mixture. Cook and stir 1 minute longer; remove from the heat. Stir in the vanilla extract; immediately cover the surface of the custard with plastic wrap. Refrigerate until well chilled.

2 MAKE THE FRUIT FILLING: In a large bowl, mix the honey and orange juice. Add the figs and raspberries; toss to coat. Let stand 15 minutes.

3 ASSEMBLE THE TRIFLE: Cut the cake into 2-inch chunks. Brush the bottom of a stemmed glass trifle bowl with some raspberry preserves and top with cake pieces in a single layer. Brush the cake with half of the sherry. Brush raspberry preserves on top of the cake layer. Spoon one-third of the custard evenly over the cake layer. Cover custard with half of the fruit, pressing some fig halves against the side of the dish in a decorative pattern. Repeat the process beginning with cake pieces, sherry, jam, custard, and fruit. Smooth the remaining custard on top. Cover and refrigerate several hours or overnight.

4 TO SERVE: In a small bowl, with an electric mixer on high speed, beat the heavy cream and honey until peaks form. Spoon the whipped cream into a pastry bag fitted with a large tip; pipe on top of the trifle to decorate. Refrigerate the trifle until ready to serve.

Nutrition information per serving— protein: 94 g; fat: 28 g; carbohydrate: 11 g; fiber: 4.7 g; sodium: 374 mg; cholesterol: 177 mg; calories: 712.

SPICED FIGS IN PORT WINE < <

Port, a sweet wine fortified with brandy, comes in a variety of classifications. To derive the health benefits of red wine, choose any type except white port, which is made with white rather than red grapes.

- 1 $^{1}/_{2}$ cups port wine
- 8 dried figs, quartered
- 1/3 cup sugar
- 1 tablespoon honey
- 1 tablespoon fresh lemon juice
- $^{1}/_{8}$ teaspoon salt
- $^{1}/_{2}$ vanilla bean, split, seeds scraped and reserved
- 4 $^{1}/_{4}$- by 3-inch-long strips orange zest, colored part only
- 4 whole black peppercorns
- 2 whole cloves
- 6 sprigs fresh thyme, plus 4 for garnish
- 2 cups vanilla frozen yogurt

1 POACH THE FIGS: In a small saucepan over medium-high heat, combine all ingredients except the yogurt and cook until the liquid begins to boil. Reduce heat to medium low and cook until the figs soften and the liquid thickens to a syrup—about 25 minutes. Using a slotted spoon, remove the figs and place them in a medium bowl. Pour the remaining liquid through a strainer over the figs and keep warm.

2 MAKE THE DESSERT: In 4 individual serving dishes, spoon $^{1}/_{2}$ cup frozen yogurt. Top each with a quarter of the fig mixture and garnish with a thyme sprig. Serve immediately.

Nutrition information per serving—protein: 4.4 g; fat: 4.6 g; carbohydrate: 75.3 g; fiber: 3.9 g; sodium: 145 mg; cholesterol: 1.4 mg; calories: 434.

RED-WINE-POACHED PEARS

- 6 firm pears, peeled, cored, and cut sides rubbed with fresh lemon
- 2 750ml–bottles dry red wine
- 1 teaspoon whole cloves
- 4 3-inch cinnamon sticks
- 2 oranges, zest removed with a vegetable peeler
- $^{1}/_{2}$ cup fresh orange juice
- 10 cardamom pods
- 1 cup sugar

1 POACH THE FRUIT: In a large pot, combine all ingredients. Cook over medium-high heat, adding water to cover the pears if necessary, and bring to a simmer. Reduce the heat to maintain a simmer and poach until the fruit is tender—about 45 minutes. Remove the fruit from the poaching liquid or store fruit refrigerated in the poaching liquid until ready to use.

2 MAKE THE SYRUP: Strain the poaching liquid into a large pot and cook over high heat until reduced to 1–1$^{1}/_{2}$ cups. Drizzle the syrup over the pears. Serve immediately.

Nutrition information per serving—protein: 1 g; fat: .8 g; carbohydrate: 62.1 g; fiber: 4.2 g; sodium: 5.4 mg; cholesterol: 0; calories: 294.

HONEY-GLAZED GRILLED PLUMS

> >

Honey, infused with the flavor of local wildflowers, makes a fragrant accent to this simple summer dessert. For an equally pleasing result, feel free to substitute almost any seasonal fruit for the plums—you need only adjust the grilling rime for the fruit.

4 firm plums (about 3/4 pound),
    halved and pitted

6 tablespoons honey

3 cups vanilla frozen yogurt

GRILL THE PLUMS: Heat a grill to medium. Toss the plums and 2 tablespoons honey in a large bowl. Liberally brush a grill rack with oil. Grill the plums, flesh side down, on the rack until lightly browned—about 3 minutes. Turn and grill on skin side until plums soften and are warmed through—2 to 3 more minutes. Serve 2 plum halves with 3/4 cup yogurt immediately.

Nutrition information per serving—protein: 7.2 g; fat: 2.4 g; carbohydrate: 62.4 g; fiber: 1.4 g; sodium: 89.8 mg; cholesterol: 7.7 mg; calories: 285.

VALENCIA ORANGE FLAN

CARAMEL:

1/2 cup sugar

2 tablespoons orange juice

FLAN:

2 cups half-and-half

2 cups heavy cream

1 cup sugar

4 2-inch-long strips orange zest, colored

12 extra-large egg yolks

1/4 cup orange liqueur

Sprigs fresh mint (optional)

1 MAKE THE CARAMEL: In a medium heavy skillet, combine the sugar and orange juice. Cook over low heat, stirring constantly, until the sugar dissolves and the mixture begins to boil. When the boiling process begins, stop stirring. Holding the handle of the pan, gently tilt the skillet off the heat to distribute color evenly as the sugar caramelizes. When the sugar reaches a uniform amber color, pour into a heat-proof 10-inch pie plate.

2 MAKE THE FLAN: Place a shallow baking pan in the lower third of the oven and add enough hot water to come halfway up the sides. Heat oven to 325°F. In a large heavy saucepan, combine the half-and-half, heavy cream, sugar, and orange zest; bring to a simmer over low heat, stirring occasionally. In large bowl, beat the egg yolks. Blend 1 cup cream mixture into the yolks. Stir the egg-yolk mixture back into saucepan and heat, stirring constantly, 1 minute. Remove from heat and stir in the liqueur. Pour into the prepared pie plate and place in the baking pan partly filled with water in the oven.

3 BAKE AND SERVE: Bake uncovered—1 1/2 hours or until a knife blade inserted in center comes out clean. Remove flan from the oven and water bath; cool on a rack, cover, and refrigerate 4 to 5 hours. To serve, run a knife blade around the edge of the flan, then carefully invert it onto a rimmed serving plate. Allow a moment for the caramel to drip onto the flan. Carefully lift pie plate. Garnish with mint sprigs, if desired.

Nutrition information per serving—protein: 7.4 g; fat: 35.7 g; carbohydrate: 45 g; fiber: 0 g; sodium: 64 mg; cholesterol: 430 mg: calories: 548.

FROZEN LIME MOUSSE WITH RASPBERRY SAUCE

MAKES 8 SERVINGS

This is a refreshing make-ahead dessert. The mousse can be stored in the freezer for up to one week; make the sauce just before serving.

LIME MOUSSE:

1 envelope unflavored gelatin

3 large egg whites

1 cup sugar

2 teaspoons grated lime zest

1/4 cup fresh lime juice

1 cup heavy cream, whipped

3/4 cup lemon low-fat yogurt

Dash of salt (optional)

Lime wedges (optional)

RASPBERRY SAUCE:

2 cups fresh or frozen raspberries

2 tablespoons sugar

1 MAKE THE LIME MOUSSE: In a small microwave-safe bowl, place 2 tablespoons water and sprinkle the gelatin over top. Let stand 1 minute. Microwave at highest setting for 15 seconds. Stir until the gelatin has dissolved. Let cool slightly.

2 In a large bowl, with an electric mixer on high speed, beat the egg whites until soft peaks form. In a 2-quart saucepan, combine the sugar and lime juice; cook over medium heat until the sugar has dissolved. Increase heat to medium high and cook, without stirring, until a candy thermometer registers 240°F (softball stage). With the electric mixer on medium speed, slowly pour the hot sugar syrup in a thin stream over the beaten egg whites and combine. Increase the mixer speed to high and beat until stiff peaks form—about 5 minutes. Beat in the reserved gelatin mixture and lime zest. Fold in the whipped heavy cream, yogurt, and salt, if desired. Divide the mixture among eight 6-ounce custard cups or ramekins. Cover with plastic wrap and freeze for at least 4 hours.

3 MAKE THE RASPBERRY SAUCE: In the jar of a blender or a food processor fitted with the metal blade, combine the raspberries and sugar. Process until smooth. Pass the mixture though a fine strainer, pressing down with the back of a spoon, and discard the seeds. Refrigerate sauce.

4 When ready to serve, pour a small amount of raspberry sauce over frozen mousse and garnish with lime wedges, if desired.

Nutrition information per serving (without salt)—protein: 4 g; fat: 12 g; carbohydrate: 35 g; fiber: 2 g; sodium: 46 mg; cholesterol: 42 mg; calories: 251.

MELON COOLER

MAKES TWO 1 1/2-CUP SERVINGS

The character of this refreshing dessert is part smoothie and part sorbet. Begin by spooning up cool mouthfuls and, once it melts a bit, sip it through a straw.

2 cups (1/2-inch cubes) cantaloupe, frozen

2 cups (1/2-inch cubes) honeydew melon, frozen

2 tablespoons sugar

1 PUREE THE MELONS: In a blender, place the frozen cantaloupe pieces, 1/2 cup water, and 1 tablespoon sugar and puree on high speed until fruit is smooth and pourable. Transfer to a bowl and keep chilled. Rinse the blender and repeat using the frozen honeydew, 1/2 cup water, and remaining sugar.

2 ASSEMBLE THE COOLER: Alternately layer about 1/3 cup of the pureed cantaloupe followed by the same amount of the honeydew melon into 2 large glasses. Repeat until all the puree is used and serve immediately.

Nutrition information per serving—protein: 2.2 g; fat: .6 g; carbohydrate: 41.5 g; fiber: 2.3 g; sodium: 35 mg; cholesterol: 0; calories: 164.

STRAWBERRY GRANITA

We use frozen fruit to make this variation of a popular Italian ice confection.

1 1-pound package frozen strawberries (without syrup)

¼ cup sugar

MAKE THE GRANITA: In a food processor fitted with the metal blade, combine the strawberries and sugar. Pulse until the mixture is granular in texture. Transfer to a bowl and serve.

Nutrition information per ¼-cup serving—protein: .24 g; fat: 0; carbohydrate: 11.4 g; fiber: .9 g; sodium: 1.2 mg; cholesterol: 0; calories: 44.

ENJOYING HOMEMADE ICE CREAM AND GRANITA

For perfect scoops, first dip the scoop into lukewarm water, which allows each ball of ice cream to be released intact. Store ice cream in wide, shallow containers, which make it easier to slide the scoop along the surface and create flawless scoops. Store ice cream containers in large airtight plastic freezer bags to keep out food odors and to prevent ice crystals from forming. Remember that homemade ice cream does not contain preservatives, so it will not keep as long as the store-bought variety: its flavor will start to fade after about 1 week.

CHERRY VANILLA ICE CREAM

If you don't use halved cherries immediately, toss them with a little lemon juice to help prevent their oxidation or browning.

1½ pounds sweet cherries, pitted

1 cup sugar

2½ cups heavy cream

1 cup milk

½ vanilla bean, split, seeds scraped and reserved

8 large egg yolks

1 teaspoon fresh lemon juice

3–4 drops of red food coloring (optional)

1 MAKE THE CHERRY SYRUP: In a small saucepan, place 1 pound pitted cherries and ⅓ cup sugar. Cook over medium heat and cook until the cherries soften—about 10 minutes. Run the cherries and any liquid through a food mill, strain the mixture, discard the solids, and return the liquid to the pan. Cook the cherry mixture over medium heat until it reduces to about 1 cup—8 to 10 minutes. Transfer to a small bowl and cool completely.

2 MAKE THE ICE-CREAM BASE: Fill a large bowl with ice and water and place a fine sieve over another medium-sized bowl; set both aside. In a medium saucepan, combine the cream, milk, vanilla bean and seeds, and cook over medium-high heat until mixture just comes to a boil. In a large bowl, whisk the egg yolks and remaining sugar together until thick and pale. Whisking constantly, add the hot milk in a slow, steady stream to the yolk mixture. Return the mixture to the saucepan and cook over medium heat, stirring constantly, using a wooden spoon, until the mixture coats the back of a spoon—about 2 minutes. Strain the mixture through the fine sieve into the bowl and place bowl in the prepared ice bath to cool.

3 MAKE THE ICE CREAM: Cut the remaining cherries in half, toss with the lemon juice, and set aside. Once the ice-cream base is completely cool, stir in the cherry syrup and the food coloring, if desired. Process in an ice cream maker according to the manufacturer's instructions. Fold in the cherry halves, transfer to an airtight container, and freeze until solid. Ice cream will keep up to 1 month in the freezer.

Nutrition information per ½-cup serving—protein: 4.2 g; fat: 23 g; carbohydrate: 28.7 g; fiber: 1 g; sodium: 33.6 mg; cholesterol: 213 mg; calories: 329.

FRESH PEACH ICE CREAM « «

MAKES 6 SERVINGS (ABOUT 1 QUART)

Luscious peaches take a starring role in this cool dessert. Just combine pureed fresh peaches, sugar, and vanilla-infused half-and-half and freeze in your ice-cream maker.

- 2 cups half-and-half
- 1 vanilla bean
- $\frac{1}{2}$ cup sugar
- 2 1/4 pounds peaches (about 6 medium peaches)
- 2 tablespoons fresh lemon juice

1 INFUSE THE HALF-AND-HALF: In a medium saucepan, combine the half-and-half, vanilla bean, and sugar. Bring to a boil over medium-high heat. Immediately remove the half-and-half mixture from heat and remove the vanilla bean. On a cutting board, with a paring knife, split the vanilla bean lengthwise. Use the back of the knife to scrape out the bean's seeds and return the pod and seeds to the half-and-half mixture. Cover and let steep for 20 minutes.

2 MAKE THE ICE CREAM: Peel, pit, and quarter the peaches. Place the peaches and lemon juice in a food processor fitted with the metal blade. Process until the peaches are pureed but mixture is slightly chunky. Strain the half-and-half mixture into a large bowl and discard the vanilla-bean pod. Stir in the peach puree and chill until very cold. Process in ice-cream maker according to manufacturer's instructions. Serve immediately or transfer the ice cream to an airtight container and store in the freezer.

Nutrition information per $\frac{1}{2}$ cup—protein: 2.3 g; fat: 7 g; carbohydrate: 22.7 g; fiber: 1.2 g; sodium: 24.8 mg; cholesterol: 22.3 mg; calories: 156.

GINGER ICE CREAM

MAKES 6 SERVINGS

Hot, sweet bites of crystallized ginger punctuate this smooth ice cream that's made with fresh ginger.

- 2 cups heavy cream
- 1 cup milk
- 1 2-inch piece peeled fresh ginger, cut into thin slices and crushed with the side of a large knife
- $\frac{3}{4}$ cup sugar
- 3 large egg yolks
- $\frac{1}{4}$ cup finely diced crystallized ginger

1 MAKE THE ICE-CREAM BASE: In a heavy-bottomed nonreactive saucepan, combine the cream, milk, and fresh ginger. Bring to a slow simmer over low heat and cook for 15 to 20 minutes to thoroughly infuse the cream with the ginger. Add the sugar and stir until it dissolves.

2 In a separate bowl, whisk the egg yolks. Strain in about one third of the hot cream mixture and quickly whisk. Strain in the rest of the liquid. Use the back of a large spoon to press the ginger through the strainer. Return cream mixture to the saucepan. Cook over medium heat, stirring constantly, until the mixture coats the back of a spoon, 5 to 7 minutes.

3 Strain the mixture into a clean bowl. Set the bowl in a larger bowl of ice water and let cool, stirring occasionally. Remove the bowl from the ice water, cover with plastic wrap, and refrigerate for at least 8 hours, preferably overnight.

4 MAKE THE ICE CREAM: Add the chilled cream to an ice cream maker. Follow the manufacturer's directions to freeze. Just as ice cream begins to freeze, fold in the crystallized ginger. Finish freezing. Serve immediately, or remove from ice cream maker and store in a plastic quart container in the freezer until ready to serve.

Nutrition information per $\frac{1}{2}$-cup serving—protein: 4.4 g; fat: 33 g; carbohydrate: 30.7 g; fiber: 0; sodium: 53.7 mg; cholesterol: 221 mg; calories: 431.

CHOCOLATE BREAD PUDDING

Serve this recipe warm or with our Irish Whiskey Sauce (recipe follows).

- 3 cups milk
- 1 cup half-and-half
- $3/4$ cup granulated sugar
- 1 8-ounce package semisweet chocolate
- 1/3 cup Irish whiskey
- 4 large egg yolks
- 1 tablespoon butter
- 1 teaspoon pure vanilla extract
- $1/8$ teaspoon salt
- 1 1-pound loaf challah or French bread, cut into 2-inch cubes
- Chocolate shavings (optional)
- Confectioners' sugar (optional)

1 MAKE THE PUDDING: Heat oven to 350°F. Grease a 2-quart baking dish and set aside. In a 6-quart saucepan, combine the milk and half-and-half. Bring to a simmer over medium-low heat, stirring occasionally. Add the granulated sugar and chocolate; stir until melted. Bring mixture to boil; cook 1 minute. Remove from heat and stir in the whiskey.

2 MAKE THE BREAD PUDDING: In a small bowl, beat the yolks. Slowly whisk in $1/4$ cup of the milk mixture. Whisk the egg mixture into the remaining milk mixture until well-combined and thickened. Stir in the butter, vanilla, and salt. Fold in the bread; spoon the pudding into baking dish. Let soak 1 hour at room temperature.

3 BAKE THE PUDDING: Bake until a knife inserted in the center comes out clean—about 50 minutes. To serve, spoon into bowls; garnish with shaved chocolate and sprinkle with confectioners' sugar, if desired.

Nutrition information per serving—protein: 14 g; fat: 28 g; carbohydrate: 59 g; fiber: 5 g; sodium: 370 mg; cholesterol: 131 mg; calories: 529.

IRISH WHISKEY SAUCE

Try pouring this spiked over pound cake or brownies as well.

- 2 tablespoons butter
- 2 tablespoons all-purpose flour
- 1 cup milk
- $1/4$ cup sugar
- 1 tablespoon Irish whiskey

MAKE THE SAUCE: In a 1-quart saucepan, melt the butter over medium heat. Add the flour and cook, whisking until well combined. Remove from heat and stir in the milk, sugar, and whiskey. Bring to a boil, whisking constantly, until thickened—5 to 7 minutes. Serve immediately.

Nutrition information per tablespoon—protein: .4g; fat: 1g; carbohydrate: 3 g; fiber: 0; sodium 13 mg; cholesterol: 4 mg; calories: 26.

SUGARED JELLY CANDIES

MAKES 81 ONE-INCH SQUARE CANDIES

While it only takes about an hour to make the jelly-candy base for these diminutive treats, you'll need three days to finish the candies. Candies are first dried and cut, then, after 48 hours, they are rolled in sugar.

FOR ALL FLAVORS:

1 pound Granny Smith apples (about 2 large), quartered and cored

1 pound pears (about 2), quartered and cored

$2/3$ cup dry white wine (such as chardonnay)

$1/2$ cup granulated sugar

1 teaspoon powdered pectin

1 cup sanding or granulated sugar

SPICED JELLIES:

$1^{1}/2$ cups granulated sugar

$1/2$ cup fresh lemon juice

1 teaspoon ground cinnamon

$1/4$ teaspoon ground cloves

$1/4$ teaspoon ground nutmeg

RASPBERRY JELLIES:

1 cup granulated sugar

$3/4$ cup seedless raspberry jam

$1/4$ cup fresh lemon juice

LEMON JELLIES:

peel and flesh from one lemon (pith removed)

2 tablespoons chopped fresh ginger

$1^{1}/2$ cups granulated sugar

$1/2$ cup fresh lemon juice

1 MAKE THE FRUIT: Line the bottom of a square 9-inch pan with parchment paper. Lightly oil the parchment paper and set aside. In a medium saucepan, place the apples, pears, and wine and bring to a boil over medium-high heat. (For Lemon Jellies, add the ginger and the peel and flesh from 1 lemon to the saucepan.) Reduce heat to low, cover, and simmer, stirring occasionally, until softened—15 to 20 minutes. Run the fruit through a food mill, discard the solids, and transfer the mixture to a clean saucepan.

2 MAKE THE CANDY: Combine $1/2$ cup granulated sugar and the pectin in a small bowl and set aside. Add the remaining ingredients, depending upon the flavor you are making, to the pureed fruit and simmer over medium heat until slightly thickened—about 15 minutes. Remove the pan from heat and whisk in the sugar-pectin mixture. Increase heat to medium high and continue to whisk until all of the sugar is dissolved—about 2 minutes. Bring the mixture to a boil and pour into the prepared pan. Place the pan on a cooling rack and let sit uncovered for 24 hours or until set.

3 UNMOLD THE JELLIES: Lightly dust a 12-inch piece of parchment paper with granulated sugar and set aside. Loosen the edges of the set jelly with a knife, invert onto the parchment, and let set for another 24 hours. At this point jellies can be wrapped in parchment paper and plastic wrap and stored in the refrigerator for up to 3 weeks or until ready to serve.

4 CUT OUT THE CANDIES: Use a knife to cut 1- by 1-inch squares or use a small cookie cutter to cut out shapes from the jelly. Dredge each piece in sanding sugar and transfer to a wire rack to dry—about 24 hours. Store jellies covered with plastic wrap for up to 1 week.

Nutrition information per jelly—protein: 0; fat: 0; carbohydrate: 9.4 g; fiber: .3 g; sodium: .5 mg; cholesterol: 0; calories: 37.5.

MAPLE INDIAN PUDDING > >

Colonists, who sometimes called corn "Indian", named this cornmeal-based dish Indian Pudding.

- 3 cups milk
- 3/4 cup maple syrup
- 1/2 cup cornmeal
- 1 tablespoon butter
- 1/2 teaspoon ground cinnamon
- 1/2 teaspoon salt
- 1/4 teaspoon ground ginger
- 1/4 teaspoon ground nutmeg
- 2 large eggs, beaten
- Whipped cream (optional)

1 MAKE THE PUDDING: Preheat the oven to 350°F. Lightly coat a 1-quart casserole dish with vegetable oil. In a large saucepan, bring the milk to a boil over medium heat. Reduce heat to low, stir in the maple syrup, and cook for 4 minutes. Add the cornmeal and cook, stirring constantly, for 6 to 8 minutes. Add the butter, cinnamon, salt, ginger, and nutmeg while stirring well. Remove from heat and let cool 5 minutes. Whisk the eggs into the milk mixture until well combined.

2 BAKE THE PUDDING: Pour into the prepared casserole dish and bake until the center is set—about 1 hour. Serve warm and top with whipped cream, if desired.

Nutrition information per serving without whipped cream—protein: 6.9 g; fat: 8.1 g; carbohydrate: 40 g; fiber: .9 g; sodium: 266 mg; cholesterol: 92.8 mg; calories: 260.

RICE PUDDING WITH MACADAMIA-MAPLE BRITTLE

The brittle is a snap to make—simply sprinkle the nuts over the puddings, drizzle with with a mixture of maple syrup and sugar and run under the broiler.

- 6 cups milk
- 1 cup sugar
- 2 tablespoons unsalted butter
- 1 cup medium-grain white rice
- 2 3-inch cinnamon sticks
- 2 large eggs
- 2 teaspoons pure vanilla extract
- 1/3 cup maple syrup (grade AA, if available)
- 1/4 cup chopped macadamia nuts, toasted

1 MAKE THE RICE: In a 4-quart saucepan, bring the milk, 3/4 cup sugar, and the butter to a boil over medium-high heat, stirring until the sugar dissolves. Add the rice and cinnamon sticks; return mixture to a boil. Reduce heat to medium-low, cover, and simmer 25 minutes, stirring occasionally.

2 MAKE THE PUDDING: In a medium bowl, whisk together the eggs and vanilla. Whisk 1 cup rice mixture into the egg mixture. Transfer the egg mixture to saucepan with rice mixture, stirring until well combined. Reduce heat to low and simmer 10 minutes. Remove from heat, discard cinnamon, and transfer to a 2-quart baking dish. Let cool at least 20 minutes or cover and refrigerate overnight.

3 MAKE THE BRITTLE: Heat broiler. In a small bowl, combine the maple syrup with the remaining 1/4 cup sugar. Press the macadamia nuts into the rice pudding, covering the top. Drizzle the maple syrup mixture evenly over the top. Broil, 4 inches from heat, until lightly browned—2 1/2 to 3 minutes. Let cool, spoon into dessert cups, and serve.

Nutrition information per serving—protein: 10 g; fat: 13 g; carbohydrate: 61 g; fiber: .5 g; sodium: 111 mg; cholesterol: 85 mg; calories: 399.

CITRUS-SAGE CUSTARD SOUFFLÉS

< <

Don't let the name soufflé intimidate you. The beauty of this dish is that it can be served straight from the oven, or, if you prefer, at room temperature. Because of the custardlike base, this dessert won't fall.

4 large eggs, separated (at room temperature)

1 cup sugar

3 tablespoons butter, softened

1/3 cup all-purpose flour

1 tablespoon finely chopped fresh sage leaves

3 tablespoons fresh lemon juice

1/2 teaspoon grated lime zest

2 tablespoons fresh lime juice

1/8 teaspoon salt

1 1/2 cups milk

8 thin slices lemon

1 PREPARE THE SOUFFLÉS: Heat oven to 350°F. Lightly coat eight 6-ounce ramekins with vegetable oil. In a medium bowl with electric mixer on high speed, beat the egg whites until foamy. Gradually add 1/2 cup sugar, 1 tablespoon at a time, beating until stiff peaks form. Set aside.

2 MAKE THE CUSTARD: In a large bowl, with mixer on medium speed, beat together the remaining 1/2 cup sugar and the butter until well blended. Beat in the flour, sage, lemon juice, lime zest and juice, and salt until combined. Add the milk and egg yolks, beating until well mixed. Gently fold in 1 cup egg-white mixture, then fold in the remaining egg-white mixture. Spoon the batter into ramekins. Top each with a lemon round.

3 BAKE THE SOUFFLÉS: Place the ramekins in a baking pan and carefully fill pan with 1 inch hot water, creating a water bath. Bake the soufflés until set—about 45 minutes. Carefully remove the ramekins from pan and serve either immediately or at room temperature.

Nutrition information per serving—protein: 5 g; fat: 8 g; carbohydrate: 32 g; fiber: 0; sodium: 92 mg; cholesterol: 122 mg; calories: 223.

‖INDEX

Angel Food Cake, Berry-Dotted, 178, 179
Appetizers
  "Bedeviled" Eggs, 21
  Citrus Gravlax, 22
  Cucumber Crudité Dip, 24
  Double-Pesto Terrine, 23
  Fig and Brie Turnovers, 24–25
  Gougères, 17
  Grilled Chicken with Citrus Sauce, 21
  Shrimp Mouse, 22
  Warm Aged Gouda Custard with Roasted Tomatoes, 18
Apple
  Apricot Compote, 113
  Brandy Gravy, 42
  Butter, 164
  Cheddar Crumble Pie, 206–207
  Cookies, Iced, 194, 195
  Cranberry Granola Spiced Apples, 220
Asparagus, Lemon-Dressed Steamed, 104
Avocado Soup, Cold, 10

Bacon and Egg Hash, 58
Balsamic-Grilled Summer Vegetables, 119
Banana-Caramel Cake, 181
Banana-Oatmeal Pancakes with Maple-Rum Syrup, 155
Barbecue Beef Brisket Sandwiches, 48–49
Barbecued Country Ribs with Lemon, 56, 57
Barely Pickled Beet and Orange Salad, 128–129
Bayou-Style Greens, 103
Beef
  All-American Burger, 53
  Barbecue, Brisket Sandwiches, 48–49
  Barbecued Country Ribs with Lemon, 56, 57
  Corned Beef Hash with Boston Brown Bread, 57
  Beef and Red Wine Stew, 51
  Cowboy Chili, 54
  Glazed Brisket with Root Vegetables, 50
  Grilled Flank Steak with Cucumber-Noodle Salad, 122
  Korean-Style Short Ribs, 52, 53
  Lavender and Pepper Steak, 51
  Prized Family Meat Loaf, 65
  Rib Roast with Mushroom Sauce, 48
  T-Bone Steaks with North African Spices, 54–55
  thermometers for, 51
Beets, Honey-Roasted, 108, 109
Belgian Endive with Walnuts, Braised, 100
Biscotti Cookie Sampler, 194
Blackberry-Cassis Jam, 165
Blackberry-Glazed Pork Tenderloin, 59

Black Raspberry Buttermilk Scones, 156–157
Blueberry and Peach Pie, 200–201
Blueberry-Bay Vinegar, 167
Blueberry Chutney, 38
Boston Brown Bread, 141
Breads
  Banana-Oatmeal Pancakes, 155
  Black Raspberry Buttermilk Scones, 156–157
  Boston Brown Bread, 141
  Carrot-Ginger Bran Muffins, 160, 161
  Chocolate Bread, 150, 151
  Cinnamon-Pecan Sticky Buns, 158, 159
  Easter Morning Biscuits, 153
  Five-Grain Bread, 138–139
  flour types for, 144
  Herb Popovers, 152, 153
  Italian Holiday Loaf, 148–149
  Multigrain Blueberry Pancakes, 156
  Olive Fougasse, 147
  Pizza Bianca, 149
  Potato Clover Dinner Rolls, 140, 141
  Prune Hazelnut Bread, 142–143
  Pumpkin Biscuits, 154
  Raisin Pumpernickel Bread, 144
  Rhubarb-Almond Muffins, 160
  Rosemary Raisin Focaccia with Pine Nuts, 146
  Saffron Bread, 148
  Savory Cornmeal Cookies, 149
  Schiacciata Con Uva, 145
  Sesame and Poppy Seed Crackers, 154
  Skillet Cornbread, 150
  Whole Grain and Pepper Crackers, 155
  yeasts for, 142
Brussels Sprouts, Sautéed, 104
Burger, All-American, 53
Butter-Basted Roast Turkey with Mushroom Gravy, 39
Butter Bean and Sausage Hot Pot, 61
Buttercup-Barley Stew, 92
Butter Lettuce with Cherry Vinaigrette, 124
Buttermilk Chess Pie, 209
Butternut Squash (Roasted) and Pear Soup, 16
Cabbage Slaw (Warm) with Maple-Bacon Dressing, 131
Cakes. See also Frosting
  Banana-Caramel Cake, 181
  Berry-Dotted Angel Food Cake, 178, 179
  Chocolate Espresso Torte, 188
  Easy Chocolate Party Cake, 190–191
  Fresh Berry Shortcake with Spiced Syrup, 187
  Hot Chocolate Cake, 190
  ingredient substitutions, 179

Lemon-Blackberry Cake, 184, 185
Maple Walnut Cake, 186
Moravian Sugar Cake, 180
Pear Upside-Down Cake, 176, 177
Pistachio Semolina Honey Cake, 188–189
Pumpkin Spice Cake, 182, 183
Rhubarb-Pecan Oatmeal Bars, 192
Stacked Applesauce Cake, 189
Toasted Coconut Coffee Cake, 176
Candied Yams with Apples, 113
Canning safety, 164
Caramel Icing, 181
Carrot and Parsnip Soup, Creamy, 12
Carrot-Ginger Bran Muffins, 160, 161
Cereal Tarts with Yogurt and Fresh Fruit, 210, 211
Champagne, Fruit, and Marsala Cream Parfaits, 222
Cheese Grits and Corn Pudding, 94, 95
Cheeses, substituting, 23
Cherries, Dried, 124
Cherry Pie, 203
Cherry Vanilla Ice Cream, 229
Chicken. See also Poultry
  Clubhouse Sandwich, 36–37
  Coq au Vin Blanc, 30
  Curried, Quesadillas with Pineapple Salsa/Peanut Sauce, 34
  Grilled, with Citrus Sauce, 20, 21
  Louisville Hot Brown, 36
  Manchego Empanadas, 35
  Mushroom Noodle Soup, 18, 19
  Potpie, 31
  Preserved Lemon Chicken, 28, 29
  Rosemary-Garlic, 28
  in salad, 122
  Spicy Southern-Fried, 32, 33
  Tomatillo Chili, 33
  Waldorf Chicken Salad Sandwiches, 35
Chickpeas, Parsley and Lemon, 105
Chili
  Chicken-Tomatillo, 33
  Chipotle-Vegetable, 117
  Cowboy, 54
  Sweet and Spicy Pork, 61
Chocolate
  Bourbon Pecan Pie, 211
  Bread, 150, 151
  Bread Pudding, 232
  Cake, Hot, 190
  Coconut Macaroons, 193
  Espresso Torte, 188
  Party Cake, Easy, 190–191
Cilantro-and-Mint-Crusted Sea Bass, 71
Cinnamon-Pecan Sticky Buns, 158, 159

Cinnamon Whipped Cream, 189
Citrus. See also specific fruits
  Gravlax, 22
  Sage Custard Soufflés, 236, 237
  Sauce, 21
  Sesame Fish Fillets, Crispy, 70, 71
Clubhouse Sandwich, 36–37
Coconut Coffee Cake, Toasted, 176
Collard Slaw, Hot, 100–101
Cookies
  Biscotti Cookie Sampler, 194
  Chocolate-Coconut Macaroons, 193
  Iced Apple Cookies, 194, 195
  Lemon Icebox Cookies, 196, 197
  Simple Shortbread Cookies, 197
Coq au Vin Blanc, 30
Corned Beef Hash with Boston Brown Bread, 57
Cornish Hens, 43, 44, 45
Cornmeal Cookies, Savory, 149
Cornmeal Fritters with Spicy Buttermilk Dipping, 94
Couscous, 92, 93
Cowboy Chili, 54
Crab Bisque, 14, 15
Cranberry Glaze, 58
Cranberry-Pear Wild-Rice Stuffing, 40
Cranberry Sauce with Orange, Spiced, 168, 169
Cranberry-Walnut Couscous, 92
Cucumber Crudité Dip, 24
Curried Butternut-Squash and Rice Casserole, 87
Curried Chicken Quesadillas with Pineapple Salsa/Peanut Sauce, 34
Curry-Dijon Mayonnaise, 79

Desserts, 220–237. See also Cakes; Cookies; Frosting; Pies/tarts
  Champagne, Fruit, and Marsala Cream Parfaits, 222
  Cherry Vanilla Ice Cream, 229
  Chocolate Bread Pudding, 232
  Citrus-Sage Custard Soufflés, 236, 237
  Cranberry Granola Spiced Apples, 220
  Fig, Raspberry/Honey Trifle, 223
  Fresh Peach Ice Cream, 231
  Frozen Lime Mouse with Raspberry Sauce, 228
  Ginger Ice Cream, 230, 231
  Holiday Fruit Salad with Pomegranate Syrup, 222
  homemade ice creams, 229–231
  Honey-Glazed Grilled Plums, 226, 227
  Maple Indian Pudding, 234, 235
  Melon Cooler, 228
  Mixed-Berry Pavlova, 220–221
  Red-Wine-Poached Pears, 225
  Rice Pudding with Macadamia-Maple Brittle, 234

Spiced Figs in Port Wine, 224, 225
Strawberry Granita, 229
Sugared Jelly Candies, 233
Valencia Orange Flan, 226
Double-Pesto Terrine, 23
Dough, 200, 216
Dressing. *See also* Sauces/spreads
    Blueberry-Bay Vinegar, 167
    Blueberry Vinaigrette, 128
    Cherry Vinaigrette, 124
    Classic Vinaigrette, 166
    Creamy Ranch Dressing, 167
    Honey Hazelnut, 130
    Honey Mustard Vinaigrette, 134
    kiwi-blended, 127
    Lemon-Feta, 167
    Maple-Bacon, 131
    Pesto Vinaigrette, 125
    Rancho Deluxe, 133
    vinaigrette secret, 124
    Warm Pine Nut Vinaigrette, 166
Duck Breast, Blueberry Chutney-Glazed, 38

Easter Morning Biscuits, 153
Eggplant Salsa, Roasted, 172, 173

Fennel and Apple, Roasted, 112
Fennel Slaw with Radishes and Red Onion, 132, 133
Figs
    Fig and Brie Turnovers, 24–25
    Fig, Raspberry, and Honey Trifle, 223
    Spiced Figs in Port Wine, 224, 225
Five-Grain Bread, 138–139
Fresh Berry Shortcake with Spiced Syrup, 187
Frosting
    Caramel Icing, 181
    Cinnamon Whipped Cream, 189
    Fudgy Cream Cheese, 192
    Lemon Buttercream, 185
    Maple-Sugar, 186
    Pumpkin-Cream Cheese, 182
    Tips, 192

Garden Herb Pesto, 77
Garlic (Roasted) Soup, 13
Ginger Ice Cream, 230, 231
Gorgonzola-Buttermilk Pasta with Arugula, 88, 89
Gouda Custard with Roasted Tomatoes, 18
Gougères, 17
Gravies, 39, 42
Green Beans with Honey Mustard Vinaigrette, 134
Green Goddess Mayonnaise, 166
Greens and Nectarines with Honey Hazelnut Dressing, 130
Grilled Lobster with Lime-Bay Butter, 74
Grilled Vegetables with Rosemary Goat Cheese Polenta, 96, 97
Grits (Cheese) and Corn Pudding, 94, 95
Gumbo, Seafood, 80–81

Ham. *See* Pork
Hazelnut-Crusted Goat Cheese Salad, 128
Herb-Crusted Boneless Pork Roast, 59

Herb Pasta, Fresh, 84, 85
Herb Popovers, 152, 153
Holiday Fruit Salad with Pomegranate Syrup, 222
Holiday Oyster Stew, 17
Honey Hazelnut Dressing, 130
Honey-Shallot Ketchup, 168
Horseradish Cream, 75
Hot Pepper Sauce, 171

Irish Whiskey Sauce, 232
Italian Holiday Loaf, 148–149

Johnnycakes with Nantucket Bay Scallops and Horseradish Cream, 75

Kiwi-blended dressing, 127
Korean-Style Short Ribs, 52, 53

Lamb
    Chops Marinated in Red Wine, 65
    Minted Lamb Patties, 62–63
    Moroccan Lamb Kebabs, 64
    Rack of, with Mint Pesto, 64
    Savory Braised Lamb Shanks, 62
Lasagna, Granddad's Special, 86
Lavender and Pepper Steak, 51
Lemon
    Blackberry Cake, 184, 185
    Buttercream Frosting, 185
    Feta Dressing, 167
    Icebox Cookies, 196, 197
    Tart, Double, 208
Lime-Bay Butter, 74
Lime Mouse (Frozen) with Raspberry Sauce, 228
Louisville Hot Brown, 36

Macaroni and cheese, 90, 91
Macaroons, 193
Maple
    Bacon Dressing, 131
    Glazed Turkey Drumsticks, 40, 41
    Indian Pudding, 234, 235
    Rum Syrup, 155
    Sugar Frosting, 186
    Walnut Cake, 186
Maque Choux, 109
Marinara sauce, 86
Mayonnaise. *See* Sauces/spreads
Measuring, importance, 180
Meat grades, 58
Meat Loaf, Prized Family, 65
Melon Cooler, 228
Minted Lamb Patties, 62–63
Mixed Berry Crostata, 202, 203
Mixed-Berry Pavlova, 220–221
Monkfish, Stewed, 68
Moravian Sugar Cake, 180
Moroccan Lamb Kebabs, 64
Multigrain Blueberry Pancakes, 156
Mushroom Gravy, 39
Mushroom Sauce, 48

Olive Fougasse, 147
Onions, 110
    Creamed Pearl Onions, 110–111
    with Parsnip Puree, Roasted, 114
    Wilted Spinach and Red Onion Salad, 130
Oregon Hot Crab, 79

Pancakes, 155, 156
Pasta

Fresh Herb Pasta, 84, 85
Gorgonzola-Buttermilk Pasta with Arugula, 88, 89
Granddad's Special Lasagna, 86
Perciatelli Carbonara, 87
Pumpkin Ravioli in Sage Butter Sauce, 85
Sage Baked Macaroni and Cheese, 90, 91
Pastry Dough, 216
Peach Ice Cream, Fresh, 231
Peanut Sauce, 34
Pears
    Cranberry-Pear Wild-Rice Stuffing, 40
    Pear Tart with Blue Cheese Streusel, 216
    Pear Upside-Down Cake, 176, 177
    Red-Wine-Poached Pears, 225
    Warm Pear and Green Bean Salad, 134–135
Pea Soup, Chilled Fresh, 10–11
Perciatelli Carbonara, 87
Pesto. *See* Dressing; Sauces
Pickled Garlic, Shallots, and Pearl Onions, 172
Pies/tarts, 200–217
    Apple-Cheddar Crumble Pie, 206–207
    Blueberry and Peach Pie, 200–201
    Buttermilk Chess Pie, 209
    Cereal Tarts with Yogurt and Fresh Fruit, 210, 211
    Cherry Pie, 203
    Chocolate Bourbon Pecan Pie, 211
    Double Lemon Tart, 208
    dough tips, 200
    Flaky Piecrust, 31
    Mixed Berry Crostata, 202, 203
    Pastry Dough, 216
    Pear Tart with Blue Cheese Streusel, 216
    Pumpkin Cream Pie with Candied Cranberries, 212–213
    Rhubarb-Custard Pie with Pecan Crust, 205
    Tarragon-Rosemary Strawberry Tart, 204
    Tomato and Camembert Tart, 214, 215
    Wild Mushroom Tart, 217
Pineapple Salsa, 34
Pine Nut Vinaigrette, Warm, 166
Pistachio Pesto, 105
Pistachio Semolina Honey Cake, 188–189
Pizza Bianca, 149
Plums, Honey-Glazed Grilled, 226, 227
Pomegranate Syrup, 222
Porcini-Pancetta Risotto, 89
Pork
    Bacon and Egg Hash, 58
    Blackberry-Glazed Pork Tenderloin, 59
    Butter Bean and Sausage Hot Pot, 61
    Country Style Ham with Cranberry Glaze, 58
    Herb-Crusted Boneless Pork Roast, 59
    Louisville Hot Brown, 36
    Shoulder Pot-Au-Feu, 60

Sweet and Spicy Pork Chili, 61
Wine and Fruit-Glazed Pork Chops, 60
Potato Clover Dinner Rolls, 140, 141
Potatoes
    Blue-Ribbon Potato Salad, 131
    Golden Mashed, 112
    Latkes with Apple-Apricot Compote, 113
    Rosemary-Roasted, 114
    selecting, 114
    Whipped Root Vegetables and, 116
Potpie, Chicken, 31
Poultry. *See also* Chicken; Turkey
    Cornish Hens Baked in Salt Dough, 44, 45
    Cornish Hens with Wild-Rice Stuffing, 43
    Duck Breast, Blueberry Chutney-Glazed, 38
    Quail with Golden-Cherry BBQ Sauce, 45
    terms, 39
Prune Hazelnut Bread, 142–143
Pumpkin
    Baked Stuffed, 118, 119
    Biscuits, 154
    Cream Cheese Frosting, 182
    Cream Pie with Candied Cranberries, 212–213
    Ravioli in Sage Butter Sauce, 85
    Spice Cake, 182, 183
Pumpkin Seed Pesto, 167

Quail with Golden-Cherry BBQ Sauce, 45
Quesadillas (Curried Chicken) with Pineapple Salsa/Peanut Sauce, 34

Raisin Pumpernickel Bread, 144
Ranch Dressing, Creamy, 167
Rancho Deluxe Dressing, 133
Raspberry Sauce, 228
Red Pepper (Fire-Roasted) Salad, 125
Rhubarb
    Almond Muffins, 160
    Chutney, Spicy, 171
    Custard Pie with Pecan Crust, 205
    Pecan Oatmeal Bars, 192
    Sauce, Chunk, 193
Rib Roast with Mushroom Sauce, 48
Rice dishes, 89, 93
Rice Pudding with Macadamia-Maple Brittle, 234
Roasting instructions, 43, 64
Rosemary-Garlic Chicken, 28
Rosemary Raisin Focaccia with Pine Nuts, 146

Saffron Bread, 148
Salad
    Barely Pickled Beet and Orange, 128–129
    Blue-Ribbon Potato, 131
    Butter Lettuce with Cherry Vinaigrette, 124
    Dried Cherries, 124
    Fennel Slaw with Radishes and Red Onion, 132, 133
    Fire-Roasted Red Pepper, 125

Green Beans with Honey Mustard Vinaigrette, 134
Greens and Nectarines with Honey Hazelnut Dressing, 130
Grilled Chicken, Mushroom, and Fig, 122, 123
Grilled Flank Steak with Cucumber-Noodle, 122
Hazelnut-Crusted Goat Cheese, with Blueberry Vinaigrette, 128
Oregano-Lemon Couscous, 93
Tomato Flowers, 127
Tomato, Watermelon, and Cucumber, 126, 127
Warm Cabbage Slaw with Maple-Bacon Dressing, 131
Warm Pear and Green Bean, 134–135
Wilted Spinach and Red Onion, 130
Salmon. See Seafood
Salt Dough, 44, 45
Sandwiches
    All-American Burger, 53
    Barbecue Beef Brisket, 48–49
    Clubhouse, 36–37
    Louisville Hot Brown, 36
    Oregon Hot Crab, 79
    Waldorf Chicken Salad, 35
Sauces/spreads. See also Dressing
    Apple-Apricot Compote, 113
    Apple Butter, 164
    Basic Mayonnaise, 166
    Blackberry-Cassis Jam, 165
    Blackberry Glaze, 59
    Blueberry Chutney, 38
    Buttermilk Dipping, 94
    Chunk Rhubarb Sauce, 193
    Citrus Sauce, 20, 21
    Cranberry Glaze, 58
    Cucumber Crudité Dip, 24
    Curry-Dijon Mayonnaise, 79
    Double-Pesto Terrine, 23
    Garden Herb Pesto, 77
    Green Goddess Mayonnaise, 166
    Honey-Shallot Ketchup, 168
    Horseradish Cream, 75
    Hot Pepper Sauce, 171
    Irish Whiskey Sauce, 232
    Lime-Bay Butter, 74
    Maple-Rum Syrup, 155
    Marinara Sauce, 86
    Mushroom Sauce, 48
    Peanut Sauce, 34
    Perfect Strawberry Preserves, 164
    Pickled Garlic, Shallots, and Pearl Onions, 172

Pineapple Salsa, 34
Pistachio Pesto, 105
Pomegranate Syrup, 222
Pumpkin Seed Pesto, 167
Raspberry Sauce, 228
Roasted Eggplant Salsa, 172, 173
Sage Butter Sauce, 85
Spiced Cranberry Sauce with Orange, 168, 169
Spicy Rhubarb Chutney, 171
Sweet-Corn Relish, 170
Tomato Jam, 165
Tomato Relish, 170
Schiacciata Con Uva, 145
Seafood
    choosing, storing, 75
    Cilantro-and-Mint-Crusted Sea Bass, 71
    Clubhouse Sandwich, 36–37
    Crispy Citrus/Sesame Fish Fillets, 70, 71
    Grilled Lobster with Lime-Bay Butter, 74
    Gumbo, 80–81
    Herb-Stuffed Grilled Trout, 68–69
    Honey Ginger-Glazed Salmon, 72, 73
    Johnnycakes with Nantucket Bay Scallops and Horseradish Cream, 75
    Maple-Marinated Roasted Salmon, 72
    Oregon Hot Crab, 79
    Paella, 78
    Salmon and Goat's Cheese Frittata, 74
    Sea Scallops and Pasta with Garden Herb Pesto, 77
    Stewed Monkfish, 68
    substitutions, 80
    Tuna-Egg Roll-Up, 79
Sesame and Poppy Seed Crackers, 154
Shrimp Mouse, 22
Simple Shortbread Cookies, 197
Skillet Cornbread, 150
Soups/Stews. See also Chili
    Beef and Red Wine Stew, 51
    Butter Bean/Sausage Hot Pot, 61
    Buttercup-Barley Stew, 92
    Chicken and Mushroom Noodle Soup, 18, 19
    Chilled Fresh Pea Soup, 10–11
    Cold Avocado Soup, 10
    Crab Bisque, 14, 15

Creamy Carrot and Parsnip Soup, 12
Holiday Oyster Stew, 17
Pork Shoulder Pot-Au-Feu, 60
Roasted Butternut Squash and Pear Soup, 16
Roasted Garlic Soup, 13
Spring-Greens Soup, 12
Stewed Monkfish, 68
Tomato-Fennel Soup, 13
Winter Root Vegetable Soup, 16
Sourdough Mushroom Stuffing, 42
Spinach (Wilted) and Red Onion Salad, 130
Spring-Greens Soup, 12
Stacked Applesauce Cake, 189
Strawberry Granita, 229
Strawberry Preserves, Perfect, 164
Stuffing
    Cranberry-Pear Wild-Rice, 40
    Sourdough Mushroom, 42
    Wild-Rice, 43
Succotash, Farm Stand, 117
Sugared Jelly Candies, 233
Summer Squash with Pistachio Pesto, Sautéed, 105
Sweet and Spicy Pork Chili, 61
Sweet-Corn Relish, 170
Sweet Potato Fries, Oven-Baked, 112
Swiss Chard, Herbed Rice Stuffed, 90

Tarragon-Rosemary Strawberry Tart, 204
Tomatoes
    Fried, with Ginger Parsley Crust, 106–107
    in salads, 126, 127
    Tomato and Camembert Tart, 214, 215
    Tomato-Fennel Soup, 13
    Tomato Jam, 165
    Tomato Relish, 170
Tuna-Egg Roll-Up, 79
Turkey
    Butter-Basted Roast Turkey with Mushroom Gravy, 39
    Clubhouse Sandwich, 36–37
    Maple-Glazed Turkey Drumsticks, 40, 41
    Roasted Apple Turkey with Apple Brandy Gravy, 42
    roasting, 43

Valencia Orange Flan, 226
Vegetable dishes, 100–119

Baked Stuffed Pumpkin, 118, 119
Balsamic-Grilled Summer Vegetables, 119
Bayou-Style Greens, 103
Braised Belgian Endive with Walnuts, 100
Candied Yams with Apples, 113
Chipotle-Vegetable Chili, 117
Creamed Pearl Onions, 110–111
Farm Stand Succotash, 117
Fried Tomatoes with Ginger Parsley Crust, 106–107
Golden Mashed Potatoes, 112
Honey-Roasted Beets, 108, 109
Hot Collard Slaw, 100–101
Lemon-Dressed Steamed Asparagus, 104
Maque Choux, 109
Oven-Baked Sweet Potato Fries, 112
Parsley and Lemon Chickpeas, 105
Potato Latkes with Apple-Apricot Compote, 113
Roasted Fennel and Apple, 112
Roasted Garden Vegetables, 116
Roasted Onions with Parsnip Puree, 114
Rosemary-Roasted Potatoes, 114
Sautéed Brussels Sprouts, 104
Sautéed Summer Squash with Pistachio Pesto, 105
Southern Vegetable Sauté, 102, 103
Whipped Root Vegetables and Potatoes, 116
Vegetable (Winter Root) Soup, 16
Vegetarian dishes. See also Pasta; Soups/Stews
    Cranberry-Walnut Couscous, 92
    Curried Butternut-Squash and Rice Casserole, 87
    Grilled Vegetables with Rosemary Goat Cheese Polenta, 96, 97
    Herbed Rice Stuffed Swiss Chard, 90
Vinaigrettes. See Dressing

Waldorf Chicken Salad Sandwiches, 35
Whole Grain and Pepper Crackers, 155
Wild Mushroom Tart, 217
Wild-Rice Stuffing, 43
Wine and Fruit-Glazed Pork Chops, 60

PHOTOGRAPHY CREDITS

Beatriz DaCosta: 91, 158 >> Dasha Wright Ewing: 202 >> Mark Ferri: 8, 25 >> Charles Gold: 236 >> Ericka McConnell: 3, 63, 111, 140, 157, 169, 178, 198, 221 >> Alison Miksch: 70, 96, 107, 123, 120, 127, 177, 227 >> Keith Scott Morton: 135, 196 >> Helen Norman: 174, 195 >> Judd Pilossof: 19, 37, 81, 82, 85, 136, 152 >> Steven Randazzo: 95, 102, 213 >> Alan Richardson: 14, 69, 73, 98, 109, 139, 143, 151, 201, 207, 235 >> Charles Schiller: 4, 29, 101, 115, 118, 161, 162, 173 ,183, 210, 214, 224 >> Ann Stratton: 2, 11, 20, 32, 41, 26, 44, 49, 52, 46, 55, 56, 66, 76, 88, 129, 132, 184, 191, 218, 230